PRAISE FOR

WHERE *the* DEER *and* *the* ANTELOPE PLAY

An Amazon Best of the Month Pick

"The book is an amiable ramble outdoors, with Offerman sharing his assorted experiences in the wild and his musings on nature, land use, labor, agriculture, and community."
—*USA Today*

"Honest-to-God advice about how to enjoy nature."
—Outside

"Offerman brings dry humor and a reverence for nature and physical labor to his growing understanding of capitalist and colonial horrors, all while maintaining hope for the future."
—*The Seattle Times*

"I found the book both entertaining and inspiring. . . . [It] has depths you may not expect from an actor/comedic performer/woodworker who goes to great lengths to entertain the audience but also has me thinking about the choices I make as I live in the world."
—John Warner, *Chicago Tribune*

"Offerman's thoughtful and hilarious musings at the nexus of human life and nature, particularly through the lens of John Muir and Aldo Leopold . . . serve another welcome reminder that nature is for all."
—*Smithsonian Magazine*

WHERE *the* DEER *and* *the* ANTELOPE PLAY

THE PASTORAL OBSERVATIONS
OF ONE IGNORANT AMERICAN
WHO LOVES TO WALK OUTSIDE

NICK OFFERMAN

DUTTON

DUTTON

An imprint of Penguin Random House LLC
penguinrandomhouse.com

Previously published as a Dutton hardcover in October 2021.
First Dutton trade paperback printing: October 2023

LIBRARY OF CONGRESS CATALOGING-IN-PUBLICATION DATA
has been applied for.

ISBN: 9781101984703 (trade paperback)

Printed in the United States of America
1st Printing

BOOK DESIGN BY LAURA K. CORLESS

To the children of the players herein, our hope and delight (plus Tom):

Molly, Bea, Isaac, Tom

Spencer, Sammy

Caitlin, Alena

Elise, Holly, Sunshine, Maggie, Harper

(sorry for the cussing, kids, but sometimes a man gets riled)

contents

PART II

PART III

INTRODUCTION

In many ways, the inception of this book occurred one score and five years ago, when I was working on a production of Sam Shepard's *Buried Child* at Chicago's excellent Steppenwolf Theatre Company. Back then, I had been well on my way to a comfortable life of blind materialism, hopefully emulating one of David Lee Roth's insouciant, musical short films I had newly come to adore on a brilliant new cable channel, simply called—get this: Music Television. Little did I suspect that by the time that play had closed, the trajectory of my life would be forever altered.

Sam himself had come to town to do some rewriting and polishing on his script, even though it had won him a Pulitzer Prize back in 1979. I guess he didn't entirely agree with the Pulitzer folks. That was certainly his prerogative, and I guess that's what made him so damn handsome, I mean smart. The production was a pretty big deal, directed as it was by Steppenwolf founding member Gary Sinise, and starring some honest-to-god hotshots like Lois Smith, Ted Levine, Kellie Overbey, Ethan Hawke, and the late, great James Gammon. Gary, a legendary actor and director, also happens to be an awfully generous fellow, if you're ever lucky enough to meet him—he always treated me quite equitably, even though the first time we met I was unaware his name was pronounced "Suh-neese," and I said, "It's nice to meet you, Mr. Sinus."

Despite that initial gaffe, Gary hired me as an understudy for the show and also as a makeup artist, to apply old-age makeup to James Gammon every night, just by way of some stippling and painted modeling with highlights and shadows, nothing fancy. I had a scenery shop in the warehouse where I lived, or I guess to be accurate I should say I had a futon and a hotplate in the warehouse where I cohabitated with my table saw and my pin nailers. I had also previously made some props for Steppenwolf, including some masks for Alex and his Droogs in *A Clockwork Orange*, a play in which I also appeared and served as fight captain. All of which is to say, I was lucky as hell to be the jack-of-all-trades gofer kid running around the theatre the night Sam Shepard corralled me, slipped me $40, and told me to go get him a bottle of Maker's Mark.

Now, I had gone to theatre school in Urbana-Champaign in the late eighties and early '90s, which means that Sam Shepard was still the biggest rock star cowboy playwright in America (not to mention Chuck Yeager in *The Right Stuff*—heart-eyes emoji) when he sent me to get him a very specific handle of Kentucky straight bourbon, which means that I was high as a kite as I sprinted a block each in three different directions to score the bottle before realizing there was no liquor store within sprinting distance. Son of a bitch! I had been gone at least seven minutes, and I was beginning to panic—if I could but successfully score him this whisky, there's no reason that it might not specifically fuel some innovative rewrites in rehearsal that night that could make the Pulitzer committee realize they had better take things up a notch and award *Buried Child* a first-ever *second* Pulitzer! Inspired, I finally streaked into the Argentinian restaurant on the corner and found a bartender to take pity on me. He fetched me the bottle, which I gingerly cradled as I cautiously high-stepped it back to the theatre.

In hindsight, acquiring intoxicants for your playwright before rehearsal begins is probably not ever a good idea. That fact began to dawn on me that very night shortly after I had deposited the Maker's Mark at Sam's seat in the audience, just before his significant other, Jessica Lange, arrived to join him. Her mood didn't seem great, and there was some quiet but stern talking happening, and it dawned on me that maybe the reason he surreptitiously sent the gofer kid out for booze was because he wasn't supposed to be having it. I honestly don't know if that was the case, or how the evening played out between them, but I recall being painfully aware of the shift in tone the experience took: what had started out as a thrilling, personal, whisky-flavored interaction starring me and America's greatest living playwright that left me breathless and blushing (I'm Sam Shepard's Kentucky candy man!) ended with the banal reality of a (terrific-looking) middle-aged couple just doing their work and dealing with whatever individual circumstances they each brought to the table that night. My few years at Steppenwolf were invaluable for teaching me that, at the end of the day, every person puts their pants on just the same as me (even if these two people were packing some *top-drawer* buttocks into those britches), and it was just one in a lifelong string of reminders that the more I focused my attention on myself, the stupider I behaved; and the more I focused on others, the likelier I was to be of actual service, because I could then apprehend the work that needing doing.

That was a good lesson, as I began to see the world a tiny bit more clearly. As it turns out, that was just the appetizer to a much meatier main course, because that 1995 play in Chicago was also the juncture in my life at which somebody first gave me some Wendell Berry stories. That "somebody" was Leo Burmester, a dearly departed, larger-than-life Kentucky actor who was also in the show and could apparently smell the hay on me, or at least a waft of manure, and, recognizing a kindred spirit, he changed my life with his gesture. The spirit running through Mr. Berry's writing, a farming and life philosophy I would come to know as "agrarian," appealed to my core and curiosity in a way that has not yet abated. Agrarianism promotes an egalitarian agriculture based on morally sound land use. Slow down, please, and read that last sentence again. Have you ever read a sentence even half that boring?

As a person who makes his living creating popular culture of one sort or another, I can absolutely admit to the absence of pizzazz in this topic. *"This is terrible television!,"* my inner mountebank barks, as I notice that I am nonetheless unable to look away from it. The marrow of Wendell Berry's writing managed to reach something in my own bones; some deep truth that was not put there by me but by my excellent mother and father, because I recognized that they were agrarian also. They had grown up on farms a few miles from each other, and the seeds of their quiet, steady lessons of thrift, service, and decency had been expertly planted in me and my siblings, but mine didn't truly begin to flower until my emergence from boyhood at age twenty-five, when the sprouting seeds were watered with Mr. Berry's vision, and I have been completely screwed ever since, goddamn my eyes.

I would never be that innocent MTV-lover again. As if for the first time, I could see clearly the folly in the shiny materialism I had so adored, and the folly in us humans as well, me, first and foremost. The plenteous golden tresses cascading down Mr. Lee Roth's bright red leotard would never ensnare my fascination again. Ever since that epiphany, with my limited cognitive capacity, I have instead been able to periodically glimpse the ways in which we industriously sell to one another our own demise. One of the most pernicious ways in which we do that is by pretending and convincing one another that the planet's resources are unlimited, and that we don't need to worry about the concerns of agrarians, because they are old-fashioned and certainly not cool.

Eventually, I befriended the Berry family and have endeavored to do my small part in supporting their work, that of stolidly sounding the alarm for some decades now, to draw our attention back to the land by which we are inescapably supported, and the neglected farm families who steward that land. This cause was lovingly detailed in a documentary by Laura Dunn I helped to produce, appropriately entitled *Look & See*. A few years ago, I had the substantial pleasure of introducing my parents to the Berry clan at the lunch table of Berry daughter, Mary, who should frankly be elected to as high an agricultural post as we can vault her. You'll hear a bit more about her later, but for now it's important to know that the following ceremony occurred as we partook of her delectable brown sugar pie:

The round oak table was peopled by Mary and her exemplary farmer husband, Steve Smith; Wendell; his winning bride, Tanya; and my mom and dad, or more importantly, four farmers and a retired nurse and a retired schoolteacher. They were kindly indulging the lunch's only trained juggler (me) as I described an idea for a new book about our population's general lack of any intimate knowledge of nature; a book that would hopefully add to the various, disparate voices reminding people that if you like to eat food, then you had best begin to give a shit about our farmers and our agriculture.

Wendell had pushed his chair back from the table and crossed his legs, having finished his pie with fresh whipped cream. He leveled his gaze at me and said, "Look. Examine the 'conservation' of 'nature,' not through the lens of John Muir, which is how everybody looks at it, but instead through the lens of Aldo Leopold."

I swallowed audibly and nodded confidently, having no idea what the fudge he meant. "Mm. That's great," I replied cluelessly, taken aback at this unexpected turn our dessert course had taken. Sure, I suppose I mentioned the book in the hopes of winning some small approbation from him, but I never could have dreamed that I would finish that lunch having been tasked with a riddle-wrapped quest by my favorite wizard-poet.

Far be it from me to shirk my chores, so I set my investigation in motion. My journey took on a few different guises, as I perambulated all over a whole bunch of nature, dovetailing Wendell's challenge into my perpetual search for the way to find nuance in every situation I can, even the ones that seem the most enraging and controversial. My tasks involved the making of mistakes, then discovering how to resolve those errors without being an asshole, a search that I now understand will never end.

There were some pretty damn charming companions in my travels, including my bromance brothers Jeff Tweedy and George Saunders, with whom I hiked Glacier National Park; James Rebanks and his redoubtable family, who showed me how beautiful farming life can be in the hills of Cumbria; and of course my own bride, Megan Mullally; our dog Clover; and our Airstream, "the Nutmeg," all of whom you'll meet shortly. Without them all I could never have put together the following pages. I thank all of them very kindly, and I'll thank you, dear reader, for making it to at least the end of the introduction.

PART I

1

KALISPELL

"JESUS IS LORD."

Uh, okay. This was the message that greeted me, emblazoned across a large billboard, as I pulled out of the Kalispell, Montana, airport in July of 2019. I mean, wow. I had just flown in from Los Angeles for a week of hiking and camaraderie in nearby Glacier National Park, and my mood at that moment could not have been better. A few hours earlier, the relatively small flight had lifted me up and away from the cacophonous LA traffic and my hectic life, over the California Sierra range, north over Nevada and Idaho—ruggedly beautiful terrain with very little civilization spoiling the majestic composition of mountains, lakes, clouds, and blue sky. I had sat looking out the window, breathing deeply to release the tension that for me seems to accompany the urban sprawl, even as my spirit swelled with anticipation for this rare, restorative break from the hustle of my life, and yes, from the bustle of it as well.

I landed, collected my checked bag full of hiking gear, picked up my rental car, and headed out to meet up with my companions at the local REI (Recreational Equipment, Inc.), to snag a couple of last-minute items. Pulling onto the main road, I was soon assaulted by a veritable *barrage* of billboards, reading "JESUS IS LORD," "CHOOSE LIFE," "LEGALIZE JESUS," "FEAR GOD," etc. It was a rather ham-fisted display that didn't seem particularly well thought out. I mean, it didn't remotely give me a feeling of love or safety or *welcome*, which is what I would think a Christian-minded organization would desire. Even a dum-dum like me recalls Jesus's saying in Matthew 25: "*I was hungry and you gave me food, I was thirsty and you gave me drink, I was a stranger and you welcomed me.*" But, no, the clear message here in Kalispell was "*Fear God (or Else).*"

If they're going to monopolize the local billboards, why wouldn't they try something less aggressive, like "Welcome to our town, we hope you safely enjoy the ways in which we will be providing you succor in exchange for your tourism dollars, and by the way, we have a church or two if you're looking for that sort of thing, but mainly just don't forget to love one another!" The whole notion came across as weird and clanky because billboards are generally employed for advertising, for either goods and services or else political causes. However, "Jesus is Lord" would qualify more as an opinion methinks, in answer to a question that I'm not aware anybody had asked, certainly not within the four doors of my sensible rental sedan. Dear reader, I have strong opinions as well that I'm happy to share, especially if you travel onto my turf, but I don't feel the need to erect a sign in my yard proclaiming "BEEF TALLOW IS THE FUCKING BOSS." Later in this volume I will examine the apparent need for my fellow humans with certain mindsets to behave in this peculiar fashion.

"Not exactly the beginning I'd expected," I thought as I drove on, exhaling the rancor that these billboards had excited within me. I shouldn't have been surprised by them, I guess, since my trip had been pretty dreamy up until that point, and you have to figure things will get complicated sooner or later, when one trucks into the realm of other people. We just don't all think the same, do we. I set out to write a book about us humans, particularly us Americans, and our relationship (or lack thereof) with the natural world, a.k.a. our ecosystem. I knew that our country's complicated and loaded history vis-à-vis the various denominations of the Christian faith would play an important part in that conversation; I just hadn't expected it to slap me fulsomely across the kisser the moment I set foot in Montana.

I drove on. As if to provide an immediate sweetening to the lousy taste these messages had left, once I had driven past the onslaught of THE ADVERTISEMENTS OF THE LORD, a whole new, much more positive visual offensive began, this time straight-up turning me on to the current availability of *huckleberries*! The huckleberry is a sweet, wild berry, a little smaller than a blueberry. Every new advertising space now pitched me this apparently plentiful, sublime local berry in the form of pancakes, muffins, jams, jellies, and pie, or for the intrepid consumer, just full-on huckleberries by the handful (visitors to the park may pick up to one quart of huckleberries per day), and this not just from the businesses of which you'd expect this sort of thing, your eateries and your lodgeries, but truly every business you saw. "*Len Grote Mufflers—you gotta try our baked Huckleberry Buckle!*" Now, this was more like it. No matter how or where I chose to participate in religion or not, I could certainly wrap my head around the glory of huckleberry pie, and plenty of it, in my near future. My smile returned.

I'm a guy whom you might know from my work as an actor in film and television, like for example as one particular guy with a healthy mustache who loved to eat bacon and giggle at a little horse, or another guy with a full ginger face-bush who ate arugula by the handful and manifested quantum realities, or maybe it was as the fellow with a Quaker beard and a propensity to drink too much beer and yell at handsome state troopers in burgundy pants. Some folks also have cottoned to my books, of which I have written four before this one. And then the best of you know me because I built some canoes and maintain a fine woodworking shop in Los Angeles, although I try not to pick favorites when it comes to my readers.

* * *

That day, the calendar read July of 2019, which means the country was a few years into the Trump presidency, and therefore extremely confused. Because I am an artist who always maintains the attitude of a student, I wanted to get out into some remote nature, away from the various channels of distraction that ever-increasingly rule my daily labors, and get to studenting. Letting the concerns of modern life slip away from my immediate attention—filling up my senses with Mother Nature's lush bounty—was foremost on my mind. Also, because I am a human being and subject to base passions, I wanted to go for a long walk in the woods so that I wouldn't punch anybody in the nose, and the same was true for my bromance partners Jeff and George.

I met up with them at the local REI, where we exchanged hugs and giggled with excitement at being reunited with nothing to do for the next week but wallow in some seriously magnificent national park vibes.

While Jeff shopped for rain gear, I modeled midweight, moisture-wicking tops for the group. There was a teal, half-zippered version from Patagonia that everyone agreed looked *too cute* on me to be denied, so I got to enjoy that special American rush of purchasing a fancy sweatshirt that I didn't know I needed when I walked in the door. More on that later, when we get to consumerism.

For now, let's meet these new players. George is George Saunders, the devilishly handsome American writer known for his masterful and wildly original fiction and his numerous contributions to rags like *GQ* and *The New Yorker*. Because I was such a serious fan of his writing, I had asked to meet George and interview him for my book *Gumption* in the spring of 2014. He generously agreed and we spent a day together in New York City, fertilizing what has become a powerful friendship.

Jeff is Jeff Tweedy, the devilishly handsome singer-songwriter and front man for the American rock band Wilco, and the author of two great books in his own right. I had been devoutly committed to the music of his first band, Uncle Tupelo, and then Wilco for the better part of two decades before we met on the set of *Parks and Recreation* in January of 2014. He played Scott Tanner (a local rock star in the town of Pawnee) in an episode that I was directing, so I actually had the surreal/daunting pleasure of getting to hire my hero. As with George, Jeff and I hit it off and we found ourselves strongly enamored of each other.

I had garnered the good fortune of two substantial new friendships, but everybody knows that the triangle is the strongest form in nature, and as a furniture maker I can certainly attest that it is the three-legged table or seat which exhibits the least wobble. It's also no secret that a grouping of three is the most effective number when it comes to establishing story structure and fomenting comedy. Just imagine the diminished value of the Two Stooges or *Goldilocks and the Four Bears. Seventeen Musketeers.* "One Blind Mice." Preposterous. Therefore, I suppose it naturally follows that Jeff and George were destined to also meet *each other* backstage at the final taping of *The Colbert Report* in December of 2014, completing the 2014 triangulation of our merry trio.

Since then, we three have shared years of fellowship and chuckles and an extremely rich text thread. This trip was the first time we got to actually enjoy an outing all together, just the three of us, and I would be remiss if I didn't mention that it was Jeff's idea. I was playing a New Year's Eve show, opening for him at Largo in Los Angeles, and when I mentioned my new book idea to him, he immediately suggested that we three go take a walk somewhere beautiful together. I am the youngest of our crew, and when we're together I often feel like my cool older brothers are letting me ride in the back of their Trans Am while they speak to me of topics like Kierkegaard and Foghat and empathy, so with that in mind, you can bet your sweet bippy that I took Jeff's idea and ran, all the way to the Montana tent store in which we now found ourselves.

When I was but a mere lad in the 1970s and '80s, my family taught me to adventure on a budget, leaning heavily on park trail maps, fishing acumen, comic books, mosquito spray, and masterful use of the charcoal grill and the ice chest, or as we called it, "the cooler," to fill our days with as many hijinks and hot dogs as possible. And while there will be plenty of seat-of-our-pants capers in part 3 of this book, I took the opposite approach on this trip and hired a company to plan our six days of arduous pleasure. It costs a bit more, certainly, but delegating most of the responsibility of such a journey to an outfitter is a highly recommended luxury if you can scrape up the dough.

One great advantage of an adventure company was that I was able to get on the phone with a real human person who could compare and contrast for me, in real time, items like lodgings, assorted topographies, and activities. At the time, we weren't even sure which park we'd choose, but I knew we wanted to go the vintage national park lodge route if possible, and I also asked for a river rafting experience and a horseback ride. We could have additionally included a fishing excursion, but my travel mates were not as keen on fishing as the Offerman clan. The question did however engender an enjoyable riff in our three-way text thread about fishing from horseback or then perhaps horsing from fishback? If that was a thing? (I have since determined that it is indeed not a thing.)

My goal was to immerse myself in one of our most magnificent national parks—what many of us have come to regard as the pinnacle of nature's glory—far from the entangling web of my responsibilities in Los Angeles and the various channels of communication and distraction that populate those responsibilities. When I was a kid and my family would pile into our Suburban and drive from Illinois to Minnesota or the Badlands or even Yellowstone, we just let the relatives and neighbors know we'd be back in two weeks or so, and to please water the tomatoes and keep an eye out for a postcard.

Nowadays I take the much more aggressive step of telling everyone in my close circle to simply leave me alone for two weeks. I relish nothing more than setting an automatic response to my texts and emails, which performs the exact same function as if I had hung a "Gone Fishin'" sign in the window of my hardware store in days of yore.

* * *

But that day in REI, our focus was gear. Jeff had decided on a sensible poncho for the rain, and we were now just lounging about in Menswear like a bunch of Caesars at the bathhouse, openly objectifying me in my adorable new fleece, speculating about the revelations awaiting us in the coming days. Looking at the three of us, I couldn't help but marvel at how much things had changed during our lifetimes. Growing up, all three of us belonged to households where your choices in "outdoor gear" would be limited to "coat—with or without hat or gloves." Now we were in a spacious specialty store that sold a vast variety of gear for every conceivable outdoor activity, in an array of colorful choices.

You can tell a lot about a person by the way he, she, or they spend money, and just such an interesting delineation was about to befall the three of us. Each of us grew up in an extremely working-class environment, clumsily learning the ropes of life alongside everybody else while setting our respective courses for what would become our disparate artistic journeys. I daresay one of the reasons the three of us get along so well is that we have Chicago in common: We all have lived and loved there, sometimes even together, and we've all vomited within two blocks of the Art Institute. We often feel like loving brothers and we say so in person and in our text thread, with messages like "I love you, brothers," but like any set of siblings we also have our idiosyncratic differences. Since I had never been out "in the woods" with either of these guys, only warmly embraced in the luxurious arms of civilization, what with her comfortably controllable climate and her readily available preponderance of food and beverages, I had no expectations going in, regarding the respective degrees to which we would outfit ourselves with gear.

Jeff and I definitely came down on the side of "into gear" or even "psyched about our gear," which methinks is both a modern delight and a dilemma. That morning, when we gathered in the homey lobby of our lodge, we quickly fell into a deep chat about Jeff's new boots and blister-proof socks and my engineered hiking raincoat and my CamelBak water reservoir system. It would have been clear to anyone eavesdropping on us that we had enjoyed that amazing, particularly modern form of consumerism by which one uses the internet to ask, "What is the recommended version of any item I might purchase?," then, after reading reviews and "five in-the-know tips" from experts, decides upon a selection. We happily partook of this luxury, utilizing some *disposable income*, exploiting, at least momentarily, our comfortable seats on the bus of the Leisure Class.

George's gear, on the other hand, sported the obvious signs of mere normalcy. He was outfitted with a backpack, a hoodie, and a quilted flannel shirt that had clearly *not* been purchased new for the trip, and bore the labels of brands that didn't even have their own app. His beat-up brown leather hiking boots also advertised years of previous enjoyment, but it was his water bottle that made me realize how his whole gear vibe was screaming "unassuming pragmatism." It was one of those cheap, janky aluminum bottles that you get at a convention or on the first day of work, when you get a tote bag and a crappy water bottle that reads "NewzMax" or some such. All of this suddenly added up and I realized, "George is a badass." Professionally, he writes and speaks very eloquently about how one's fiction requires mainly rewriting and editing and rewriting and editing and so on, and I think that he has been able to apply this discipline so effectively to his own life that he is able to simply engage only in what is necessary. He had boots, he had warm layers, he had water. Boom. Let's hike. Those three hours

Nick and Jeff spent shopping? Fun, maybe. But not necessary. He lives right.

I think that a downside of the kind of shopping Jeff and I enjoyed is that perhaps it can fool a person into creating an actual deficit in life—"I can't go have fun doing [x activity] because I don't have the proper gear." Of course, one should absolutely invest in safety and responsibly attack any activity with common sense and curiosity, but if you've been around the block (like George), then you might realize that you can hike a national park trail without dropping a few bills on a fancy new pair of boots. I've never to my knowledge finished the ups and downs of an arduous, daylong hike, arriving back at camp only to lament, "Man, that was so fun, but think how much better it could have been if only my middle under-layer was self-wicking! Damn!" To each their own, I say, because I can certainly understand both sides of the issue, based on my own hard-earned experience.

When I was eleven years old, heading into my sixth-grade basketball season, the Minooka Junior High School athletic department handed us boys a ditto-copied form to take home and have our folks sign. The form was a purchase order for Converse high-tops, and on it we would fill in our shoe size and whether we would prefer the canvas or the leather version of said shoes. I think the canvas were about $16 and the leather were closer to $40. Naturally, I had a screaming fit with my parents over why I needed the leather shoes, but of course their frugality won the day and I got the canvas. I had a fine, not remarkable, season, racking up an impressive tally of rebounds, which was apparently my specialty, and I am dead certain that my play would not have been improved one tiny whit if I had executed it in more expensive sneakers, but goddammit, I would have looked so much cooler.

When it comes to footwear, I have since spent a lifetime choosing it for its functionality rather than its fashion. All things considered, I'm grateful because my parents were right on that count, and it was from lessons like that one that I learned to become the practical person that I am. Then again, if they had relented and bought me the doper shoes it would have saved us all from having to listen to a sobbing eleven-year-old boy. If that option *had* occurred, it would most certainly not have been even remotely the first time that an expenditure of honest, hard-earned cash had been gladly forked over by parents to prevent a bout of caterwauling. So, I suppose you could aver that either side was right. Nuance.

That day in the REI, our concern was less with the nuance of the moment than it was with matching the right gear to our impending medium-intensity adventures. We wanted to be comfortably and safely attired so that our attention could be free to muse and percolate on the ways in which we humans relate to nature, as it were. Jeff mentioned a couple of day hikes on the Appalachian Trail, and the deep solace he had felt there. This made him wonder aloud, "Do we feel such an overwhelming peace when we enter the woods because the chaos of nature is a balm to the rectilinear order of mankind?"

George countered, "Or is civilization the chaos, and nature's inscrutable design the respite because of its older-than-the-hills systems and patterns?"

I shook my head and smiled at the random, exquisite moment we were sharing there in an REI store. I nodded and took mental notes, as I so often do when these two lovely thinkers set to musing. In his book *A Swim in a Pond in the Rain*, George said (through the lens of a Turgenev story), *"Emotional power is the highest aim of art and can be attained even in the face of clumsy craft,*" and I was moved. I felt seen. Once I read that I immedi- ately pronounced it to be the motto of our gang, because I aspire to the degree to which Jeff and George are able to consistently achieve "emo- tional power" in their work, despite their sometimes clumsy attempts. They are among the teachers from whom I have learned that when you make art with confidence, then clumsiness doesn't play as clumsiness, but panache.

I imagined myself grabbing the mouthpiece to the store's PA system, hopping up on a fake boulder, and confidently busting out with,

> "*And so I go to the woods. As I go in under the trees, dependably, almost at once, and by nothing I do, things fall into place. I enter an order that does not exist outside, in the human spaces. I feel my life take its place among the lives—the trees, the annual plants, the ani- mals and birds, the living of all these and the dead—that go and have gone to make the life of the earth.*"

> "*I am less important than I thought, the human race is less im- portant than I thought. I rejoice in that. My mind loses its urgings, senses its nature, and is free.*" Wendell Berry, *A Native Hill* (1969).

Dozens of people would have gathered around me, I dreamt, in awe, adoring me with wet eyes, and when I finished speaking they would have covered their mouths with their hands almost in disbelief, then warmly applauded, looking at each other, nodding, quietly mouthing the words: "He did it."

I wish I had done it. It would have been *so* cool, and the perfect send- off to chapter 1 of my book. I always wished that I had a bunch of such literary gold packed away in my melon, to be brandished casually, aston- ishing all within earshot. This is how I often feel when spending time with George and Jeff. Their particular talents are for generating wildly original content of their own in the form of ideas, words, and music, whereas my skill set has more to do with artfully manipulating my eyebrows and leveling an oak tabletop. When art speaks directly to a deep part of my being, as theirs often does, I think some version of, "Oh, man, this is so good . . . this is how I will write *my* fiction, or cut *my* rock-and-roll record," forgetting momentarily that those are not my fields of study.

But that day in the actual REI, I merely mumbled something in agreement and said we should get out of the shopping center and check into our lodge so we could get an early jump on the other birds in the morning, worm-wise. I had a momentous feeling that if we could leave the plastic and asphalt trappings of the human-made world behind, the coming days would present us with the opportunity to take on board some real religion.

2

LOGAN PASS/HIDDEN LAKE

A man on foot, on horseback or on a bicycle will see more,
feel more, enjoy more in one mile than the motorized
tourists can in a hundred miles.

—Edward Abbey, *Desert Solitaire*

Our guide for the week was a well-read fellow in his early thirties named Jon, who absolutely looked the part of "Western states trail skipper": thin beard (connoting youth); barrel-ish, beefy frame draped in outfitter-style garments topped off with a cowboy hat. As he drove us into Glacier National Park, he regaled us with information about the history of the enormous space, which was established by President Taft in 1910, converting what had previously been the Lewis and Clark Forest Reserve. The breathtaking topography of its 1,583 square miles was available for us to skip about in thanks to an uneasy agreement between the US government and the Blackfeet tribe, a subject which will require more scrutiny in later pages.

How had we ended up in Glacier National Park? Excellent question.

Back when I was planning the trip, I'd called the outfitter Jon worked for to get some guidance on where three pilgrims might find some gorgeous hiking. The answer, according to the experts I consulted, was Glacier, which seemed to have just what the doctor (me) ordered in terms of pristine wilderness in close proximity to relatively comfy hotel beds.

I wasn't sure where exactly to start, but I felt that this was as good a place as any to begin my search to solve the conundrum of Wendell's advice. He had told me to frame our perception of "wilderness" less through the lens of John Muir and more through that of Aldo Leopold. So here I was, about to jump with both feet into a substantial example of John Muir's "pristine wilderness." That titillating phrase, in association with his name, brought to mind classic iconic park scenes of the American West, like El Capitan in Yosemite and the Grand Canyon. We were going to spend a week marinating in the splendor of such verdant outdoor settings, historically unsullied by human presence, except of course for a trail here and there. But hang on. Was Glacier, or *any* national or even state or local park, actually the pristine wilderness I'd been imagining? Or did we only consider it to be virginal for an all-too-common American reason? (Because we said so.)

I came into this trip as a casually comfortable consuming citizen, a.k.a. "ignorant"—simply into the park mainly for all the beautiful reasons I could see on the cool posters that the national parks print. It was an amazing place to go hiking with my two friends. But once I began unpacking the history of this majestic real estate, I was in for a surprise, and the fact that I could still be surprised by such a revelation speaks to my ignorance. In our very first SUV ride on the very first day, our guide, Jon, who had extensively studied the local history, both geographically and sociologically, began to illuminate the situation with the Blackfeet.

As he explained, this enormous area was far from unsettled before it became the Lewis and Clark Forest Reserve in 1897 and subsequently Glacier National Park in 1910. The Blackfeet, a "tribe" which actually consisted of four or more smaller tribal nations, had been living all over the park area for thousands of years. As the early opportunists of the burgeoning United States began to invade the territory, the Blackfeet were expelled from their own land, and eventually forbidden to hunt there as well, a situation that has lasted until even today.

I was taken aback to hear this, but why should this have come as any surprise to me? When I thought about it, I realized that we modern Americans would be hard-pressed to come up with a single scenario in which we treated the Indigenous peoples with anything remotely resembling fairness. It's laughably shameful. I mean, think about it. Have you ever read a historical account of the settlement of North America in which the English/Spanish/French/etc. dealt with the Native tribes inhabiting a certain area in any way that was remotely cool?

Then, as now, greed ruled the day. Besides the outright pillaging, genocide, and brutal warfare, even when the white folks managed to pull off a "negotiation" that was halfway peaceable, it was still flagrant robbery in broad daylight. These tribes saw the lands they called home invaded six ways to Sunday by foreign hordes. Those natives would have been perfectly justified, according to the "Stand Your Ground" laws that we now have in more than thirty of our United States, in killing each and every prospector and trapper and surveyor who came off the boat and over the hill. Don't get me wrong, they certainly tried their damnedest to fend off the whites, but the tribes were simply far outstripped by our capability and capacity for violence.

My specific astonishment in Glacier came from hearing the Europeans' rapacity described simply. Their first response upon seeing the land was the old standard: "What here can we sell?" I mean, sure, there was probably a momentary revelation of "Whoa, this place is dope as hell. Lookit that lake!" But that can't have lasted very long, I mean we're talking about the first American capitalists here, so once the appreciative pastoral murmurings died down, then likely followed, "Okay. How can we sell it?" The answer involved voracious hunting and trapping. Suddenly, a "Hang on, guys" echoed through the pines, as the new breed of Americans paused to attend that timeless and inevitable maneuver: "Is there gold?" They immediately applied themselves to finding out, bringing with them the ruination that accompanies any rush for precious metals in the form of boomtowns and the desecration of the landscapes and waterways. Soon enough, it was, "Aw shit, hold up, y'all—there's no gold!" but no matter. Despite a thin, sporadic stream of income for our "settlers" thus far, the previous inhabitants had nonetheless been beaten off their land, bullied and cajoled into treaties that our government then failed to honor, and finally saw their survivors placed into the reservation shuffle on lesser terrain to the east of what became the park.

Maybe there's something to be learned by looking at the way this history was written, and by whom. I'll say one thing for sure: It wasn't written by the Blackfeet. Once the tribes were "safely relegated" to their reservations, and it became clear that there was no gold or silver to be mined, the park was free to become what it became: a park. Enter the likes of John Muir, and George Bird Grinnell, who is generally credited with "founding" Glacier. There is also Gifford Pinchot, John Muir's "frenemy" who was conservation minded in general but with more nuance than that simple term connoted. Brandishing the mercurial trait known as "human nature," he also insisted that forest lands specifically should be put to commercial use.

There was and will be more contemplation on such issues to come, but at that moment, the focus was setting off on our first hike. Despite our early morning, the parking lot at the Logan Pass/Hidden Lake Visitor Center was completely full. Jon dropped us off to get a head start while he slowly circled, waiting for a spot to open up, making his morning just as fun as a trip to the grocery store the day before Thanksgiving. We cruised through the gift shop, enjoying the people-watching more than the Going-to-the-Sun Road signs and the Pendleton blankets on offer, although I will say that I always find the items for sale in a national park souvenir shop to be more substantial and honest (and therefore desirable) than the crap in similar retail spots in more commercial locations.

I saw that Jon was still making slow, maddening loops through the parking lot, so I set off with Jeff and George on the trail to Hidden Lake Overlook, knowing Jon would catch up to us since the trail was of the out-and-back variety. Of the seven-hundred-odd miles of trails in the park, this was the most popular, the most likely to be traversed by tourists of every stripe, commencing as it did from the main gift shop. It was a moderate, mostly uphill walk over a broad, very nicely maintained trail, with a lot of wide boardwalks and terraced steps designed for an easier, more accessible strolling experience. The original plan had been to hike down to the actual lake, but that option was temporarily closed to the public due to some grizzly bears' indulging in a "fish feeding frenzy" on the lakeshore. Dangerous to begin with, the bears were apparently to be treated with even more cautious distance when engaged in a trout-eating contest.

We found ourselves amongst a scattered gaggle of way too many fellow hikers, half of them family groups who seemed more suited to a day at Disneyland, exhibiting little to no reverence for their surroundings, not to mention for their fellow walkers who were definitely there to revere some shit. Some of them chatted loudly as they ambled, or shouted at their children to "stay on the trail!" or "slow down!" or "speed up!" or "don't you eat that!" They called to mind all of the ill-mannered people I've encountered hither and yon who absolutely give Americans a reputation for being loud, rude, and stupid: the woman at Stonehenge yelling to her man, "Oh my god, they look totally real!," or the Updog guys, oh shit. I had to share this doozy with Jeff and George.

This is a favorite story at our house, of a remarkable experience some years ago that befell me and my bride, the fabulous Megan Mullally. Back in 2002, Megan and I were in line with our parents one Christmas Eve checking into a fancy Santa Fe restaurant for dinner. The wait was growing tedious because the group of three frat guys in front of us, red-faced, wearing way too little clothing for the freezing weather, were loudly horsing around with some bit.

"Man, it totally smells like Updog in here," said one of the guys, Brody (I imagine).

"Oh, rad, Brody, it does. Heh. Sick. Smells *just* like Updog," answered Rafe (presumably).

"Whoa, heh heh, definitely Updog," added Tripp (unquestionably).

This was quickly getting old, when the maître d' finally bit: "What's Updog?" he innocently asked, words which he had barely gotten out before the jabroni three *erupted* into jubilant shouts of "What's up, dog? Ya-ha! What's up, dog?! Ha ha ha ha!," slapping each other high fives.

The crazy part of that instance was that, as annoyingly as the whole episode came off, we actually really enjoyed the joke, as did everyone around us. These surfer-voiced party bros, at whom we had all been rolling our eyes moments beforehand, now had us all smiling and nodding at one another begrudgingly. Americans. Nuance.

The loudmouths at Hidden Lake were not quite so cute, I'm sorry to report, but just like on so many bad days on the internet, there were adorable animals coming to our rescue. The stars of the walk were a number of very cute silver-bellied marmots, furry midsize mammals with the personality perhaps of a curious beaver. Of these marmots, a thirtysomething dad up ahead on the trail kept erroneously but enthusiastically yelling to his group, "A badger! You guys, check it out! A badger!" He was so loud, the epitome of an audience member oblivious to the grief he was causing his fellow participants. We three brothers looked at one another, narrowed our eyes, and increased our pace to escape the dumbass.

* * *

I t was an easy walk that morning. It occurred to me that our guide, Jon, was testing us with this opening maneuver. From our reactions to the day's scenery and level of difficulty, he would have a much better chance of correctly discerning our degree of relative comfort in the rugged environs of the park, thereby suiting the rest of the week's activities to better fit our needs and preferences. This was also a brilliant bit of psychological strategy from a professional outdoorsman who preferred to rise early and beat the crowd in every possible circumstance, but might find his propensity for promptness hampered by the soft morning habits of the city folk in his tender. By turning us loose on the Glacier Park trail populated the most like a shopping mall, he could then say going forward, "Oh, you didn't like the guy hollering 'Badger'? Well, then we'll need to get up and hit the trail by six thirty a.m. to avoid those folks." He needn't have worried in our case.

Many of the pedestrians we dealt with on that morning were utilizing a gait that in fact reminded me of well-fed mall-walkers, grazing along with no particular need to achieve an objective beyond gazing upon the displays of retail capitalism. I have been given to understand that the average visit to a national park is only half of one day, which I guess is not that different from a day hanging out at the mall, except that this bullshit park lacks a proper food court and a babyGap. This half-day statistic gets at the heart of what I think is wrong with the way we look at nature, because we treat it like an attraction at a theme park.

"Hidden Lake? Can we see it from the car? No? How far do we have to walk? Not too far? Okay, cool."

I feel like national and state parks of all sizes, as well as national seashores, preserves, and forests, can come across to our simple brains like any random "sight," as in "We should take in the sights."

"Have you seen the observatory? It's so dope, and there's an Egon Schiele exhibit at LACMA, oh my god and you have to see Joshua Tree. It's so cool, these rocks?"

Now, although my tone may sound a bit derisive, I am reasonably sure I have uttered these words, and others like them. I'm not sure we know, sometimes, the difference between going to the woods and going to M&M's World in Times Square, and perhaps we could reexamine the ways in which we apprehend "the outdoors." If nothing else, we could start with understanding the difference between "works of nature" and "works of humankind"? I was once hiking solo in Arizona, lost in a red rock reverie as I trudged along, intoxicated by the smell of the sage. My quietude was pretty quickly ruined, however, as a large pink Jeep full of eight tourists came roaring up a very rough road across the washed-out river gully I was skirting. My first question would be "What in the hell is the enjoyable part of being jostled by boulders and potholes until the fillings have all fled your teeth?"

It's kind of like the difference between seeing the miniature Eiffel

Tower in Vegas versus the actual structure in Paris, which is a city in France. I've argued with folks in my hometown when they are singing the praises of Las Vegas in general, and specifically getting to see things like a facsimile of said tower, or the mini version of New York City that is the New York–New York casino, complete with a one-third-scale Statue of Liberty. I have piped up and said, "Well, you should check out the real thing in either of those cases," and they have looked at me like I was an abject idiot, like I was the one missing the whole point, and I suppose I was. For them, I think the attraction is that someone has gone to the trouble of *reducing* these larger, messier, *real* destinations and then lined their simplified avatars up conveniently in a row on the Vegas Strip, where they can be briefly and efficiently ogled from the comfort of a three– to five–Busch Light buzz. They will gladly pay to *not* go to New York or Paris, and instead enjoy the several sinful delights available in the radius of a few Vegas city blocks. I describe to them a Parisian street crêpe and they remind me that they already know how to make pancakes where everybody speaks English, thank you very much, and I have to remember that that's okay. Everyone should get to like what they like, and that's perfectly fine, but for my part, I'd suggest that much greater pleasure can be derived if you get *out* of the Jeep and discover your own experience of the trail, or the forest, or the mountain.

It didn't take too long for the morning's populace to disperse along the mile-and-a-half route to the overlook, so once we put some distance between us and the other hikers, the real show started, and that main event was the jaw-dropping scenery. After traveling into Montana from our respective homes (Chicago for Jeff, Syracuse for George, and LA for me), hustling our gear into the charming old lodge the night before, meeting Jon, and masticating our way through a breakfast lousy with (you guessed it) huckleberries, then driving a solid forty-five minutes into the park and ending with the obstacles of parking lot and people, all of the hurdles were finally out of the way.

The mountains. The sky. The clouds. The trees. The marmots (!) and eventually the lake were arranged in such a way as to render us silent for long stretches as we merely hiked and gaped at them. Have you gone out to a restaurant for an amazing meal of a few courses, a repast that you have perhaps heard about, even seen pictures of, but before the first appetizer even comes the waiter brings warm bread rolls and some soft, salted European butter that looks and smells so delicious that you eat a heavenly bite and declare, "Oh my god, I could just have this," in the indulgent knowledge that there are more delights to come? This walk was the buttered rolls of our impending Glacier feast. Turning away from the parking lot—the last visual outpost of manufactured human ugliness—we felt the wind and sun upon our faces and were transported as we saw the mountain goats skipping nimbly up the slopes, do-si-do-ing between ponderosa and lodgepole pines as we traversed below them.

This feast to my senses washed over me completely, as though the mountain breeze were actually washing the accumulated grime of daily life from my very spirit. I smiled at Jeff and George and described to them why this scene felt surprisingly familiar. It reminded me, I said, of a special moment that takes place during the trip my family has taken every summer since I was six years old, a fishing vacation in northwestern Minnesota. As soon as I can every year upon arriving, after we have unloaded our groceries and put the trailered boats into the water, I get onto the lake with my dad and others, and we motor out to an appropriate spot to begin our yearly offering of nightcrawlers to the pike and panfish gods. We shut off the motor and drift, or drop an anchor, depending on the breeze, and our boat undulates slowly in the silent flow of the lake, as we almost melt. Our troubles certainly do. We unstring the everyday worries that hold our necks and shoulders taut, and cast our eyes upon the lush conifer forest, sandwiched by the blue-green expanses of water and sky. The air is fresh and sweet, and we sip great drafts of it through our teeth (minding the bugs), and our bodies seemingly transform from the practical, robotic machines that drive our cars and wash our dishes and type our emails, into furry mammals that feast and fart and belong upon this water and in these woods.

It was a markedly similar sensation that struck me there upon the trail to the Hidden Lake Overlook, and not just because I slapped a mosquito on the back of my neck. What occurred to me was the sensibility that seems to be shared by most, if not all, of the people I know when it comes to achieving the distinct pleasure I was now feeling. I have felt it in many places, scenically and geologically disparate places, but although far apart, the characteristic that these places share is simply the way in which they present the natural world, at some distance from home, in a place that is free, happily, from the trappings of convenience that somehow simultaneously free us and shackle us to our spots.

The aforementioned John Muir was instrumental in establishing this notion in our country with his great love of the mountains and deserts of the American West. In 1903 he persuaded president and fellow nature enthusiast Theodore Roosevelt to join him on a three-night camping trip to an exceptionally picturesque valley in California's High Sierra range, known as Yosemite. With eloquent articles in publications like *The Century* magazine and *The Atlantic*, Muir extolled the virtues of nature's masterworks and broached the idea of preserving these areas as accessible parks for the public. While generally a wonderful inspiration on the surface, the establishment of parks would cement the eradication of Indigenous people from their historical land and call for the removal of livestock (he actually referred to sheep as "hoofed locusts"). With the ardent support of President Roosevelt, Muir made what has been called "America's Best Idea" a reality. Today, there are sixty-three national parks, and while their histories and Muir's "hoofed locusts" perspective certainly contain quite a bit of trouble, the grandeur he so ardently advocated for preserving is certainly never in question.

I solemnly comprehended what John Muir meant when he said of this park in which I now trudged, "*Wander here a whole summer, if you can . . . and the big days will go uncounted . . . it is easily and quickly reached by the Great Northern Railroad. Get off the track at Belton Station, and in a few minutes you will find yourself in the midst of what you are sure to say is the best care-killing scenery on the continent—beautiful lakes derived straight from glaciers, lofty mountains steeped in lovely nemophila-blue skies and clad with forests and glaciers, mossy ferny waterfalls in their hollows, nameless and numberless, and meadowy gardens abounding in the best of everything. . . .*" (I looked up *nemophila* and was rewarded with the discovery that it's a genus of small blue and white flower mostly found in the western part of North America, and that most of the species named in this genus contain the phrase "baby blue eyes.")

Halfway back to the parking lot, Jon finally caught up with us and, hearing the tale of our hike, was gratifyingly incensed at the badger guy. He began to lay some more of his park "knowledge" on us, as though we hadn't just been powerfully transformed into Montana magi by gazing into the unfathomable cyan depths of Hidden Lake. There were no grizzlies to be seen, incidentally, until I realized that I was being too literal. The grizzlies were *within* the three of us, harvesting the trout and salmon leaping from our creative streams, and munching gloriously upon them in a way and for a reason that made this metaphor even slightly worth it. I had a feeling it was going to be a good week.

3

AVALANCHE LAKE

It was still fully dark at six thirty a.m. when we set off on the six-mile out-and-back trail to Avalanche Lake, and you can bet your Yeti thirty-six-ounce Rambler water bottle with Chug Cap that we were the only ones on the trail. Or so we thought, until we immediately ran into a lanky solo hiker with a huge pack, shining his headlamp on the trail map in its substantial wooden frame at the trailhead. He told us his name was Mark, and as we bid him good morning, he mentioned how relieved he was that we weren't "power hikers" so he could maintain a "visual distance."

"What the fuck was that supposed to mean?" Jeff asked as we set off through the moon-dappled forest. We three had no idea what a power hiker was, but that ignorance did nothing to prevent us from taking offense at the suggestion that we visibly didn't qualify as such.

Jon explained that Mark would stay far enough behind us so as not to worry either our experience or his own, while keeping close enough that we would be handy to him in the case of injury or a bear. This prompted some quick questions on our part about safety, specifically of our bodies, when dealing with bears, specifically the occupants of this very park, black bears and grizzlies. A portion of our insecurity stemmed from the local tradition of answering such queries with dark humor. For example, I heard from a teenager in the lobby of our lodge, who was setting out warm cookies:

"When you spot a bear, you know how you tell a black from a grizzly? The first thing you should do is climb a tree to get a good look at it, and from the bear's behavior you can determine the species. If it's a black bear it'll climb up the tree to get you, but if it just stands up and shakes the tree until you fall out, it's a grizzly." The cookies were very good, anyway, thank you very much, Trevor, you sadistic bastard.

Jon was no stranger to this practice of unnerving bear comedy, and his tale was all the more hair-raising, delivered as it was on a dark and chilly predawn trail. Even as he spoke, bears could have been all around us, ready to enjoy some semisoft, liberal artist breakfast carpaccio!

"A couple novice hikers ask the wizened lady running the hiking shop if there are bears in this area. She replies, 'Yes, you're heading into bear country. We got black bears and grizzlies, so you'll want some bear bells, which are golf-ball-size jingle bells you hang from your backpack so that the bears can hear you coming and ostensibly avoid you. Then, in case those don't work, you should have some pepper spray to fend off an attacking bear.' The hikers paled a bit and then asked the woman how to tell the difference between black bears and grizzly bears.

"'Well,' she said, 'it's easy. Look for their scat. If it's full of bear bells and smells like pepper, it's a grizzly.'"

After relishing the pall of terror he had just cast over our group, Jon then reversed course with some comforting guide-speak about how we might *see* bears in the park this week, but the chances of a dangerous or scary encounter were remarkably slim. Since 1967 there had been only ten bear-related fatalities in the park, with only a few of them involving hikers, and because we were four medium-to-large males sometimes engaged in gripping conversation, our noise and scent presence would go a long way toward protecting us. Basically, Jon told us, the best way to *invite* a bear attack is to go alone, then run on trails as silently as possible to up your chances of surprising a bear or a family of them.

This was reasonably good, reassuring intel, but just as we were feeling that things might turn out okay for us, and that perhaps even lonely, thin Mark would survive his idiotic solo jaunt eightyish yards behind us, Jon then gave us the straight dope on the only deterrent that has proven even slightly effective in repelling ursine attackers, commonly known as "bear spray." You might recognize this product as the substance famously used by rioters in the attack on our nation's capitol on January 6, 2021. Jon sported a can of the stuff in a holster on his belt. There is a triggered nozzle atop the can allowing the user to spray a steady cone of fog between them and the charging animal, and the most badass version of this product yielded by an internet search tells me that a 10.2-ounce can will shoot this liquid forty feet for "8 seconds of spray time!"

"So, let's just think about this for a moment," said Jon, holding his pretty wimpy-looking can of spray in an "action" position. "You stumble onto a mama grizzly and her two cubs, and she is immediately enraged and charging you to protect her babies. While absolutely shitting yourself, you pull this can out and deploy this foggy cone for about the length of two pickup trucks. It would take a she-bear about two strides to cover that ground, and she's on you." On top of that, he pointed out the medium-light breeze blowing across the trail at the moment and said that it would render the spray useless if we attempted to shoot it right now at a bear crosswind up the trail, so like much of life, it's an absolute crapshoot.

Jon cited a 2008 study that said bear spray is effective about 90 percent of the time in stopping an attack before contact occurs. But, again, that's if you wait for the bear to get close enough for the spray to hit it before it blows away. I think it's worth noting that Jon doesn't pack a firearm when guiding in the lower forty-eight states, which made me feel more comfortable than any of the information he was relaying. His gunless belt said to me that he didn't think we'd be in danger. That said, Jon did assert, "If the conditions are less than favorable for spray, six shots of forty-four Magnum can do a pretty good job of persuading the bear that the meal is not worth the cost. Bear spray is effective on nine out of ten bears but you'll be happy to have a firearm for that one, especially if it's a griz."

He went on to point out that anytime food is involved in a way that makes a bear feel protective of it, the bear will be more dangerous. However, if the bear is overstimulated while trying to get food, a human will not even blip its radar. A bear feeding on a winter-kill elk in the spring: Stay very far away. A bear gorging itself during the salmon run: You can get surprisingly close without alarming them. Apparently bears can become besotted with overeating and they have been known to wallow in their kill, consuming more and more meat and fat, even once it has turned rancid, whereupon they will puke it up, then sleep it off awhile, then wake up and resume stuffing their faces, vomiting, etc.

Jeff said, "I've been known to do that with pizza, on tour. Everybody knows you get two hotel beds, one's yer sleepin' bed and one's yer eatin' bed."

We laughed a little too readily through countenances that bore the hard-boiled admission that we had all known such depravity as the scene at which Jeff had just hinted . . . and then some. I glanced at George for support or solidarity, but he could not meet my gaze. Sensing the day suddenly teetering toward the glutton's mozzarella darkness, Jon then skillfully salvaged the mood with the sort of deft hand on the mood tiller that makes a great wilderness guide and pointed to the skyline of peaks. "Check it out. What's really cool about this mountain range is that we're in a single fault line. It's a pretty big park, and it's a pretty primitive park. But it suffers from some of our management issues that you'll see at the earlier national parks."

We then turned the conversation to Teddy Roosevelt, a favorite historical character of mine, and learned that most presidents named two or three national parks or monuments during their presidencies, but Theodore (who despised being called Teddy) Roosevelt Jr. named about eighty-five of them. According to Jon, there was a meme that the rangers kept posted in their office: Teddy Roosevelt walks through the woods and slaps signs upon them reading "Monument! Monument!" every time he sees a tree he likes.

Unfortunately, but keeping well within our theme of human nuance, Roosevelt had some terrible ideas as well. As Jon told it, there are two ideas he had that dictated his sensibility of the national parks. One of which the park staff still follows, and one they don't. The one they don't follow, thankfully, is his vision of public land on a national scale being like the hunting preserves that the queen of England has, but for the common man. "Can you imagine trying to hike in a national park, being blasted at wherever you go?"

"We need," Teddy wrote in 1893, "in the interest of the community at large, a rigid system of game laws rigidly enforced, and it is not only admissible, but one may almost say necessary, to establish, under the control of the State, great national forest reserves, which shall also be breeding grounds and *nurseries for wild game; but I should much regret to see grow up in this country a system of large private game preserves, kept for the enjoyment of the very rich. One of the chief attractions of the life of the wilderness is its rugged and stalwart democracy; there every man stands for what he actually is, and can show himself to be."*

On one hand, he had the foresight to understand that lands in which wild species could continue to flourish must be set aside and preserved. Initially, this "preservation" was pretty counterintuitive—conceived to allow the beasts of the field and birds of the air to survive in healthy numbers so that Roosevelt and other like-minded hunters could then have the pleasure of killing them. The nuanced hits just keep coming. Fortunately, that idea came and went, as it became clear that the blossoming American population would quickly drive every species to extinction, like we nearly did with the bison.

"Still," Jon continued, "many of the parks unfortunately suffered from a very long period of planned de-predation. In the early 1900s, we knew just enough to get in trouble. We know these animals hunt these animals, so let's kill all these first animals. Glacier Park fell victim to that, particularly its large grizzly population." So, whether hunters were killing game in the mountains or killing off the pestilent bears, cougars, and wolves that were guilty of too-successfully harvesting the prizes that the hunters sought, fortunately the practice was hugely curtailed before these creatures were completely eradicated.

The second great idea Jon was referencing, which we still hold to today, is that these places are our crown jewels. "Teddy came up with that great line. The natural beauty of this country is our crown jewels, and we should put them on display. It's a common misconception that the primary purpose of our parks is preservation. It's really preservation mixed with access."

Access for whom, though? Reflecting on Jon's words now, that's the history we know, that it was America's Best Idea. We're taught to think of John Muir and George Bird Grinnell and their ilk almost as folk heroes, for all of the substantial gifts they gave to this country. But as I was learning, both then and now, we had to deeply revise history to think of national parks as places that "man has never been," as the popular misunderstanding goes. Because in reality, many people had already been there who loved that land, and who were using it more respectfully than it has perhaps been used since, but who regardless were forcibly removed from it.

* * *

Back on the trail, we began to hear the sound of rushing water growing near, which always thrills me anyway, but it was particularly welcome as a palate cleanser to the imagination after picturing Jeff's furred back glistening with orange-red tomato grease as he coupled in a writhing tryst with an extra-large stuffed-crust meat-lover's. Soon enough, the stream's cacophony was so loud that we had to shout at one another to be heard over it.

We came upon Avalanche Creek, the Platonic ideal of what I would have pictured when reading the words *mountain stream*, except the color of the water itself was beyond my comprehension, or at least beyond the reach of my paltry arsenal of adjectives. Where the flow ran shallow enough, the water was crystal clear, allowing the multicolored creek stones in reds, ochres, and a few scattered blue-greens to pleasantly twinkle. Deeper than six or eight inches, though, the perpetual, wet barrage took on a frosty light green hue that bespoke a definition of *fresh* that every toothpaste and soda pop commercial in history has tried and failed to evince. If it were a sample chip at the paint store, it might be called "Elrond's Mouthwash" or "Faerie Spunk," which may or may not be redundant. Let's just say it was luminescent and bewitching.

The fellas patiently stood by while I sat on a rock and lost myself in the sight and the sound and the smell, and inscrutably, the feel of this exciting rush. It stands to reason, say I, that even though you can't credibly *demonstrate* the exceptional motion of the humidity swirling 'round within and without your body, the phenomenon also cannot be denied. It's damn bracing, says me, and also says John Muir: *"The rivers flow not past, but through us, thrilling, tingling, vibrating every fiber and cell of the substance of our bodies, making them glide and sing."* This creek made me feel the way I've seen some fellow humans appear when staring at a Taylor Swift video. *Smitten* don't quite cover it.

As we followed the creek uphill and therefore upstream through a forest of ancient western hemlock and red cedar, we came to a strange clearing in the trees. It appeared as though a giant had swung her Brobdingnagian hiking boot back and kicked a long, shallow trough through the trees, piling up the accumulated trees and root balls in a massive heap at the end of the alley of destruction.

"Avalanche chute," was all Jon said, and a somber awe settled upon us. Imagining the sheer force of what must have been an enormous mass of snow, ice, and debris thundering down the adjacent southern slopes of Mount Cannon, enough to bulldoze an entire section of forest in one sweep, was sobering.

Every few years on our family fishing trip, we misgauge the weather and it blows up a blustering storm while we're well out on the lake, a mile or three from the safety of our dock and cabins. Fortunately, we've always managed to make it back to shore, sometimes motoring almost only by feel in the thrall of blinding, driving rain, navigating larger swells and chop than one should ever attempt to master on a clumsy pontoon, all while the muscular wind heartlessly impels us in any direction but home.

I thought of that feeling, and the good fortune we'd cashed in, every time we got safely out of such a situation. As I comprehended the aftermath of this mighty avalanche, wandering in the resultant wound itself long after the weaponized snow had disappeared, it brought to mind the way in which our species, the first-world populace especially, has grown so inured to the natural forces that inexorably blow the fire of life into all creatures, and just how quickly that flame can be snuffed as well. I appreciate a regular reminder from Mother Nature that, because her power is unfathomable and her whims unpredictable, she demands the utmost respect. Humans like me who operate deep within the protective shell of civilization can easily forget that we are not ultimately in charge of things on planet Earth. As Wendell Berry says, *"Whether we and our politicians know it or not, Nature is party to all our deals and decisions, and she has more votes, a longer memory, and a sterner sense of justice than we do."*

To have my particular home screen refreshed with this message is a great comfort to me. One of the most persuasive aspects of the nature tourism of John Muir, I think, is relinquishing the usual control that technology has over our lives. There is something deeply pacifying about traveling my body, with or without compatriots, to remote areas for the purpose of stripping away all the distractions that worry my everyday to-do list; to bask instead in the meditative solace of Nature and her elements; to coddle myself in the knowledge that I have used my common sense, and the sense of those who have gone there before me, to not only survive but relish the feeling of safety that comes from wearing the right gear and packing the right supplies for a place that demands hands-on know-how when something goes south. I love getting out into places where the "channels" can't reach me—where my problems can't be remedied with a quick google to consult a listicle like "7 Cutest Ways to Avoid Being a Mountain Lion's Brunch" or "Splint or Amputate? 5 Top Designers Weigh In on Compound Ankle Fracture Fixes for the Spring."

By this point the sun was up and Mark had decided to roll the bear dice and blow on past us up the trail. We never saw him again. So it goes. When we eventually emerged from the forest at Avalanche Lake's lower end, my jaw dropped at yet another few unbelievable variations of teal and aquamarine in a perfectly calm lake. The deep green conifers across the way were reflected in the mirrored water to add to the magical quality of the scene. Beyond the lake and a band of pines to the south, Bearhat and Little Matterhorn Mountains continued to rise, forming the distant top of this small watershed. Beyond Little Matterhorn lay the Sperry Glacier, out of sight yet evidenced by the handful of snowmelt streams and waterfalls cascading down the rock faces to supply the lake with its water, and subsequently my beloved Avalanche Creek.

Our gang took a seat on some driftwood pine trunks that served perfectly as benches, and we watched a chipmunk getting up to some hijinks. One of my favorite things to do, no matter where I am, is to locomote my hirsute bod to a location like this, sit down, maybe enjoy a cup of black coffee or tea from my thermos, and listen. This is a pursuit that really doesn't get enough play on our modern corporate-driven channels. You rarely see messaging encouraging one to sit still, breathe, and please don't think about buying anything at all.

This is one of the most important aspects of what I think of as "wilderness." It's a place where I can marinate in the silence created by the absence of my technology. Do you ever feel that low-key anxiety when you're away from your phone, that you're potentially missing some life-or-death message? That can't be great for us, which is why I make space in my life to be away from that connectedness. Whether it's on a big trip like this or just sitting on a stump out behind my woodshop, I find that when I render myself unavailable to the channels, I am calmed beyond any silence that I can reach while in touch with the world.

If and when I can achieve some level of this, I might still hear distant traffic or an airplane, but in the immediate vicinity, a world of sounds will occur to me that moments earlier had been entirely outside of my notice. These sounds are fascinating and beautiful and whether the players are frogs or insects or birds or rustling leaves, their melody is one of health and bounty.

My usual, workaday economy of thought is rooted in a sort of commerce—weighing the pros and cons of every move and action, tallying the spoils or deficits of a given hour, day, week, or year. When I can sit in the woods and be silent and breathe and listen, this mental adding machine is switched off, and I become much more ready to be delighted by what Mother Nature has wrought, like, for example, a chipmunk.

4

HIGHLINE TRAIL

The Highline Trail is about twelve miles of awe-inspiring, high-altitude scenery that is understandably very popular. For much of its length it traces the Continental Divide, which means it's aptly named, commanding scenic views of several snow-dappled Rocky Mountain peaks for many miles around. This was our assignment for the day, and the prospect was quite thrilling compared to some of the other routes we assayed, which were also lousy with jaw-dropping eye candy, but this route took us to the top of what the Blackfeet called the "backbone of the world."

On our way to the charming picnic area next to the appropriately named Lunch Creek, Jon pointed out that most of the roads that we had driven on were supported by stone archways that were built in the 1930s by the Civilian Conservation Corps, a venerable organization created by the New Deal administration of President Franklin D. Roosevelt, along with his similarly revered WPA, the Works Progress Administration.

Both programs were specifically created to address the massive number (twelve to fifteen million) of unemployed Americans in the few years following the stock market crash of 1929. They were mostly comprised of young people, who were put to work creating and maintaining public works like parks, roads, and forests, and the WPA took on similar challenges but featured older Americans, including more artists.

Both programs were massively successful, putting eleven or twelve million Americans to work over the eight or nine years of their existence. The list of their accomplishments is simply staggering, with the CCC posting highlights like planting 1.5 billion trees, blazing 13,000 miles of park trails, and laying 125,000 miles of roads. The CCC established 711 new state parks, and all of these nationwide locations featured flood and erosion control, fire towers, lodges, cabins, shelters, and lakes. The list goes on.

Its sibling the WPA has a commensurate list of its own, including the construction of more than 4,000 school buildings, 130 hospitals, 29,000 bridges, and 150 airfields. They also paved and repaired 280,000 miles of roads. These numbers for both organizations are especially amazing when you realize that they were accumulated in less than a decade. Unlike the CCC, however, the WPA also employed tens of thousands of actors, musicians, writers, and other artists. In our modern age when even most public schools have done away with arts programs, as well as shop classes and home economics, it's pretty heady to imagine the government funding arts programs in any substantial way. They had numerous initiatives, like the Federal Art Project, the Federal Writers' Project, and the Federal Theatre Project. Taken together, these programs were known as Federal Project Number One, and their aim was to foment creativity among the citizenry while boosting morale and just providing some much-needed escapism during the Depression.

I've enjoyed so many beautiful, lasting works of taste and quality created by the CCC and WPA across the country, eighty or ninety years later. Not only did I enjoy the shelters and lodges and trails, on that day and on various other trips with my family, but in the course of touring the nation several times for humorist shows and book events, I was always moved when I saw these accomplishments, from the Hoover Dam to the restoration of the Statue of Liberty, to the San Antonio River Walk, to any number of the 1,371 incredible murals that were painted by 850 artists, including Diego Rivera, Jackson Pollock, Lee Krasner, Mark Rothko, and Willem de Kooning. One hundred sixty-two of the artists were women, which is notable for the time period but still pretty shameful, although not nearly as damning as the paltry number of Black artists: three. Most of the murals were in post offices or other federal buildings, and, fun fact, they inspired the murals done in *terribly* poor taste in the hallways of Pawnee's city hall at my old job, the TV show *Parks and Recreation*. The scenes depicted in our murals were meant to point out, lightheartedly, the ways in which we white folk have been just reprehensible to every other group of people over the years. In fact, a mural depicting 850 muralists, with 162 of them women, and 3 lonely Black artists off to one side of, let's see here . . . 685 white guys, would have fit right in, in the hallway of reprehensible behaviors we have exhibited over the years, including—fun fact—this year!

Right now is an especially interesting time to think once again about the CCC and WPA, considering the Biden administration's plan to create some new version—one focused upon preparing for and alleviating climate change, both the change that's coming and the storms, be they fire or ice, that are already here. Both financially and in overall scope, Biden's plan for jobs is but a mere fraction of what FDR managed to achieve, but it's a start, and as a great man once said, you miss 100 percent of the shots you don't take. Biden's plan also has the opportunity to improve on those 1930s numbers and include a much more diverse collection of Americans. However it turns out, I'm in favor of "making." I think that a government that funds creative social programs like the WPA and the CCC is going to deliver a much-needed dose of medicine to an extremely bifurcated population. Theatre is the mirror held up to society, and any self-improvement course must begin with an honest recognition of one's own failings. These programs were pretty amazing the last time we did it, so I wholeheartedly vote that we follow FDR's lead and put our unemployed to work on the American infrastructure, in all its iterations, including some artworks this time, too.

Jon went on to detail the different projects required to make this glorious but vast acreage slightly more accessible to the public, but not too accessible. That meant building only a few roads; a handful of re-mote chalets to provide hikers with shelter from the elements, but few other amenities; and the occasional park-sponsored pit toilet, or out-house. Successfully utilizing any public bathroom facility depends upon your cleanliness and your kindness, as well as that of your neighbors. If those who came (or "went") before you have decent manners, then you might avoid the main terror of park toilets: OPPPTYB (Other People's Poop Particles Touching Your Butt). We were advised that, for those of us who would rather eschew the outhouse, we could also engage in the use of either "cat holes" or "hot-bagging." Those two terms are, I believe, sufficiently self-explanatory. All cringing and kidding aside, the proper disposal of personal waste (or "wolf bait") is a very important health and safety issue on the trail, for reasons of water pollution and the potential spread of pathogens.

Let's return to something more appetizing. Not only was Jon our hiking guide, (potty) trainer, and local historian, but he was our lunch daddy as well. After some mild consultation the night before to discover that we were all three of us pretty game eaters, he showed up with a cooler full of cold cuts and other sandwich fixin's, which he spread out on a table-like flat rock. I don't know about you, but there are few things that get my motor running like sitting out in the crisp air near a creek that is not quite chuckling but certainly tittering, and eating a respectable ham-and-Swiss sandwich on rye with lettuce, red onion, pickle, and mayonnaise. This meal, including potato chips (straight-up sea salt Kettle chips; what kind of asshole do you take me for?), is simple, delicious, and fortifying. These tried-and-true comestibles are winning because their quality is undiminished by eating them out of a cooler on the side of a mountain. This grub was also guilt-free, since we were about to burn more calories than we had consumed by hiking an arduous distance and/or incline. Lunch Creek is where it's at.

After the first quarter mile, the Highline Trail becomes an absolute ledge cut into a vertical rock face. The path is only six to eight feet wide for three-tenths of a mile or so, with nothing but air between you and the Going-to-the-Sun Road one hundred or more feet below. The park has attached a hand rope along the inner wall of the path so you can hold tight to safety in the case of disorienting acrophobia (fear of heights). We found the dangerous stretch to be no big deal, although lightly thrilling, so long as we watched where we put our feet.

In fact, it occurred to me that this circumstance was precisely what I was after on this trip, or on almost any trip I take into "the Great Outdoors." So many decisions that I make in my life have to do with establishing safety and comfort for myself and my loved ones, which I think is sort of the default human setting, right? When presented with a choice, we tend to choose the option that will make us generally feel physically better, right? Really, like all life on Earth, we're programmed to keep ourselves and our bloodlines alive, so as to perpetuate the successful proliferation of our particular genes.

That's why, when we get ourselves out of that so-called comfort zone into an exhilarating situation like sauntering along a mildly scary mountain ledge, we exclaim, "Whew! Now I feel alive!" Domesticity is a funny thing. I'm certainly a fan. It's a consolation, generally, to be sought, but then once attained, it can immediately flip the script and become stifling. If we're lucky enough to have some perspective, we understand that our choices depend upon a great deal of nuance. We strategically time our "getaways" to coincide with the sands of patience running out in the hourglasses of our civility, so we're able to reset those calming qualities before we "punch" our "fists" through our "closet doors."

Now, in the case that you're *unable* to leave town before the volcano of your roid/road/Zoom rage goes boom, here comes some keen self-help advice: Break up your cycle. Get out of your rut. Find a way in your normal setting to "feel alive." One thing I'll do is get up early and see the sunrise from my yard, or for some bonus points, from my roof or a nearby hilltop. Jump in a chilly swimming pool! If it belongs to your neighbor, experiment with not telling them. Don a thong and maybe a midriff tank and head to the post office. I have not tried that one yet but I'll bet it won't be boring. Goosing myself out of normal, daily redundancies helps me to stay open and curious to the ever-shifting world around me.

* * *

Speaking of comfort zones, the conversation with my comrades that day led my thoughts to the long-running national debate about the cultural appropriation and racist representation of Native American culture and imagery, especially in sports, an argument in which I was soon to participate, concerning my own beloved Minooka High School and our mascot of the "Indian." The school paper is called the *Peace Pipe Chatter*. The kids' football league is the Chanooka Braves. The breakfast diner where my grandpa Ray presided over his group of friends known as the Liars' Club was the TeePee Hut. So, we're deep in it. Here in 2021, it's not exactly news that this symbology is unquestionably offensive to the Indigenous peoples of this nation. So I was not surprised to learn that there was a petition happening to change the mascot in my own small Illinois town. At the behest of one of my five charismatic nieces, I weighed in on the topic on social media, or perhaps I should say I waded in—to the cesspool of opinion surrounding it.

The particular issue at hand, on a massive, national scale, involves the depiction of Native Americans as warlike entities in sports, most clearly evinced in the teams known as "Warriors" or "Braves" or "Savages" or the like, or the simply racist "Redskins." I confess, I had not given the matter much thought over the years beyond being aware of it and agreeing with what seemed like the obvious program of social correction. When I was at the University of Illinois in the early nineties, there were protests directed at the school's mascot—the sports teams are the Fighting Illini, and the specific complaint was with the mascot Chief Illiniwek. When I was there, the Chief was portrayed by a compact, redheaded male gymnast, clad in a buckskin suit with a lot of ceremonial-looking beads, moccasins, and a massive feathered headdress. It's one of those many nuances of (white) society that many people don't really think about until someone points it out, like performing in blackface or making slanty eyes to mock Asians, for example. It simply never came up in the 1980s, before we had the internet to make us aware that we were being extremely shitty to a large portion of the population, no matter who we were stereotyping.

Somebody, presumably a Native American person, said, "Hey, that little white dude doing back handsprings dressed as though he's supposed to somehow represent my elders who were nothing but fucked over by this country? That's pretty fucked up." Then, those of us with ears heard that, looked at him, and said, "Oh, wow, yeah, that's totally insane." I would have assumed that the Chief had been given the heave-ho summarily, but I just checked, and it took the school another sixteen or so years until they dumped him, in 2007.

"But there are a zillion teams with those names! And these schools actually honor their mascots!" are a couple of the main arguments coming from the ignorant, a group in which I, I repeat, belong. This tribal ignorance, I feel, is one of the most important aspects of recognizing the good and bad effects of our own human nature, and we'll see it pop up again and again in this book.

Put simply, it is in our "nature" to make ourselves comfortable as a people. For example, we'll settle in a region of the Midwest and prepare it for agriculture by clearing trees and brush, and eliminating the apex predator animals like wolves and bears—oh, and also killing or driving off the Indigenous peoples who were already living in the region. Then we'll put down our roots, build our split-level ranch houses, our Starbuckses and our Jiffy Lubes, and we'll open our schools and name the sports teams after appropriate creatures that are known for their vicious, violent natures. Cougars, bears, gators, and eagles, and so forth. And Indians. And include a lot of "scalping," don't forget that—"Come on, Indians, scalp the Coal City Coalers!"; tomahawks are also prevalent. Later in this book we'll hear a bit about scalping, but only a very little bit, because it's truly fucked up, and I am a humorist, not Cormac McCarthy. The reason we're able to casually suggest that we scalp one another, or goad the sports crowd into performing a mimed tomahawk attack with a chopping arm is because we have long since forgotten that there are actual people involved. Historically, we absolutely *had* to vilify the Indigenous peoples in order to justify our depraved actions toward them. By diminishing the Native Americans thus and reducing them to cartoon bad guys (the opposite of good-guy cowboys) we allowed ourselves to disregard them. By now, our refusal to change these mascots is simply our way of saying that *those* people don't matter. We long ago drove them from the county and now have the temerity to ask, "If they care so much, why aren't we hearing from them at the county board meeting?"

My hometown of Minooka, Illinois, counted eleven thousand souls, give or take, in the latest census, including about 92 percent white people, and between 2 and 3 percent Black people, leaving a solid 5 to 6 percentage points to be divvied up between the other nonwhite folks. The US Census even lists "Native Hawaiian or other Pacific Islanders" as 0.2 percent in this small burgh an hour southwest of Chicago, but Native American? Zero. They are not even listed, at least before the 2020 census, when the population jumped to .1 percent. So, this place that we consider to be our place, as in "We own this land. It is our property," that we acquired from the previous occupants through any means but decency or fair play, to this day fails to house a single ancestor of the families that once hunted its woods and fished its streams—the same families that are represented on the sides of the football helmets and in the war cries and "Seminole chops" of the sports fans in the bleachers of our games.

Solipsism is a wonderful word, and it is perfectly applicable to we European-spawned Americans who hear and dismiss any complaint about the peaceful state of affairs in a given community. The dictionary defines *solipsism* as "extreme egotism," referring to one's inability to comprehend or credit anything that does not directly apply to oneself. So, when we hear about a petition protesting our school mascot as racist, we think that the mascot has not ever bothered us. This petition can't be sincere, it must have some dastardly ulterior motive, because I don't mind one bit the Indians depicted on our school gymnasium walls and football helmets, in a "noble" profile, resplendent in their ceremonial feather headdresses. It's the Noble Savage, isn't that a thing?

In order to escape the aforementioned ignorance of which I have been a participant, as a former citizen of this place, I need to step outside of my solipsism. I must open my ears and listen to the grievances of the Indigenous folks, the Black folks, the gay folks, the Latinx *familias*, and anyone else who does not reside within the group that has traditionally been, by far, the majority in American communities throughout our young history: again, the straight, white, Christian people.

Once outside the group of Americans who believe that our civilization was designed for their benefit exclusively, I find it much easier to walk a mile in the shoes of others, and if those others are experiencing discrimination, I find that fact much easier to comprehend once I don't make it about me. Many angry replies to my Minooka petition sentiments suggested that I should simply "shut up," but I would counter that a) that only makes you sound guilty, and b) the path to justice and equality for all Americans and ultimately all earthlings is going to require *all* of us safe, white, unoppressed softies to shut the hell up.

Scattered throughout this thread of angry comments were occasional flashes of reason and rationality, especially from one very patient fellow who doggedly attempted to refute all of the ignorance being hurled at me and at the issue. He kept urging all of the people hating on me and on the issue to watch a video by a fellow named John Kane, entitled "We Are Not Your Mascots," so I watched it. He's a Native

American activist, a member of the Mohawk tribe, and he states the case quite plainly from the point of view of the only people we should be asking about this issue—the Native Americans being depicted.

Here is where I would urge all of the non–Native American people with strong opinions about this subject to break out of our solipsistic bubbles and simply do a little homework. I kept reading—it didn't take long—and I found a few more great citations from people like Adrienne Keene, a citizen of the Cherokee Nation and faculty member at Brown University's American studies and ethnic studies department. She said, "I would be honored and respected as a Native person if our treaties were honored, if our sovereignty was recognized, if our lands were taken back into Indigenous hands. Those are the type of things that honor me as a Native person, not a stereotypical image combined with a racial slur. I think what happens is that when Native youth or Native people are look-ing at these images, even if they're not a wild-eyed, grinning caricature, it limits the possibilities of what they can see for themselves and reflects what broader society thinks of them as a Native person. So it doesn't matter if it is an 'honorable' image or representation, it still is limiting."

There are between two thousand and three thousand sports teams with mascots of this ilk remaining in our country, but many have al-ready been successfully changed over the past few decades, including the recent step into decency for the Washington pro football team and the Cleveland major league baseball team. At last report, no towns or col-leges or pro teams were bankrupted or otherwise damaged by the re-quired rebranding of jerseys and helmets. Apparently we humans are able to feel just as much pride in our volleyball-spiking Eagles as we once did when they were called Braves. All we had to do was listen to an op-pressed group and respond with empathy.

If we are going to ever be great as a nation of people, this step will be an imperative part of our improvement, and it will necessarily always need to remain a living step—an ever-evolving process, just as any living organism is ever-evolving.

None of us should be insisting we are 100 percent right about these issues, especially because the dominant, white culture that has been in power so long has been wrong in almost every way, and finding out what actually is right will require a lot of listening and then the instituting of new ideas.

Meanwhile, we'll need a new sports team in my hometown! I'm pitching the Minooka Dovetails, Minooka Sledgehammers, Minooka Hedgehogs, Minooka Woodchucks, Minooka Beavers, or Minooka Bacon-Wrapped Shrimp.

Back to the trail—instead of the somber, more cloistered feeling in the forested areas of our first two hike locations, we were now atop the world, doing our best to fully take in the fully un-take-in-able grand scope of the views. As we traipsed along in the sun and the breeze, full of ham, we were absolutely on cloud nine (a figure of speech that is said to have originated in London in 1896, when Sir Ralph Abercromby's attention coincided with the newly published *International Cloud Atlas*. The scientific document listed the cumulonimbus as cloud number nine, the tallest possible cloud. I love it—it wasn't enough to say "*I'm on top of a cloud*," but it had to be qualified by specifying that one was on top of the categorically *tallest* of clouds).

The perfectly serviceable ingredients in our recent lunch had led to a conversation about the sourcing of food items in our lives, because although we were a very long way from a Whole Foods, or a *good* organic grocery store for that matter, all four of us had a healthy curiosity about the subject. Most of the intelligent people I run into agree on what are the big-ticket, modern questions to which we should be devoting our collective attention. One is obviously climate change: the consequences of our unhealthy exploitation of fossil fuels, and how we can convince ourselves, our leaders, and the rest of "the people" that we should take action sooner than later.

Another topic is our ever-increasing ignorance when it comes to knowing about where our food is produced and sourced, how, and by whom. Since I pretty much knew the score regarding the "enlightened" urban grocery shopping of Jeff, George, and myself, I was especially curious how a rural outdoorsman like Jon saw the topic. His answer was interesting, because sure enough, he's a lifelong hunter.

He said that he was raised as a hunter, not because his family had no other choice, but because they knew that meat they harvested themselves was much healthier than what was on offer at the local grocer's. Jon's favorite thing about hunting with his dad every year is specifically the sense of responsibility and proficiency they display when it comes to breaking down a buck and using every possible part of the animal. They maintain an understanding of the local deer population and the importance of culling the overpopulated species. He and his dad know the satisfaction that comes from providing one's own sustenance in a conscientious way, whether it's venison or turnips. They deal directly with the bounty of Mother Nature, cutting out all of the middlemen and -women, and thereby a lot of pollution and carbon footprint.

Jon was deer hunting with some friends in Oklahoma, and he almost came to blows with them over the way they processed their animals.

"They took the backstraps and the hindquarters, and that was it," he said. Jon told them, "There's at least sixty pounds of meat you're wasting, leaving it like that," to which the friends replied, "Oh, where are your Birkenstocks?"

George laughed and pointed out that using nature economically was hardly a liberal notion—Jon was defending a purely frontier (agrarian) morality, simply that nothing should go to waste whenever possible, especially with regard to a local game mammal whose life had been sacrificed so that the hunter's family might prosper. This sort of economy is literally conservative, and I, a very liberal thinker, am all for it. I do love the smell of nuance in the morning.

While it's rare that I would be with someone who would make the statement "I love to kill animals," I do have friends, and an uncle, who would say "I love to hunt" in much the same way that I love to fish but would not say "I love to kill fish." They are simply regular, consistent hunters, a practice which comes with a strict set of moral rules. My family loves fishing, and my folks freeze and then eat the fish we catch in Minnesota all year long. My uncle learned to hunt from his dad and uncle, when he was a teenager. He is a retired schoolteacher and my aunt is a retired librarian, so they weren't exactly swimming in income. Hunting has always been a way for him to provide plenty of the highest-possible-quality organic meat for his family, while spending many hours silently communing with nature. He's just a very good guy, and I powerfully admire his discipline and commitment to the morality of both hunting and fishing.

Speaking with Jon that day reminded me of the overwhelming lack of nuance in the national gun conversation—how people like him and my uncle exist in a sphere wherein their gun ownership as hunters makes perfect sense, as much sense as owning a fishing pole. But that is only one facet of a many-sided story. Both Jon and my uncle also own and maintain firearms for self-defense, which is another ball of wax entirely. A body cannot shoot up an elementary school with a fishing pole.

I heard something strange on the trail several yards behind me and turned around to see a good-sized mountain goat striding doggedly in our direction. Now, first of all, I had only seen these stately critters from more of a distance earlier in this trip. This fella was approximately the size of a small pony but built a little more like a 1970s tight end. With its rangy stride and tufted white coat, it exhibited a strong Muppet vibe, if Muppets could lower their heads and butt you off the mountain.

There wasn't much room into which we could clear off the trail, maybe one body-width, and as we stepped aside to let the goat pass I felt a combination of thrill at his proximity and unease at his proximity. The eight-to-ten-inch curved black horns atop his snow-white head had something to do with the fact that the three of us newbies held our breath.

Once the goat had passed us by, picking up his pace into a little jog, Jeff muttered a quiet, "Yeah . . . I thought so," at the volume you use to make your friends laugh while remaining absolutely certain that the goat won't hear you and abruptly come back and get in your face to ask, "You say somethin'?"

I asked Jon if that handsome goat would be good eating, to which he replied, "Come November, after a full season of grazing, it would be pretty good. 'Specially in a cast iron skillet, drizzled in butter with just a pinch of brown sugar and baked to one thirty-five. Otherwise, like now? They're still shedding their winter coats and recovering from a pretty harsh winter, very thin and not much fat on them. They would be dry and gamey."

This probably sounds funny to most of us. But just like I think that woodshop and welding and baking and sewing and so forth should be taught in our public schools as imperative parts of the curriculum of life, I also think it would do our society a world of good were we made to participate in a hunt. This would include the competent processing, or butchering, of the kill. Similarly, I believe that if we were all made to participate in the raising and subsequent butchering of a farm animal, it would quickly foment a massive shift in our national agricultural policies. Because it would serve as a poignant reminder of how this particular food stream works, like what parts of the animals we use and what happens to the "waste." For that matter, shouldn't we all also have some knowledge of where all of our waste goes? We really are inured in modern American society from being required to face not only how our food is produced and delivered to us but then how our domestic waste is transferred back into the natural cycle of decay.

I take great satisfaction in cleaning the fish I've caught. My dad taught me to do it forty years ago, and I love how clean of a system it is. In a Minnesota lake setting that appears as crisp and inviting as any beer commercial you've seen, we catch healthy panfish and then, with a fillet knife and a (relatively) skilled pair of hands, glean all of the muscle from the fish, before adding the remainder of the fish's guts to the compost pile.

5

RAFTING THE FLATHEAD RIVER

By now we had experienced a rather overwhelming amount of scenery, weather (mostly chill and lovely), and walking. It was high time for these three amigos to get out of our hiking boots and into a relaxing river raft. Or so I thought.

We met our rowing guide, Demi, along Moccasin Creek, just outside the park, where we all lent a hand lifting our raft into the calm stream that fed into the river. The sixteen-foot inflatable rubber raft was designed to carry up to ten passengers, but we were just the three of us plus Demi. Since we lacked a full complement of rowers, she attached an oar rig high up on the stern which would allow her to steer the boat with much more power than she would normally bear. I sat in the front starboard corner (right) with George in the front port corner (left) and Jeff just behind him (in his lee). I'd say we were in the bow, but I'm not certain that rafts have a bow.

As we gently propelled ourselves from the trickling creek into the middle fork of the Flathead River, Demi steered us into the current and we were off, gliding through the scenery on this small, ridiculously picturesque river that none of us (except our guide) could ever have imagined would soon plunge us into veritable maelstroms of hell. I paddled along, dazzled by the ever-shifting play of light and color in every square yard of the river, enraptured by every inch of the experience as our threesome chatted gaily. This was when Demi said, "Okay, let's start getting ready for Fluffy Kitten Rapids."

For decades, friends had been insisting that I should really try my hand at some river rafting—that I would "love it to bits." This suggestion was predicated upon the knowledge that I hail from a family of boat people, even beyond our yearly fishing trips. Whenever we can, weather permitting, we get in a boat and get out on a lake or river to engage in fishing, waterskiing/tubing, or meditative sightseeing, depending on who's at the tiller. It's a big family, so it might be any combination of siblings, aunts, uncles, and cousins. On top of that, for most of my life I have maintained an enthusiasm for paddling a canoe, which manifested itself powerfully when I built two cedar-strip wooden canoes by hand about fourteen years ago.

So, ironically, the very reason it occurs to people to urge river rafting upon me—that I love to paddle about in boats—is also why I never get around to it. If I have time that I could otherwise devote to a rafting trip, I have likely already arranged to be fishing, canoeing, or building a boat or other goodness in my shop. On paper, rafting just never sounded that different from what we were already doing. Reader, let me please advise you that it is indeed *mighty* different, and incredibly so. Take the feeling of conditional security that comes with the proper operation of a watercraft and douse it in a bucket of the stomach-churning exhilaration of a roller coaster. Imagine that log ride at a theme park, but then take it literally off the rails and occasionally plunge it beneath the mighty surging veins of current in a crystal-green, freezing-cold river.

I'll pause to point out that despite the aforementioned thrills, river rafting, even those routes described as "white water," is an extremely safe outdoor sport, logging less than one fatality in one hundred thousand participants on average. I'm no adrenaline junkie, but I do think that there is some value in experiencing a certain level of risk when visiting "the outdoors." As part of my personal campaign to prevent myself from becoming a fully soft, modern urbanite, I regularly explore places and activities outside of my comfort zone, as it were. By planning such trips, which for me have recently included hiking, cycling, skiing, running, fishing, rafting, and canoeing, I am able to test the limits of what my body can endure and how it will perform in various circumstances. This profoundly affects my health and my self-confidence, and my knowledge of navigating my existence, both at home and abroad.

As the world emerges from the widespread lockdowns of COVID-19, I think it's especially important to reestablish our relationship with risk, lest it become reduced to something resembling agoraphobia. Thanks to an understandable reticence toward getting out into the world during the pandemic, I would not want any further timidity to set in with myself and others, merely because we had not "ridden a horse" for so long. Seeking acceptable levels of risk, I think, is a great way to get "back on the horse" and reclaim our individual powers.

It was not yet clear how acceptable today's level of risk would be. The ironically named Fluffy Kitten Rapids is the first of approximately sixteen sets of rapids, varying in intensity from Class II to III, that have more accurate, satisfying names, like Can Opener, Bonecrusher, and Toilet Bowl. Demi did a terrific job of making us comfortable with the approach of each pulverizing scenario and then steering the raft with her oars to keep us safe while simultaneously working in concert with the river to thrill our pants off. The orientation of enormous boulders beneath the surface is what causes the mighty flow of virgin glacier-melt to behave in every goofy way you might imagine. My favorite ones involved the current's plunging straight down suddenly, then doing a bit of a backflip, so as we dove straight toward the river bottom, tons of brisk water washed back across us in an attempt to swipe us clean off the boat.

The breathless, blinking elation I was feeling was not too dissimilar from past live music experiences, when I had felt lost in the pleasurable sensations evoked by dancing and feeling the blood coursing through my limbs, although those moments were always assisted by one intoxicant or another. The gusto to be savored on the raft, however, required no help whatsoever. The commitment required was so encompassing that we could only spare one another the occasional glance, grinning complicit smiles in the knowledge that we were *all in* for the duration of this ride. Shouting laughter to the point of screaming punctuated each one of these thrilling and joyful obstacles, followed by sucking inhalations and exclamatory triumphs of one sort or another once the waters calmed yet again to friendlier behavior.

At one point early on, George removed his glasses and reached inside of his life jacket to place them securely in the breast pocket of his shirt. Evincing a gingery charisma that was part John Denver, part Edgar Winter, flipping the sopping locks off his forehead, he nodded sagely at me, to which I responded, "Smart." Back into the fray we plunged. As we were then coming clear of the next churning chaos, and the gallons of water cascaded off of us, I looked to my left to see George's glasses now sitting impossibly on the round inflated side of the raft *behind* his rear end, just as Jeff casually noticed them and nimbly grabbed them before the wild torrents could return to sweep them away. He had them!

The entire moment was pregnant with magical reality, fully *Through the Looking-Glass*/opening credits of *Land of the Lost*–type stuff. I mean, everything was already more twinkly and delightful than my senses could fully comprehend *before* we saw George secure his glasses in his pocket. The atmosphere was such that if you had told me the river had prised the eyeglasses from beneath his vest, sluiced them into his gaping mouth as we dove into the depths, and manipulated them through his body until, as we crested the river top once again, he neatly pooped them out of his bottom, complete with a cork-popping noise, I would have merely stated, "Aha. I was wondering." The actual fact then, that the serpentine mischief of the waves somehow transported the spectacles from their safe burrow to see them puckishly alight before Jeff, only to taunt him before snatching them away to ruin George's mojo, and subsequently our good time, shifted our expedition firmly into the realm of Faerie.

Or so they thought. Because these river dryads had not met our Jeff Tweedy. Sure, it might *seem* as though Jeff had merely looked down in front of him at a fortuitous time and had the wherewithal to pick up a pair of eyeglasses in peril. I would have sworn it was not a big deal but a perfectly ordinary feat, requiring the barest minimum of strength, coordination, and cognition, but apparently I was wrong. As Jeff pointed out to us, repeatedly, for the remaining couple of hours we paddled on the Flathead, it was a deceptively heroic achievement on his part. We weren't quite suitably astonished, in his view, and we "might just want to think again about the athletic prowess [he] exhibited in [his] golden grab, reflexes that any self-respecting cat would have been glad of," and like that. George was certainly grateful to have his eyeglasses rescued, but by the time we had heard Jeff recount his hyperbolic blow-by-blow commentary more than twice, I think George would have gladly rather spent the balance of the trip half-blind.

To be honest, George is precisely the kind of guy who could handle a ramble through the woods *without* his glasses. In fact, he'd likely come out of it with a pithy 3,500-word essay about how it took losing his glasses to bring the plight of the American honeybee into focus, or some such jewel. All three of us were pretty well traveled thanks to our respective vocations, but I daresay George's work as a journalist occasionally found him in much more precarious "real-life" scenarios than the venues where Jeff and I were generally transported to perform for people or cameras. Whether he was sleeping alone in a Fresno homeless camp or under the stars with Texas border patrol guards, or swimming in a Sumatran river so full of monkey shit that it laid him sick in bed for weeks, George's writing assignments regularly took him much farther from the realm of material comfort that we all usually enjoyed.

Think about it like this: When Jeff and I travel abroad to do our work as entertainers, the exchange of goods delivered (our music/mirth/medicine) to the recipients (audiences buying tickets plus beer/merch/bratwurst) is much more immediately realized than when George travels to gather experience and evidence to fuel or support whatever he happens to be writing, whether it's an essay for *The New Yorker,* or a short story, or what have you. In the case of a writer like him, the money does not depend directly upon the travel. With Jeff and me, however, if we don't get to the *church* on time, nobody gets paid. Therefore, we are ridiculously pampered by people whose income depends on our successful conveyance from place to place, and so if they could, the promoters would lay our pale, fleshy bottoms on climate-controlled velvet pillows and see us carried gently from place to place so as to ensure the best possible chance of seeing their own paycheck.

George, however, is usually on his own. And he *needs* to be, to successfully blend into the background of whatever scene he's scrutinizing. His destination and the people there are his artistic quarry. He cannot let his appearance, or his rental car, or any other superficial signal, betray to his potential subjects that he is going to capture them with his eyes, ears, and heart, then represent them with compassion and accuracy as best he can when he writes his intended piece.

As a person who worked for many years as a laborer, I am now painfully aware of my spotless, new white Ford Expedition when I pull into my own woodshop and park among the vehicles of my employees and neighbors, which are rarely new or spotless. I have a well-beaten Ford F-250 that lives at the shop, and when I drive it around town, I'm instantly aware of the difference in the way my fellow motorists and pedestrians perceive me.

George seems to have developed a quiet mastery of this ability to disappear amongst the people, which allows him to travel far off the beaten path in search of his literary gold. What gave him this spark for adventure? Was his innate curiosity somehow also connected to his tendency to embroider into his writing a sense of empathy?

This thought occurred to me as we got to know our guide Jon better and better each day. Although we were from very different upbringings in vastly disparate parts of the country, we found that we had much more in common than not, and we could agree on most commonsense issues. Then again we were, all four of us, cisgender, middle-aged white guys in America. One wouldn't have to travel very far at all outside of our country before looking back to find us appearing indistinguishable from each other in the middle distance. It stands to reason, then, that from the greater distance of Asia, the Middle East, or South America, we would just appear among the masses of rich white people who are not starving.

One would need to travel all the way to us, and experience us in the context of our lives, before being able to fully take the measure of us as individuals in each of our particular circumstances. By the same token, I feel like it's important for everyone to travel to other countries and experience the ways in which we humans are all the same, as well as the ways in which our cultures differ. When we can see our fellow humans in other parts of the world doing their best to do their work and love their families and have fun together one way or another, it makes empathy much easier to come by. For the many instances in which we can't travel to foreign lands, we have documentary films and writers like George to help us relate to all of humanity.

Later in the raft ride, with only a few rapids remaining, we entered a large eddy in which the swirling current slowed to feel more like a pond for a few dozen yards. Demi announced that this was an ideal place to jump in the river, should we care to feel the thrill of swimming in forty-eight-degree pristine water that had until extremely recently been frozen in a glacier a ways upstream. This sounded pretty great; she sold it well, but then again, we were pretty wiped out from the many rapids we had braved thus far, and maybe we didn't need to jump into the freezing, opalescent drink.

Jeff spoke first, citing once again his Homeric accomplishment with the eyeglasses and the toll that particular decathlon had exacted upon his reserves. He said, not unwisely, that he would pass on jumping into frigid water and then suffering the consequence of sodden clothing for the duration of the journey. This was a fair point. We were by no means dry by this juncture of the trip, but a full soaking in the river did seem perhaps a step too far.

I was about to voice my agreement with this vote for less swimming and more comfort when George turned to me and veritably twinkled his eye. It really twinkled! Veritably! He said, "Let's do it."

And I said, "Of course. Hell yes."

The river was quite deep in this segment, so our dives yielded no bottom, nor did our swimming about, above and below the surface. For a long few moments I was actually lost in the utterly exhilarating sensation, so new and stimulating it was. Cold water wakes you up to begin with, so to apprehend that bodily jolt that's better than the best triple espresso in the midst of the most picturesque water-rocks-forest-sky scenery imaginable in the company of two loving brother-friends (like sister-wives but with fewer babies) was not only a trip highlight but a life highlight. I'll never forget that sensory pinnacle of our trip to Glacier National Park, and more important, I'll never forget the inherent lesson in George's insistence that we say yes to life as hard as we could.

6

GRINNELL GLACIER HIKE

This is the big one. Everything has been leading up to this. Jon had planned the week so that our distances and inclines gradually increased in difficulty in order to condition us for today's hike to the Grinnell Glacier. Covering 10.5 miles round trip, and a rise of 1,600 feet, we art boys had our work cut out for us. If that wasn't clear already, it really hit home when Jon huddled us up in the parking lot and delivered a sedate guide speech.

"This hike is going to differ from the others in that it will put us more than two hours from definitive medical care, which means this is a backcountry hike, as opposed to a front-country hike."

He went on to basically explain that he would establish a "sphere of acceptable risk," as in "You kids stay near me," and that we would all now agree to trust his guidance when it came to navigating hazards, from crossing snowy slopes, to pushing through fatigue, to possible bear encounters. We all agreed, with minimal wisecracking, and we mothered each other through an assessment of our clothing layers, since we were starting in shorts and T-shirts but would end up in the snow on a glacier (!). After double-checking our stores of water and food, we set off.

It was about seven a.m., which meant we had few other hikers with whom to share the trail, and those who were there were as serious about this endeavor as we were. In other words, nobody was shouting "Badger!" The first section of the hike required us to perambulate through a shady aspen forest which bordered first Swiftcurrent Lake, then Lake Josephine, and the conditions could not have been more idyllic.

As we approached the far end of Lake Josephine, a charming lake boat came cruising up to a dock to unload twenty or so passengers. Jon informed us that we could have taken the boat from a lodge at the far end of Swiftcurrent Lake at the start of the jaunt, instead of walking the first couple of miles. As I've said, we Offermans love a boat ride. No matter where we are in the world, if we're deciding between two routes and one of them includes a ferry, then the decision is made. I think it's because we're a hardworking people and we don't vacation perhaps as much as we ought to. So, when what amounts to simply our commute happens to get us out on the water of a lake, river, or bay, where we can take in some scenery and feel the breeze and smell the rich, heady mix of diesel fuel and fish, well, it feels like we're getting away with something. The fact that on many ferries one can get some sort of grub and a beer also does not damage our affection.

Despite my boat-ist leaning, I was glad we had walked through the aspens, firstly just for the pure enjoyment of the setting—hearing the morning birdsong while ambling along with friends, admiring clear lake waters through trees. On top of that, I have this stubborn propensity for being a completist. For example, if I say to my bunkmates in a prison camp that I can "eat fifty eggs," even if it causes me great physical distress, you best believe I'm going to eat fifty damn eggs, with no cheating either. This has proven to be extremely the case with me and hikes for which I have a map and pertinent statistics. For some reason I apparently take it as a challenge when an app tells me that such-and-such moderate route is seven miles, and it should take three hours to finish. It's not that I want to race the suggested time, I just want to feel like I've consumed the entire feature, which also means that I eschew any proffered shortcuts. So if our guide takes us on a ten-and-a-half-mile hike, and we were to spend two miles sitting on our duffs in the extravagant pleasure of a boat, I would feel somehow cheated. Megan, my bride, loves this quality in me, when she says, "Can we go back now? I have a blister," and a look of intense consternation falls upon my mug, as I have to gently talk myself out of the idea that my wife is asking me to fail.

Once the path took us above the forest and the lakes, we entered a couple of gorgeous miles of vegetation, including cow parsnip, my beloved huckleberries, and bear grass. There was some disagreement in local opinions on whether bear grass was so called because bears like to eat it, especially the blossoms, or because bears use the leaves and stalks to line their dens. Either way, it was right pretty and quite prevalent. We did see a moose cow eating some later in the day, but I would want to collect considerably more data before suggesting we change the name to "moose grass."

Our progress proceeded relatively unhindered as we strode higher and higher up the side of the mountain valley. We passed a cool woman standing off to one side of the trail on a rock, painting the magnificent view on a small canvas perched on a little easel. She looked a bit enchanted, like she was always there, greeting passersby with mirth and mellow vibes. Her mere appearance had me half wondering, "Why am I not doing that with my life?"

We came upon a section of trail that featured a tall, sheer rock wall on the right side and a pretty good drop-off to the left of the trail—an extremely dangerous fall, if not lethal. The path was simply a horizontal shelf of the shale and limestone bedrock, maybe eight feet wide. It felt relatively safe but would have been undoubtedly safer had it not been for the waterfall tumbling down the rock wall and splashing across the footpath. The circumstance required carefully placed steps, especially once the ice-cold water began to heavily fall upon you. With calm focus, one at a time, we crossed to safety. I never felt particularly in danger, but a powerful exhilaration at the combination of the waterfall's effects and the potential hazard.

Nearing the top of our hike, we were able to look down below us at a view of Lower Grinnell Lake, and it was truly exquisite. The saturated turquoise color, surrounded by conifers, slopes, and mountain peaks, all beneath a cerulean sky patched variably with puffs of cloud, imprinted itself in my memory so effectively that I am still able to recall the exact scene and the shadows of the clouds playing across the lake's surface, rendering it endlessly fascinating to look at.

For me, this was the epitome of what John Muir was talking about in his championing of such singular natural scenery—here was a visual sensation that could only be achieved in this very anomalous and specialized location. Nature is, by definition, all around us, no matter where we are, but here was Mother Nature achieving something exceptional even for her, or so it seemed to us humans. Why is that? I wondered. What is it about this random arrangement of elements, pushed and molded into this particular configuration, that made it so much more glorious to my eye than a seemingly more mundane miracle, like watching a "plain old" tomato bloom and grow into a delicious, pendulous ball of juice and flavor?

While I was photographing the fluctuating light as it dappled the lake, Jon and George had distanced themselves up ahead a ways. Jeff was engaging in that age-old, unintentional comedy bit of trying to find a spot to safely pee when no one is coming up or down the trail. I know the proper trail etiquette says to get anywhere from fifty to two hundred feet away from the trail to "water the moose grass," but on these mountain trails one was lucky to find a safe spot even ten feet off the path, due to the steep terrain. You know how this goes: Every time Jeff would try to fire up the bilge pump, a through-hiker's head would appear from below, and he would have to uncomfortably halt the stream while pretending to nonchalantly admire some adolescent western larch.

"Hmm. Oh, hello!" he would assert, like their appearance had startled him from a botanist's reverie. "Beautiful!" he would add, about nothing in particular.

The stranger would pass and Jeff would resume, working to prime the sump pump once more, only to be thwarted again, and so on. His laments were hilarious, since it was his bladder in peril and not my own.

The laughter died out a bit soon thereafter, however, when we arrived at the top of the hike—the so-called Grinnell Glacier. When the fellow for whom this once-enormous mass of ice was named, George Bird Grinnell, arrived in this valley on a hunting expedition in 1885, he looked up and gazed in wonder upon the full 710 acres of the glacier's nineteenth-century breadth. Of course, after a century and a half of slow (and then not-so-slow) climate change, that area has shrunk to about 152 acres currently. At the end of the Little Ice Age in 1850, the area that would become Glacier National Park boasted 150 named glaciers. Today, the number of active glaciers has melted down to twenty-five, and continues to dwindle.

No matter how bleak the overall story may be, this was our *first* glacier, and so we were quite taken with it once we stopped and put on our down coats. Observing the remains of the glacier itself, tracing the topographical effects of the glacier and its runoff on the vast, entire view, and then straight freaking out at the insane rock formations beneath the glacier filled an hour with wonder and excited exclamations from us, like we were a few boys let loose in the woods for the first time.

"Awesome! You guys, come here, check it out!"

It was a lot to take in, and we were glad to then sit down on a comfy rock and put away a *bunch* of calories. My mainstays were almond butter, beef jerky, string cheese, trail mix, PB&J, and locally baked energy bars. And as I have said, there's nothing like a chilly spot for a thermos of coffee/tea. The warmth you maintain while hiking can quickly dissipate when you stop, but then when you pause for that needed rest, maybe the nurturing beverage warming your fingers and your belly is well worth the price of admission, and then some.

Well rested and fed, we repacked and shouldered our bags to begin the descent. We reapplied sunscreen, especially necessary when walking on/around snow, because of the reflection. The fast-moving, heavy clouds and the change in time only served to reinforce the truism that the scenery on the way back/down looks like an entirely new route every time. I was feeling the tax of our morning's lengthy climb in my legs, but we took our time with the pace and did our best to land each step gently.

> *You're walking. And you don't always realize it*
> *But you're always falling*
> *With each step, you fall forward slightly*
> *And then catch yourself from falling*
> *Over and over, you're falling*

And then catching yourself from falling
And this is how you can be walking and falling
At the same time

Pretty soon, the repeated landings reminded me of this, and never had these Laurie Anderson lyrics rung so true as they did that day. Even the most benign of steps would involve a drop-off of ten or twelve inches, which meant our knees, ages forty-nine to sixty, were repeatedly catching our entire weight like a shock absorber. Now, if you're a young whippersnapper of thirty-eight or forty, you probably can't yet fathom what I'm talking about, but for those of us over that healthy-and-plentiful-amount-of-connective-tissue hill, well, your knees begin to hurt when you use them thus.

Nonetheless, we took it easy so that we could continue "walking and falling" without it becoming only "falling." On the way up, we had crossed a couple of steeply pitched snow fields that were twenty or thirty yards across, by digging our boots into the icy snow sideways, so that the "uphill" edge of each boot dug a good grip into the stuff. Taking our time, it was easily done.

By the time we had returned to that spot, however, the sun had warmed the mountainside enough that the snow was softer and less ideal for the boot-edge-digging technique. Jon was understandably a bit nervous about sending the three of us across the slope, but we had all exhibited enough capability thus far that he decided we could go for it. Jeff went first, slowly and gingerly bedding his boot edges in the existing tracks from all the morning's previous hikers. The steepness of the hill made it almost possible to keep your left hand, the uphill hand, on the incline as you went, with the ground slanting away drastically downhill.

Jeff, therefore, had his Yeti water bottle dangling in his right hand, which seemed like it could become a problem if Jeff should lose his balance and need that hand to stabilize himself. Jon clearly thought as much, as he rushed up after Jeff had taken his first couple of steps and said, "Give me that bottle."

I understood Jon's anxiety, but he probably should have let him be, as it turned out that Jeff's water bottle was actually acting as a sort of counterweight in his precarious balancing of the hazard. We all froze as Jeff wobbled, ever so slightly, which was all the wet snowpack needed to fail him and allow his boots to slip out. He slid frighteningly fast on mostly snow and some gravel, handling it coolly, spreading himself out to lower his center of gravity and increase the friction drag on his extremities. Thankfully he slid to a stop after about forty feet, and we all shouted words of shock and relief. It was goddamn scary, but for just a few seconds.

Jeff was a little shaken up but quite manageably crossed the lower slope and rejoined the trail a few dozen yards on down. We all hugged him and inspected him for injuries. Nothing broken, but his right knee and shin exhibited what we used to call "road rash" (they were well abraded and bleeding, like he had wiped out on his dirt bike on pavement). Jon produced an ample supply of hydrogen peroxide, gauze, and bandage, the immediate value of which was a great endorsement for carrying first-aid supplies when embarking upon a ramble.

Once the shock wore off and he realized that he was going to survive, it dawned on our midtempo troubadour that his defiance of death was yet further evidence that he was the absolute hero of the story of this epic trip. After we helped him wash off his leg and continue back down the trail, he insisted that his achievements, namely the rescue of George's glasses and now this Evel Knievel–caliber action, should be celebrated. He should be lionized, he crowed. So much so that he had us wishing that maybe things had gone a different direction back up on the snow slope of death.

Soon enough we came upon the Platonic ideal of a tumbling little mountain spring, falling and splashing past us, on down the mountain. Jon was extremely proud of what he was about to announce.

"You can drink this icy-cold, crystal-clear glacial melt, as it's literally been frozen for millennia up until today, when it melted and flowed down this valley side. Because we're so close to the source, and the source is so pristine, you can drink from this creek without fear of giardia, and . . ."

Meanwhile, as Jon continued to wax on about the outstanding qualities of the water, I stooped in to the small cascade and filled the bowl of my hands to gulp some down. Wow. He was right. Swallowing this unadulterated stuff of life was almost like drinking pure light. I filled my hands a couple more times and splashed my face and beard before stepping away to give someone else a go. Jon was still extolling the virtues, and I was hardly inclined to disagree. The holiness of the moment was shattered, however, as George drank from his hands and said in a whiny little-kid voice, "Mine tastes like sunscreen."

We continued heading down the mountain, walking in reverential silence now, out of respect for the religious experience that had been the day's adventure thus far, broken occasionally by Jeff's suggesting good spots to perhaps assemble a plinth or cairn commemorating his worthy feats. The going was a bit dogged, as the path was rocky, relatively steep, and often wet. One state of affairs that had my attention was the now-and-again occurrence of small boulders situated so that they acted as uneven, descending steps, which was neat and fun, so long as they were dry. Each step down was like a mini-jump, landing one's boot accurately and securely on each stone. When they would sometimes be wet, however, resulting from any of a number of small streams flowing onto the path and then off again, they struck me as potentially treacherous.

No sooner had I completed this thought, than right in front of me, I saw Jeff's boot slide off of just such a boulder, causing his feet to slip right out from under him. His full weight fell onto the offending boulder via his right buttock, and then he toppled from that seated position off onto his side on the ground. It was scarier than the snow tumble, because we saw his body sustain what looked like a much more damaging blow.

Trying not to panic, we immediately gathered around Jeff. Jon, to his credit, kept a cool guide's head and knew all the right questions to ask. Jeff maintained an impressive calm as we got his pack off him and he lay across the trail. He asked us to help position him so that his head was below the rest of his body, so we configured him thus that a slightly lower rock would act as a pillow. Breathing deeply to maintain his equanimity, Jeff explained that he suffered from a panic disorder, and to make matters worse, anxiety could cause him to simply pass out cold due to a condition known as a vasovagal response. His doctor had instructed him to keep his head lower than his body in instances like this— potentially serious injury, with a safe outcome yet to be determined—so that the quick drop in blood pressure wouldn't exacerbate his condition, possibly causing a blackout.

Mind you, we still had a couple hours of this arduous walking in front of us. I know that Jon, George, and myself were all pretty worried about the possibility that Jeff wouldn't be able to fully hoof it on his own power. I was already imagining methods by which we could assist him, if indeed he did need to be carried out. When Jon had given us his safety talk at the top of the day, he'd mentioned that in the case of bodily injury severe enough to require extraction, a rescue chopper could be hours away, so things were slightly tense for a few minutes.

Hang on. Everybody just take a breath. Fear not, gentle reader. Let's not forget who it is we're dealing with here. In what seemed like no time at all, Jeff said he felt like he was okay, like we could keep heading down the trail. We helped him to his feet; he made a few jokes at his own expense, like any true hero; and he slung his pack back upon those shoulders that now seemed like they could bear any weight whatsoever that the world might dump upon them.

He really did march all the way back down the trail without complaint, and now it was our turn to sing his praises. Our positivity was about 85 percent sincere and 15 percent that parental psych-out, wherein you tell your child, "Wow, what a big, brave boy! You walk the best of all the boys!" in the hopes that your Jeff will be convinced to press on even in the face of minor pain.

Eventually he began to wonder aloud about having any *internal* injuries from the jarring collision of his body and the small boulder. Jon explained that, from his observations of how Jeff hit the rock, he would most likely end up with only a "contused glute," which is a scientific term meaning "real sore ass." Jeff replied that he felt like he was in danger not so much physically as psychologically.

I thought this was a very healthy example of a person suffering from anxiety using his knowledge and experience to reason himself away from panic. He named his fear out loud to us, his compatriots, and asked us to help him talk himself off the ledge. I don't know about you, but I've certainly had mysterious symptoms upon some night in the past, and made the mistake of asking the internet to weigh in on what my condition might entail. Without fail, no matter what variegated details I offered up, the answer always came back, "You'll soon be dead, please be sure your affairs are in order." I have found it to be *quite* easy to terrify myself thus, and I don't remotely suffer from anxiety, so I doffed my cap to Jeff for keeping his keel so even.

I have hiked a lot of trails in a lot of different places on the planet, but for the time being, when someone mentions anything like "getting out into gorgeous nature," it is this magnificent day hiking to the Grinnell Glacier that springs to mind. Grinnell himself and his buddies Theodore Roosevelt and John Muir knew just what they were about when they successfully advocated for the preservation and upkeep of such pristine locations (just don't ask the Blackfeet), and while I am extremely grateful, I also wonder if there is a way for us Americans to better understand that this heavenly scenery is but a tiny part of the nature in which we live every day. Indeed, the nature of which we are an intrinsic, inseparable part.

7

RUNNING EAGLE FALLS

The final feature of our Jon-curated week presented itself, appropriately, very much like a dessert. Running Eagle Falls, named after a badass Blackfeet female war chief, the rare woman who led the tribe on buffalo hunts as well as into war, is one of those jaw-dropping, gorgeous displays of the sort of random luck that occurs when running water flows off a decline or hill so steep that gravity causes the water to plummet, forming a "waterplummet," which was later shortened to "waterfall" to fit on TLC CD cases, which is a nineties joke, kids.

Before we set off on the short walk to the falls, we took the option of traversing a tangential nature walk: a cleanly maintained, handicapped-accessible path through a somber forest populated by the charred-but-still-standing remains of moderately tall lodgepole pine trees, peppered with a few white-barked aspens. Our pace had a little more pomp and circumstance to it, since we knew this route was not

long or arduous but that it was our last of the trip. Through the blackened tree trunks, the skyline of the western Rocky Mountains lent a
proper sense of grandiosity as we chatted about the week's adventures.

The welcoming quality of the nature trail and the falls meant we
were back in the realm of simpletons hollering "Badger!" and such. But
one thing that adheres Jeff, George, and me together is the immediate
kinship we feel with people from all walks of life, *especially* the badger
types, because we can never stop knowing that, one way or another, we
all actually *are* the badger people.

The three of us were all fully forged while matriculating around different parts of Illinois at the less lucrative end of the working class, and
we haven't forgotten it. Despite having won the lottery when it comes to
"earning a living with the talents Mother Nature gave us," we all are still
constantly reminded of our failings as humans—a circumstance from
which I daresay we draw most of our artistic inspiration. For example,
my latest song is entitled "Us Dipshits Gotta Stick Together," or, recalling
that brevity is the soul of wit, simply "Dipshits." It's born of the understanding that we're all just doing our best, although we're selfish, clumsy
humans, to get through each day with the slightest semblance of grace.

With that in mind, I made a habit of greeting people we'd pass on
the trail, as did our whole group, by and large. I have been given to understand that this is either a small-town thing or a Midwestern thing,
but I'm not positive that's the case. In my little hometown of Minooka,
Illinois, even when I was growing up and everybody truly seemed to
know damn near everybody else in our population of around two thousand, there were always people who wouldn't return a wave or a greeting: taciturn people, recluses, shy people, hustlers and bustlers, as well
as our share of assholes, just like any place.

It turns out that I have pretty strong feelings about this topic, as I learned when I became a runner about five years ago in my neighborhood in the hills of Los Angeles. The varying width of streets, the sharp curves and changes in elevation, and the lack of sidewalks all mean that utilizing these hill streets as a pedestrian can be a dangerous proposition. The speed limit is generally twenty or twenty-five miles an hour, which seems relatively sedate when behind the wheel but *plenty* fast when it's the speed of the oncoming vehicles you're navigating on foot, like a slaloming skater.

The frequency with which I greet the people I pass in the street never really occurred to me as anything other than normal. As a kid, not only would one certainly greet your fellow walkers, but one would also wave at fellow drivers, since the odds were good that you knew them.

We called this behavior simply being neighborly. A salutation was offered, either vocally or in the form of a gesture, to establish a level of reassurance that we were all in agreement with each other—we wouldn't commit acts of violence against one another, nor hornswoggling or other chicanery.

A friendly wave and nod, to say, "You're good by me, and I'd like to be considered the same by you, please."

Forty years later, in Los Angeles, a city known for being difficult to canvass by foot, I took up running for my health and to manage my burgeoning metabolism (waistline) as I approached half a century of age. Running four to five miles a day in the hills was extremely gratifying on every level except when I habitually clicked right back into the (apparently) pesky old habit of greeting others.

You could have blown me over when I began to register the responses from the various motorists. Appropriately, some of them waved, always with some degree of friendliness. Often these greetings would be punctuated by a benign surprised delight, as if to imply, "Hey, I did not expect a friendly gesture, but man, now that you have sent one my way, I really like it!" or "Ho ho, I remember this! Just like my mom and dad used to do!"

Now, here's something crazy: These positive responses occurred less than *half* the time. My estimation would actually be closer to a third. The remainder of the drivers fell into three possible categories:

1. Eye contact only, no acknowledgment.
2. No eye contact, fully ignoring me.
3. Terrified of my appearance, shrinking down behind the steering wheel out of sight.

The eye-contact crowd would just infuriate me, because eye contact is a form of engagement. I would wave, they would be alerted so far as to lock eyes with me, then they would choke! Come on! You just have to do so very little much more!

I would wave again, a little obnoxiously this time, to say, "Yes, you saw right, I greeted you with the universal gesture for hello, I'm not an asshole!" This just drove me up a tree. Another key to successful waving depends on the *second* wave in any exchange, and that response wave is to say, "I am going to return your gesture so that you don't feel like an asshole for waving. Life is tough, and we're all out here on the road just trying to keep 'er between the ditches."

So, do the math. These drivers depriving me of their life commiseration were making me want to feel like some kind of asswipe, but I wouldn't give in to it.

The zero-eye-contact cars were a different vibe altogether. The most generous interpretation of their abject ambivalence was that I truly just existed outside of their sphere and they literally didn't notice me. They were driving on the section of road that they had been apportioned by the "rules of the road," and on the periphery of that paved lane that claimed their focus were shrubs and parked cars and mailboxes and the occasional coyote and me. It was not a very wide road. Three car widths, tops. So the fact that a person could be so zoned out to their surroundings as to miss a good-size waving man was a tad unnerving.

The alternative explanation for the no-eye-contact-ers was kind of the one I'm driving toward, and it's that they just didn't give a shit. In my experience in modern-day America, we have been encouraged more and more to be the opposite of neighborly, because there is arguably no demonstrable financial benefit to acting warmly toward our fellow humans. We have been taught it's a "dog-eat-dog world," and that "time is money," so who cares about the neighbors, and anybody else.

When these cars would pass me by, I would be angered. I would holler, "Suck ass!" or something even more likely to be flagged by Standards and Practices. Then it occurred to me, "Hang on, buddy. Don't forget nuance." It occurred to me, eventually, to think about the other reasons that the drivers might be otherwise occupied than that they were just assholes. What if they had a lot going on, to the point of being stressed out and just barely keeping their shit together? What if they were reciting lines for the audition to which they were speeding? What if it was my *Dungeons & Dragons* ex-friend Cedric, who says that I'm invisible in real life because he's still holding a grudge after my thief stole his invisibility cloak, his bag of holding, and a vorpal dagger that his cleric had stolen in the first place, so you can still fuck off, Cedric; I know you're reading this.

There was another substantial reason for my snubbing that was staring me in the face once I got over myself for a minute: Many of the drivers were women, and I was a middle-aged white guy with a beard, i.e., a potential danger. I was reminded yet again of the privilege within which

I have existed my whole life, in the way that it had never occurred to me to be frightened of any runners I had seen, for any reason. Once I started to see them all as fully complicated humans, with rich emotional lives much like my own, I was able to grow less mad at them.

Of course, there were still plenty of asswipes. Here's a PSA just in case any of you (or your brothers) gets within reading distance of this book: If you have tuned your car, truck, or motorcycle to growl, roar, or vroom in any way louder than is necessary, when you rev your engine and treat everyone within a quarter mile to the aggressive noise you have spent time and money to broadcast, you only sound incredibly sad. It's indistinguishable from a baby screaming on an airplane or the subway, except the baby is not doing it on purpose. To further pollute the public airspace that we all share in that manner is to be a bad citizen. Please think about what you're doing. It's painful and violent, and I would ask you to consider working out your insecurities in some other way, like *Dungeons & Dragons*. Cedric, I'm obviously still talking about you.

I could go on and on, because of the myriad types of people represented on the roads of my neighborhood, but these ideas of neighborliness apply everywhere. In Glacier National Park, we successfully managed interactions with all sorts of folks on the trail, and I'm pleased to report that, based on my numbers, the kind of people who will hike a national park trail are much more apt to return a friendly greeting than the citizens of greater Los Angeles.

* * *

But that morning, as we came off the nature trail and headed for the falls, we crossed a sturdily built wooden footbridge that spanned the outlet stream between Two Medicine Lake and Lower Two

Medicine Lake. The guidebook called it an "outlet stream," but near the bridge it seemed much more a rushing, plunging, albeit small, river. Some torrential falls of eight or ten feet above and below the bridge had people pulling up a seat to watch the exciting power of the cascading jade water in the deafening soundscape. For some reason, this noise was more appealing to us than the souped-up exhaust system on somebody's Camaro in Hollywood. PS: I love motorcycles. I love Camaros. I also love the benevolent parts of Christianity, but then the aggressive billboards hit me as much more similar to the loud motorcycle. What is behind that impulse to shout, exactly? "Hey, guys, our motorcycles are so kick-ass, for maneuverability and gas mileage, and just feeling the wind on our faces, but check this out: What if we make them sound fucking horrible? I mean, like, painfully loud?! Right?"

We enjoyed *this* assault on our ears and eyes as we communicated those classic signals of a good time when it's too loud to hear one another: grins and nods and pointing at particular details and features. Our guide, Jon, eventually beckoned us past the bridge, and when we could once again hear human speech, keeping the mood buoyant, he explained that drowning and water-related accidents were surprisingly the most prevalent danger in the park. The churning power exhibited that day by the relatively small stream next to us made that easy to believe.

As we trekked another half mile, we paused at a few different turnouts off the main trail which provided alternative viewpoints from which to see the falls. For a relatively short walk, the scenic bang for our buck was quite substantial, which lent the day a pleasant gravity as the culmination of our week was at hand. Even so, it was reminiscent of our first day at the Hidden Lake Overlook with the feeling once again of strolling amongst bovine shoppers at a mall or theme park sightseers.

When the curving trail finally brought us through a tall, dark hall-way of pine trees and massive boulders out into the arena of the main event at the foot of the falls, the beefy cataract was truly magnificent in that way that a three-dimensional organic phenomenon can be: exuding a visual magic, a version of nature's masterpiece that you can do your best to try to capture on film in a photo or video, but the magic just never translates to seeing it in person. Like so many clouds or snowstorms at which I had gaped, this waterfall scenario was also being enhanced by the wind's blowing a spray of rainlike droplets off the water at the top of the cliff, so that everything appeared to wetly sparkle. As we stepped closer to the action and spun slowly around, shavings of rainbow also came and went in the mist, upping the sensation of magic even more.

Running Eagle Falls has also been called Trick Falls, due to the peculiar fact that the water can plummet from forty feet high during the spring runoff, when the volume is high, or else from only twenty feet up when the volume is lower and the water up top flows into a sinkhole and thus out a lower exit. So you could see the falls at the normal height of twenty feet, then come back in the spring to marvel that they had somehow doubled in height. Hence, "Trick Falls." I picked this tidbit up from one of those informational plaques near the trailhead, which is also where I first took on board the name of the aforementioned Running Eagle, and had my interest piqued by a Blackfeet woman so notoriously dominant that she had a waterplummet named after her.

Meanwhile, Jeff and George and I were blissing out in the bright sun below the waterfall, chilly in the heavy mist that rained upon us. It was a wonderful sensation, only slightly hampered by the fact that the next group of people were waiting to come stand in the plum middle spot where we were now standing, just like we had waited our turn before this. There were no instructions posted, nor park rangers present keeping the peace, just us hikers/cheeseburger enthusiasts maintaining our own space for what we all deemed to be a polite enough length of time. As our replacements slowly encroached upon us, we gently commandeered one of them to take a picture of us.

We look very at peace, we three, with a self-satisfaction representing all the victories and defeats in a week well lived, capped off by this moment right now, lit by a glorious afternoon sun. We had done well in our lives, against all odds, and this trip was evidence of that. The "odds" I refer to would be our propensity as middle-aged, straight white guys to somehow hobble or ultimately destroy ourselves under the influence of the enormous privilege we lived with. We had earned enough income to spend a week in Glacier National Park and pay a high-quality guide to make certain that our diversions would be safe and comfortable and therefore as pleasurable as possible. People don't realize how hard it can be to accomplish the simplest of responsible tasks when there is so much insobriety, infidelity, and insider trading being seductively slapped up one side of our heads and down the other. But, for the three of us, this time? We did it.

* * *

The cherry atop the cake of our trip was our final dinner, where we took a moment to review some of the week's highlight reel. With heavy reluctance, Jeff reminded us that mere days ago we had been in the throes of a terrifying maelstrom of river water while rafting. As he told it, "We were being churned and jostled to the point where I couldn't tell if I was facing up or down. We were taking on lots of water. I was freezing. It looked like night was about to fall. Dark clouds rolling in. And out of the corner of my eye, I caught this glint of beveled glass. Are those my glasses? It couldn't be—my glasses are still on my face!"

"Yes," George replied, resisting a smile, "it was fraught, and you should also remember that I'm pretty much legally blind."

"So those must be George's glasses!" Jeff continued. "They're about to go in the drink, straight down to Davy Jones's locker. So with all my might, I lunged forward and scooped the glasses out. At the same time, I kept rowing. Because our taskmaster of a boat captain was screaming at me to keep rowing, and I knew it was a matter of life and death, because if I stopped rowing, our side of the boat would be powerless!

"I got the glasses, but I wasn't out of danger yet. They slipped out of my hands just a little bit. This is God's truth. And I saw them just going over the curve of the boat into the water. So I lunged even farther forward, stretching farther than I'd ever stretched before in my life. Farther than you've probably seen anyone ever stretch!"

We all laughed, but soon, the conversation turned more serious, or "sappy," as my buddies down at the gravel pit would say. Jeff, putting his tales of derring-do aside, finally said, "Nick, thank you for putting this together. I was scared to take this trip. Turns out I was right to be a little scared. But I'm better now."

"Thank you guys for coming," I replied. "It was exactly what I'd dreamed of. But fully twice as good."

It was George's turn to think about the bigger picture. "I'm coming away kind of jazzed about America. The countryside, of course. But weren't the people on the trail nice?"

I agreed. "That's why I could leave my phone on a rock" (to shoot an hour-long time lapse). "Hikers aren't going to steal my phone. If they notice it, they'll just look at it and see that it's there on purpose."

George nodded. "But sometimes it's a little more complicated. I'm sure some of the people we passed on the trail were Trump supporters. But they were really nice."

Jeff said, "There are a lot of people just not participating in all the bullshit, one way or another. I mean, unfortunately, I think a lot of them don't vote."

George: "Being nice is different than being . . ."

Jeff: "Good. Or maybe being nice is the *same* as being good, but not everyone has been taught to be good in the abstract. They can be good directly, and that's very, very important, but that's the trick of it—liberals are constantly trying to get people to be good in the abstract. Be good to people you don't know, even if you don't know what their lives are like. To be good to people you don't care about."

At the risk of opening a theological can of worms here just as I'm trying to tie a nice bow on part 1 of the book, I do believe that the behavior Jeff was suggesting was simply one of the cornerstones of Christian thought. Voicing it thus, to my way of thinking, only goes to show how far the ideology of our country's so-called conservatives has strayed from the values upon which their beliefs were supposedly founded. It's almost as though those "values" were never sincerely revered in the first place. John Fugelsang put it quite succinctly when he said, "The only way you can follow both Trump and Jesus is if you've never read either of their books."

As for George and Jeff and me, this conversation was exactly the kind of content I was after. Together, with Jon's guidance and expertise, we had (mostly) enjoyed a deep dive into how American citizens might use the lands that our government has set aside for preservation. We three middle-aged white guys, ever aware of our privilege, had taken pretty full advantage of the recreation available in the glorious acreage that some other white guys had set aside for just that purpose.

With regard to Wendell Berry's challenge, I believe that we made a substantial beginning. On the spectrum of land use, we fulsomely inhabited the John Muir end, getting ourselves "out into nature" and truly reveling in her glory. Our country still has a long way to go to reconcile these magnificent parks with the way in which they were acquired, but that said, I am extremely grateful for the great idea that they remain. Hey, what if we were to use the wealth of the parks themselves to make reparations to the Indigenous tribes from whom they were brutally torn? Could that be an even greater idea?

In any case, it was time for me to turn my investigation toward the other end of the land-use spectrum and poke my nose into what Wendell was getting at when he pointed me toward Aldo Leopold. Knowing Wendell, I suspected that answer would be somewhat agrarian (having to do with the *cultivation* of land), which would be great, because it is a subject I have long adored. Little could I have known, however, to what strange new places this quest would lead me, or that I was about to make another amazing new friend.

PART II

8

ALL ROADS LEAD TO THE FARM

I know what you're thinking.

"Great balls of fire, when are you gonna spill some of that *showbiz tea* you've been hoarding in your cupboard, buddy?!"

Well, first of all, thank you for patiently wading through all of that touchy-feely badger talk in part 1 to get to your sizzling reward, right off the bat here in part 2! That's right, loves, it's Rob Lowe hot goss.

Now, hold up a second. It seems rather unlikely, but maybe there are some of you who have come to be readers of mine without having crossed paths with any of my several jobs as an American actor on screens of all sizes, and some stages as well. Could it be possible that you only signed up for this mildly challenging reading experience because you have seen my woodworking, and perhaps even came down on the side of approval? If so, then please bear with me briefly as I seek to satiate the low palates of the remainder of my dozens of fans—citizens who, like myself, occasionally (even frequently) consume recorded playacting stories like television and cinematic films. As is my constant aspiration, let us decide not to judge one another for whatsoever proclivities we tend to enjoy when it comes to tickling our free-time selves.

Now. Here's the scuttlebutt: When I began dating my wife in the year 2000, or, more accurately, when my wife began tolerating me on a regular, medium-to-heavy schedule, we each rattled off a litany common to romantically involved thespians. You talk through your past acting jobs of note/lovemaking partners to deduce whether you share any past allies or enemies or if there are any historical tryst participants who need to be avoided going forward, as they might represent a land mine of jealousy or resentment. It's really for the safety of everybody involved.

This is how I came to be gently informed that Megan had engaged in a muscular French-kissing scene with Rob Lowe in the 1986 film *About Last Night*. Mind you, this bomb was dropped on me several years before I would meet the same Mr. Lowe on the set of the comedy program *Parks and Recreation*. When she told me about it, he was just a major heartthrob from films of my youth. Perhaps *the* major heartthrob, or second only to Patrick Swayze. Thankfully, I've always been pretty good at letting this sort of information roll off my back. Whenever I have felt a twinge of jealousy in the past, I've simply examined my relationship and doubled down on my partner's happiness and satisfaction. If I give her no reason to look elsewhere, then I need not worry about her straying. If, however, she were to stray despite my sincere attentions, then it would mean it wasn't meant to be in the first place.

All was well as we embarked upon the first few years of our courtship and then our marriage, until one fateful day when I was putting on a suit for a banquet we were attending that evening. We were at a hotel in New York, and the TV was just randomly on in the next room. As I began knotting my tie I suddenly recognized Megan's voice coming from the television, so I rushed in just in time to see her in about thirty pounds of eighties hair, lip-wrestling Rob Lowe like it was an Olympic event, in that aforementioned film.

Such is the degree of my wife's acting skills, and, it must be said, the magnitude of Rob Lowe's allure, that this vision shook me from my usual firm foundation. I raised my voice to the next room in a plaintive query: "Honey? Do you love Rob Lowe?"

Well, of course not. That unnerving, unholy even, scene had been filmed almost twenty years earlier, and Megan had been through all kinds of relationships and substantial life changes since that day in a movie when she had *so clearly been in love with him*. I took a deep breath and regained my usually plumb disposition, treating all hardships with the mellowest vibes I could muster, but I never quite got back to perfectly straight. Something about Megan's kissing Rob Lowe kept me just a degree or so off balance whenever it crossed my mind, which, I'm afraid to say, was often.

Life continued for us in a relatively blissful progression all the way right up until 2010 or so, when, of all the crazy coincidences, that dark prince of the cheekbones Rob Lowe ended up on *Parks and Recreation*, a quality program upon which I already played a role. It was a very intoxicating time, with firecrackers banging off right and left all about the place; and adding a powerfully successful Hollywood person like Rob, who was upon his arrival immediately dubbed "RoLo" by Amy Poehler and Rashida Jones, felt significant.

I do my best to mind my manners in general, but often, when things start going great and moving fast, I feel more susceptible to screwing things up. Everywhere I turned, wonderful things were happening, mainly thanks to the amazing writers and producers of that program. Those many of us along for the ride just did our best to hang on for dear life and scarf down all the bacon that life kept setting in front of me—I mean us.

The carousel ride had been accelerating from *Parks'* season two into season three, faster and faster, 'round and around, until halfway through that season came an episode called "Eagleton," during which Rob Lowe's character, Chris Traeger, discovers that it's my character Ron Swanson's birthday, and grabs me by the face and gives me a big kiss on the mouth.

I've never been to Burning Man, but from what I've been given to understand, getting a smooch plastered on my piehole by that world-champion lover made my sensory perceptions explode in veritable ejaculations of light, sound, yea, and fury too, that I would deem to be commensurate with that high-desert art-festival freak-out. It was Burning Man turned up to 11 inside my soul and my brain and my breadbasket. The film crew led me to a chair, where I had to sit and breathe deeply like a spent mule as I waited for the tears to cease their flowing and the hallucinations to subside. And mind you, I was being paid handsomely for this wet and wanton act of mouth sex. When I could see shapes again, our compassionate PA Lorenzo led me to the craft services table, where I chugged a full gallon of Cran-Raspberry and made a large onion sandwich to wash the memory of that man from my kisser and my conscience.

Now that I think about it, given some slight allowances for time and space, you *could* technically say that RoLo, Megan, and myself had a threesome. Given the state of his dance card across the decades, I'm sure we're only one three-way of dozens, but I'm happy to report that our marriage survived this unexpected dalliance, and I never worried about Megan's straying again. The tit-for-tat tally had been made even.

Now that I have undoubtedly satisfied your craven hunger for loose talk, let's veer back toward the object of this tome, as I launch us into part 2. There is some crossover appeal here, because it's my work as an actor that indirectly led me to the remote corner of the world of agriculture I'm about to unwrap for you. You're also about to witness my falling head over heels (or ass over teacup, as he might say) for another fellow who may not be the lady-killer Rob Lowe is, but I *have* seen ladies by the *score* come running at him like he was all four of the Beatles and Harry Styles, to boot. The braying, adoring females were none of them wearing knickers, either, because they just happened to be his happy ewes (lady sheep, for the uninitiated).

This particular obsession started back in 2017. My involvement on social media tends to be spotty, and I generally find that I'm happier *off* of it, then as well as now. That said, I do pop onto Twitter and Instagram to see a few people who make me laugh and/or to glean the state of the world from a selection of brains that I've curated to translate the news of the day for me: "Here's what the evil people are lying about, and here is why lying is still very bad." I look at some chairmakers and boatbuilders and a BBQ chef. I try to cull just the good bits from my feed and then jump out before I run into the rampant shitstorm of negativity that can flare up in any quarter.

It was around that time in 2017 that I became glued to the feeds of James Rebanks and his wife, Helen, a couple of "fell shepherds," as they are known, for the mountainous hills, or "fells," that their sheep inhabit in England's Lake District for part of each year. I could already see that the two of them did an amazing job of balancing a progressive farm life, living off-grid with four kids (now ages three to fifteen), growing and cooking a lot of their own meal ingredients, then masterfully sharing the whole circus with their following via social media. Oh, and James is also now a massively bestselling author of a few books, including *The Shepherd's Life* and *English Pastoral* (*Pastoral Song* in the US).

Their farm was a place that I had come to know well via my online browsing, as though regularly viewing it through some sort of science fiction portal. Normally, such a two-dimensional observational practice would be visually pleasing but cold and a bit lifeless otherwise. James and Helen, however, did such a replete job of keeping their followers involved in the farming day to day that it sometimes felt like I was there with them. Their reporting on the state of the sheep herds, or the state of the land itself, and working with new plantings, hedgerows, streams, and pastures, left me understanding the nature in their little part of England more fully than that of my own Los Angeles street.

Later that year, I found myself casually chiming in on some of James's posts. I had originally been drawn to his account because of his aforementioned quality content as well as our shared appreciation for the writing of (you guessed it) Wendell Berry, whom he often referenced in his posts. And the more I read, the more I fell for the charming personal stories about James's family and his flock of Herdwick sheep set on the historic fells in the far northwest corner of the country, but also his overview of topics like the "rewilding" of our planet's developed agricultural spaces or the food and farming policies of the British government, as well as those of the United States.

Before long, James dropped me a DM (Dad Mandate), or I guess he "slid into my DMs"? That sounds maybe too sexy for a couple of aspiring barn builders, regardless of our love of hip-hop dance and crunking. Let's just say he got in touch, to say, "If you're ever in our neck of the woods, do come see the farm."

Well, that was mighty friendly, and I replied, "Sure thing, you never know when I might get to your neck of the woods." But after immediately looking up his location, I saw that it was not convenient to London nor Glasgow, which meant it wasn't going to be an easy fly-by while I was out touring with a comedy show. Still, you never do know. My calendar with each passing year yielded more and more surprising delights, as I continued to book gigs as a film and TV actor and as a touring humorist. Various jobs had seen me working in recent years in such far-flung locales as New Zealand, South Africa, the remote jungles of darkest Canada, Tasmania, and the rest of Australia, plus all over the British Isles and United States.

So sure enough, just a few months after James invited me to the farm in early 2018, I landed a terrifically plum job on a science fiction series called *Devs* for a sublime British filmmaker named Alex Garland that would bring me, geographically, quite close to the Rebanks farm. I'm a pretty down-to-earth thinker, mainly because I don't have a lot of high-right-brain capacity. But even though I don't often think on a creative, new age plane, that doesn't mean I discount it, especially when things like this occur. You can call it mojo, or kismet, or serendipity, or whatever you like, just don't call me late for dinner. But seriously, folks, I wanted to go meet a shepherd, and I wanted it real bad, and it inexplicably and beautifully was about to happen.

This will get a tad serpentine, but trust me, it all comes back to a more open-minded version of how we view nature. Let me back up to getting this acting job: After several years of extreme good fortune in landing gigs, I had taken a pause on accepting new work, stepping off the hamster wheel, if you will, to nibble some cheese and watch the world go by. This was purely a gut decision, fueled by a suspicion that things in my life might get more interesting if I considered other goals than those offered by pure capitalism.

Taking the seemingly less lucrative path has, somewhat surprisingly, worked well for me so far. Choosing to pursue a career in live theatre, for example, is never a good idea if one is seeking a pile of wealth, but it's where I met my wife, inarguably the richest gold-strike a prospector panning for *life value* could hope to seek. Likewise, starting a fine wood-working shop would be extremely inadvisable as a financial investment, but the dividends my shop has paid me in peace of mind, quality hand-crafting, and pub avoidance are priceless. Therefore, by passing on some more conventional acting jobs, I had cleared some daylight on my calendar, or perhaps more on theme, it was like I had harvested all of the produce and pulled all the weeds in my garden, then left the fecund soil simply available to nature's whim. Rather than letting "Jesus take the wheel," I let Mother Nature take the trowel.

And sow she did. Before too long, she had cultivated my life with some completely unexpected new bounty, and I was now working with a filmmaker I greatly admired, not to mention a top-drawer cast and crew of collaborators. The program would shoot in and around Santa Cruz, California, for the first half of the six-month schedule, depicting nearby Silicon Valley, where the show was set. Once our shooting at all of the American locations was completed, we would move to sound-stages in London and Manchester, England, a hardworking city that happened to be a ninety-minute train ride south of James Rebanks and his idyllic farm. I mean, come on.

Santa Cruz, where we began filming in late 2018, was in many ways the epitome of a California beach town, including an amusement park on the pier, but with a little extra funk. The sexy Brat Pack vampire film *The Lost Boys* was shot there in the eighties, which is a testament not only to the Hollywood good looks of the community but also to an easily accessed, mysterious dark side. Dramatic cliffs and beaches are framed by towering redwood forests, undulating up and down the mountainous topography. Just outside town is a gravitational anomaly known as the "Mystery Spot," where your perceptions of the "laws of physics and gravity will be questioned"! I even stayed at a hotel named the Paradox.

Maybe it's because Santa Cruz is far from any major highways, so it's lacking any of the superficial attempts at freshness that one sees next to any given freeway off-ramp these days—the gaudy sparkles of consumerism. Whatever the reason, I found the town to have a really groovy vibe, like it never fully made it out of the seventies. I reveled in my time shooting scenes at the University of California–Santa Cruz, a cluster of modern concrete and glass structures from the midsixties nestled into the redwood forest on the hillsides above the town.

During my breaks, I would run along the ocean, or ride a rented mountain bike on the miles of paths through the many neighboring parks. The campus was dotted with deer, docilely munching on greenery as they strolled about. The farmer's markets in town and the restaurants were very hooked into the local agriculture and seafood situations as well, which always gives me a much more substantial sense of getting to commune with the local occupants. I found myself at the Live Oak Market investigating some Michoacán fare I had heard about from Eddie, one of our transpo drivers, and the kind woman who served me my tacos then recommended a roadside shop in the nearby mountains with a butcher famous for his locally sourced sausages, and so on.

In one section of the college, we shot a scene in which another actor and myself cross a wooden trestle bridge away from the campus, uphill to the deeper redwoods, and eventually emerge in a clearing where my character has built a huge research facility named Devs. Things would eventually get pretty sci-fi in that futuristic building, where in the story we had developed a quantum computer that allowed us to more fully investigate the quantum "many-worlds" theories (like seeing into other dimensions, or alternate realities kind of stuff). Knowing that we would later shoot the interior of this magical building in England made the scenes in Santa Cruz extra fun, approaching the doorway as opening onto something great that we hadn't yet countenanced but could be pretty certain would be astonishing.

Adding to the uncanny feeling of living in a fantasy quest, one of the philosopher-elf-kings from mere pages ago, my dear friend George Saunders, was staying in Santa Cruz as well. He and his charming wife, Paula, took me on a hike that ended at a Buddhist prayer stupa deep in the forest. We had a really great talk about our unlikely paths from Chicagoland laborers to successful artists, but how, even though we both had our rent or mortgage comfortably covered for the time being, we both still felt inescapably human, still just trying to get things done right every day. We were just now lucky enough to be doing it with more clean socks in the drawer.

George is one of our most exceptional living thinkers, by the way. I would say "award-winning," which happens to be accurate, but I feel like that phrase has lost its luster in the same way as *organic* and *cage-free* have lost theirs. One proof of his wisdom is that he claims to be trying his best *not* to think. Just check out his commencement speech from Syracuse University in 2013, entitled "Congratulations, By the Way," now available in slender book form. It's a gentle, humorous treatise on kindness. All of this to say that I really like listening to George talk, whether he's reading his own writing in an audiobook, or holding forth in one of his creative writing classes (which I've had the distinct pleasure of auditing), or just rappin' about the Buddha.

We were in this ideal sylvan setting, with clusters of sunlight playing leafy shadows across the stupa in the light breeze, and George spoke about the idea in Buddhism that one's thoughts are actually constructed concepts of the world. We can never comprehend *all* of the information

WHERE THE DEER AND THE ANTELOPE PLAY   111

in any given circumstance, so the brain creates little false, constructed scale models to allow us to function, but they're all incorrect. Because of all the information we're missing, the more complex and substantial your imagined scale models become, the more deluded you actually grow.

Thus, when we step into nature and use our senses to try to take on board all the information we can, we necessarily fail every time, especially if we do engage in too much thinking. Because what God is saying to us in the scope of her creation is this: "Here is a glimpse of what I, God, can think, but you, human, can never remotely comprehend it. So don't think too much." This was a pleasurable ladleful of meditative notions in any case, but it was made extra savory in the knowledge that it was all part of the synchronicity of my Alex Garland dream, brought effectively to bear by my nibbling of some cheese.

Then George took me down the road to grab lunch at his favorite place, and wouldn't you know it, it was the famous butcher sausage shop. I had the bratwurst and it was amazing.

* * *

Santa Cruz had clearly enchanted me, and I would have been much more reluctant to leave had it not been for the rest of our filming awaiting us in London and Manchester in late 2018. The cast and crew all went to our respective homes for the Thanksgiving holiday, which I believe is referred to in England as "late November," then we reconvened in London for some chilly December work. One of the first nights I shot there took place a couple hours southwest of "The Big Smoke," in a botanic garden that actually housed an entire hillside of redwood trees. The enormous conifers, exclusively indigenous to the coast of

Northern California and Oregon, had been brought back to England and transplanted about 150 years earlier by a British botanist, and they had grown into a stately grove that perfectly mirrored the woods in Santa Cruz.

For various reasons, it made sense to split up the shoot this way, and here I offer to you the way one of my favorite aspects of filmmaking-magic works. So in the first episode of *Devs*, we see my character (Forest) leading the character Sergei off campus and across a wooden trestle bridge into the redwoods. We then cut to the English forest, as we see Sergei and Forest, chatting while they stroll through the woods en route to the Devs research building. Cut back to the golden-grassed clearing in Santa Cruz where Sergei and Forest come into view of the astonishing Devs building. Forest describes to him the groundbreaking ingenuity with which he designed and built the place, as they slowly approach the entrance portal. As they step through the square opening into a long antechamber/hallway, we then cut to the soundstage in *Manchester* where the interior of the Devs building had been crafted. Finally, once inside the hallway, the two characters are able to look back out through the portal and see a reconstructed view of the autumnal Santa Cruz field, with redwood trees in the background.

I'm pretty simpleminded to begin with, but at that moment, I really was transported. Standing inside the gorgeous set piece that was the Devs building interior, having been present for each of the discrete locations filmed so as to seamlessly become this dramatic walking sequence, and looking out the set door at the (manufactured) fading California sunlight in a Manchester soundstage made me tear up. It struck me as an interesting parallel to the subject matter of the *Devs* show itself, part of which was concerned with the effect on our lives and choices of being able to view through a portal other versions of our own reality.

Now cut to me, on my first extended free weekend in Manchester, hopping on a train for ninety minutes to go see the Rebanks farm! A place, an entire flesh-and-blood reality, that I had only theretofore glimpsed through the portal of my iPhone screen, or even more tenuously, through the portal of my imagination when I read James's first book, *The Shepherd's Life*.

I mean, what would any normal Joe do with a handful of days to kill in England, just an hour east of Liverpool, birth town of the Beatles? Go snap some selfies on Penny Lane? Skip about in a radical socialist reverie in search of the red gatepost in Woolton? Or go rogue, ferry across the Mersey, and seek alleyways where Frankie Goes to Hollywood might have enjoyed a wee slash?

Hell no, mate. I was hauling my ass to Cumbria to see some sheep.

9

RACY GHYLL

I have not yet had the giggle-tastic pleasure of visiting the Shire set from *The Lord of the Rings* in Wellington, New Zealand, nor the Kiwis' illustrious Weta Workshop, where so many of the denizens of Peter Jackson's (and Tolkien's) Middle-earth were molded, sculpted, or sewn, nor have I ever set foot in Hogwarts or Narnia, but I have visited these fantastic locales so often in my mind and on my screen that I feel like I have been there.

So, when James picked me up at the train station on a freezing-cold January morning in 2019 and drove me twenty minutes to Racy Ghyll Farm, it felt something like I was going to visit the hometown of Galadriel, Tumnus, or Hagrid. The Rebanks homestead, set on its rolling hillside adorned with comely sheep all around, was finally going to appear before my own eyes instead of on the screen of my smartphone or imagined through the pages of James's books. I hadn't stopped grinning since the moment I stepped into the station and James and I shook hands.

Part of the reason for my glee was simply the effect that his truck had on me. He drove what in the States would be considered a pretty small SUV, there was a sleeping one-year-old in a car seat, and it was *filthy*. It told the story, with immediacy, that six people used this vehicle to assist them in their labors as they husbanded sheep and a few cows and many laying hens and three of them attended school as well and rode horses and went down to the lake for fun on the water, all while sometimes scarfing down a "biscuit" (cookie) or other form of snack or lunch.

It reminded me of visiting the house of a new friend that happened to exhibit the chaos resulting from parenthood and the bustle of work and school, compelling the friend to "apologize for the mess." To this I always reply with an admonition: "Are you crazy? This scene clearly has written all over it that you are living! This speaks of health and vigor. If this place was impeccably spotless and resembled the cover of a design magazine, then I'd be worried about you."

James's truck was the same. It wasn't the dirty vehicle of the lazy or the slovenly. It bore the mud and crumbs and the one small, orphaned sock of people who are getting shit done.

We pulled up to the house, which was a former stone barn that James and Helen had converted into a ridiculously charming family home, perpetuating the storybook quality of the experience thus far. After meeting Helen and handing off a now awake and hollering young Tom to her, James said to me, "You want to mend a stacked stone wall?"

Of course I said, "You bet your sweet ex-rugby-playing ass I do," as he tossed me a light jacket and briskly strode out into the wet, shin-deep grass on the not-half-steep hillside, accelerating his pace as he turned up the incline.

"This is great!" he shouted as he began to point out different features of the farm, stone walls and hedgerows and tree plantings. "Mind the beck!"

A beck is a small stream, in the parlance of Cumbria, and this one took all I had to leap successfully across it. "Jesus," I thought, still grinning. "I did not think that today would be the day I perish, and death by shepherd, no less."

In all my years, I have known a lot of impressive workers, but I have never seen anyone leap to their work like James bounded up that hillside. The salient point, one that I'd gathered watching from afar and now saw in person, is this: It's not that he loves the actual act of building stone walls, or splitting firewood, or checking sheep's hooves for infection. The reason he appears to hop to each and every task is because he loves farming, and these are the menial tasks that comprise farming. The more of them he gets done, and done right, the healthier his farm becomes, and the more he and his family and their animals and every bit of his farm prosper. And *that* is what he loves.

We arrived at the section of stone wall that had been knocked half down by the Herdwick sheep, which I have to say was no small feat. According to James, once they have grazed a pasture to the point they feel is sufficient, it sometimes occurs to them that there must be better, newer grass on the other side of a given wall. They eyeball the aged expanse of wall to discern a weak spot, then begin to rear up and knock at the wall, slowly beating the heavy stones out of alignment until they actually impel them to tumble away into the neighboring paddock, leaving a U-shaped breach through which they can jump. The youngest of these walls is 150 years old, but some of them date back many centuries, and the English countryside is just lousy with thousands of miles of them, all in various states of repair and disrepair, thanks to both time and the sheep.

James sent me to the other side of the wall so that we could work together from either side to repair the void (and so that my rookie stacking wouldn't be visible from the house). He explained the system by which the carefully selected blue slate stones had been hand-shaped decades earlier to fit together, puzzle-like, without mortar, complete with "through-stones" tying the wall's thickness together, from about three feet at the base tapering up to a foot and a half thick at the "capstones" (larger, heavier, attractive stones to top off the neat stack and hold down the assembly beneath). If we wanted the repaired section to appear indiscernible from the rest of the standing wall, it was imperative to find and realign the weathered, moss-covered facets of the stones that had been facing outward, and restore them to that original orientation.

As you may have surmised, this work was not easy, especially at a temperature of thirty-eight degrees. Oh, and a freezing drizzle had begun to blow, with me in only an unlined springtime jacket. But I couldn't have been happier. I know of no better way to make a friend than to pitch in on hard work together, and the shittier the conditions, the faster the friendship forms. My stacking required a decent amount of correction from James, but we made good progress despite it.

The setting could not have been more conducive to talking about our dads, who taught us the values of hard work and perseverance and pride in craftsmanship, and their dads before them, and of course our mums as well. James went on to describe the many generations of his family who had shepherded in these very hills before him, and I wondered which of them had touched these stones before me and whether the sharp stone edges had hurt their hands as well. Jesus, it was cold.

I also thought about the fact that we weren't wearing gloves. Testing the fit and placement of each peculiarly shaped brick of stone required the full complement of hand, wrist, arm, and shoulder capabilities: prying, nudging, shoving, twisting, punching, and so forth. Even in warm weather, stacking these stones would have qualified as glove work for most of the crews on which I had labored, crews that were hardly wimpy, I might add, consisting of hardy nailers and shovel jockeys, all. Manchester had given a hint of this as well, displaying a Northerner's obstinacy in her citizens' ambivalence to the elements, with young revelers out in the freezing cold with no outerwear, the young ladies outside the pub smoking in miniskirts and laughing about it. In any case, this was my audition for the role of "person worthy of farming" for James, so I was going to be damned if I was going to squeak about my hands or anything else. Some call this quality "hardy," "game," or "dependable" . . . but most call it "stupid."

James looked at my last eight stones, smiled kindly, and instructed me to pull them off and start again. No room for politeness in this work, the result of which he hoped would last for decades more. As my education continued, we bonded over our love of books in general, but especially the agrarian ilk of Wendell Berry and Rachel Carson's *Silent Spring*, and how funny it was that that love had brought me all the way to this wintry Cumbrian pasture to perform hard, wet, cold labor and consider it a good time. Jobs like this, he said, were perfectly meditative, giving him a window of opportunity to work out notions and through-lines he would incorporate into his writing. I told him that was the equivalent of sanding in the woodshop: the repetitive chore that allowed part of one's mind to work on creative construction.

I could not have been more powerfully chuffed at how this was going down. We were engaged in my favorite pursuit—making something with our hands—and we were doing it with a method that people had been employing for millennia. Many, many generations ago, the locals had determined that the animals best suited to the climate and the terrain were sheep, in a handful of specific, sturdy variations. By merely tending the sheep—keeping them safe and occasionally feeding them when the winter snows cut them off from any forage whatsoever—the shepherd families were able to raise wool and meat while having a very minimal impact on their environment.

When they decided they wanted to relegate their flocks' movements to a certain area, but they didn't want to engage in the use of electric fencing, mainly because they didn't want to truck with the fossil fuel corporations and also because electricity wouldn't be invented for hundreds of years, the shepherds simply gathered up the free stones that were available on and around their land, knocked them into practical shapes with a bit of hammer and a bit of chisel, and stacked them into a serviceable structure. This act carries a similarly heroic charisma to woodland humans learning to chop down trees, cure them, then stack the logs into a cabin to protect themselves and their loved ones, meaning their cured meats, but also probably their children.

I described to James the development of the birch bark canoe by the Indigenous tribes of the Canadian North Woods, who could walk into the forest with a knife and a little fire and paddle out in an eighteen-foot canoe. The history of the canoe had been a favorite subject, I told him, which started when I read John McPhee's wonderful *The Survival of the Bark Canoe,* to which James said, "Oh, you must read his *Giving Good Weight,*" and so we checked another box confirming we were the kind of book nerds who could spar for hours armed with only McPhee titles.

I am a disciple of these crafts because they cannot be improved upon by modern technology. No 3-D printer or factory assembly line can build a finer stone wall or log cabin or weave a basket or skin a canoe than the hands of women and men. Crafting with sustainable, organic, natural materials requires the human genius of hand-eye coordination to properly and efficiently utilize what nature provides us. This requires us to pay close attention, in perpetuity, to the landscape from which our materials are gleaned, so that its health will continue to support our own.

All of these crafts, bark canoes, dry stone walls, and log cabins have required little to no improvement in tools or techniques for centuries, a fact that made James feel connected to his forebears with an immediacy when he participated in the tradition, and I felt that way too, a bit, as I gave up my stone wall virginity with icicle hands. I had certainly felt it powerfully when I built my first canoes (with cedar and fiberglass instead of birch bark) and paddled them, one in New York Harbor and the second on the Russian River in Northern California. Crossing the obstacle that is a body of water in any large format, in a watercraft of one's own making, because of that primal, instinctive urge to "get over there to the other side" because "I think there's a Taco Bell over there," has been uniting humankind with our sustenance for eons, answering the ancient call of the chalupa.

The development of the canoe form, by the way, not to mention the kayak, was a great example of evolutionary thinking that crossed over cultural lines. When Europeans arrived in North America, they already had a substantial boat-building tradition, obviously, since they arrived via ocean-sailing ship. The smaller watercraft of Europe were traditionally built with a sturdier, heavier construction than the canoe, with lapstraked wooden planks on frames in the rowboats, punts, and tenders that typically populated the harbors, rivers, and lakes of yore. To their credit, the French and English quickly recognized the efficacy of the Native American canoe and switched to that design for a great deal of their travel and cargo-hauling in the Hudson Bay and Great Lakes regions, thereby respecting the technology of the Indigenous tribes even as they profoundly disrespected its creators.

As is well argued by Bruce Pascoe in his book *Dark Emu*, the Europeans had a terrible track record for arriving in a new world (Australia, in the case of *Dark Emu*) and, as we all know, devastating the Native tribes by varying methods of genocide, or at least brutal displacement. In order to treat other human souls so viciously, this behavior on "our" part required a certain degree of denial. This was achieved by treating the American Natives, or the Aboriginal tribes in Australia as less than human—vermin, really—that required extermination, so that the proper, "civilized" humans could set up house. Pascoe succinctly points out that when the English made their reports detailing the progress of their settlements Down Under, they therefore had to necessarily ignore the complex civilizations of the local tribes entirely, despite their methods of surviving amicably in concert with nature that had been developed over millennia. Housing, farming, fishing, complete economies: eradicated. Wiped off the face of Australia. "Nothing to see here, your highness, except some random savages!" Next, of course, the English heroically shipped in herds of grazing sheep and cows and attempted to plant their wheat and other continental grains, and then looked on stupidly as they all faltered and died in inhospitable soil, within an ecosystem that was entirely alien to the biology of their plants and animals. They exhibited all the common sense of hijacking a plane for its cargo of riches and then killing the pilots without gleaning any of their imperative knowledge. We're all in so much of a hurry, then and now, to make money, that we never bother learning to land the son-of-a-bitching plane.

* * *

Reprieve finally came to us pasture mates when we had completed the meticulous repair job on the wall, puzzling each stone back into our best guess at its original location. The good news was, the breach was gone—entirely filled in, even though James said it was not "our best work." It looked pretty damn handsome to me, albeit through the eyes of the uninitiated. The bad news was we had about seven stones left over and no rug under which to sweep them. I guess James docked my pay per stone, because based on the *zero* quid he gave me, I must have broken even.

We went inside and got washed up for lunch, historically one of the most glorious sensual pleasures known to woman and man alike. The phenomenon is specific to the winter, and the colder and wetter one can become before reentry into the cozy warmth, the more profound the payoff. By that measure, based on the light jacket and the mitts of ignominy (a.k.a. "no gloves") that I had endured all morning, I was poised to receive the full flush of paradise.

It began with peeling off wet garments just inside the kitchen door to the garden patio—rain pants, boots, and jacket were left in the mud area. I went into the powder room and ran some lukewarm water to soap up my poor paws, the soft, fragile thespian's gesticulators cruelly impelled to perform the rugged labor of a prison chain gang. My assorted flesh wounds and contusions sang with painful delight at being alive! These hands would live another day, to be brutally used again by the asshole operating the soap.

I emerged, freshly scrubbed, and headed straight for the large dining table, where I was reacquainted with Helen and one-year-old Tom, who continued to delight and terrify, depending upon the direction of the breeze. With the other children at school, he ruled the roost, and I spoke to him of mischief, namely that he and I might get up to some, if not now, then one day soon. He cackled conspiratorially, saluting with his spoon, and nailed me with an openmouthed wink. Sometimes, even at the tender age of one, a person can communicate so clearly that they

will be my leader, and I understand with a clarity that could not be more obvious. They are the general in whose army I have the pleasure of serving. I have a niece who does this as well. God help us if she ever gets together with Tom.

What a marvelous day I was having, and it was only just lunchtime. The earlier mention I made of a pleasurable assault on the senses was about to peak. Helen brought to the table a pot from the stove to finish off the preparation of—and I might suggest you slowly say this out loud—*ham and bean broth and fresh baked bread and butter.* Let's keep cool. Deep inhale through the nose. Let it out through the ham-hole . . . I mean . . . I mean. Now you might understand my earlier comment—the colder and wetter you can stand it outside, the more goddamn amazing the ham and bean broth is going to go down.

* * *

While the scene I'm sketching took place in the UK, it couldn't help but remind me of the very American journey I'd been taking back at home, and of Wendell's question, and of the fellow he had mentioned, Aldo Leopold. Since that time and even today, I've been perusing Leopold's legend, and his own territory, my own beloved Midwest. I can scarcely imagine a better location for the rearing of a future agrarian legend than where Aldo sprung from, the forested bluffs of Iowa, overlooking the Mississippi River. Similar to James and myself, Aldo Leopold had the benefit of a dad who took him to the woods and taught him the ways of woodcraft; to look and see what was there, and to discern how he might make use of it. Young Leopold became a skilled hunter and observer as he explored the environs of Iowa and Illinois on their respective banks of that mighty river. Similarly to our twenty-sixth president, Theodore Roosevelt ('member him?), Leopold spent an impressive amount of time cataloging the local bird populations in his area.

This fascination with the forest and the creatures inhabiting it led him to pursue his secondary education at Yale's brand-new school for forestry, founded not-so-coincidentally by Gifford Pinchot, a contemporary of Roosevelt, Grinnell, and John Muir, whom we met earlier. In 1905, at the dawning of the twentieth century, Leopold worked diligently to be accepted into the nascent forestry program, and despite his tendency to spend more time in the woods around New Haven, Connecticut, than in the classroom, he managed to survive the indoor portions of his schooling well enough to achieve his goal of being hired by the US Forest Service by 1909.

His first postings were in the territories of Arizona and New Mexico, both on the verge of achieving statehood in 1912. First at the Apache National Forest, then the Carson National Forest, Leopold brought his lifelong curiosity to bear and he developed a substantial comprehension of the area's flora and fauna. When I read "Forest Service," it makes me think mainly of ranger stations and Smokey Bear and log-cabin-style fire lookout towers, but this governmental agency within the US Department of Agriculture is of course much more complex than that when it comes to its responsibilities. This was even more the case in Leopold's day, when the service oversaw areas of concern that were later split off into other subagencies, like the Fish and Wildlife Service and the Bureau of Land Management.

Thus, the Forest Service bore the responsibility for managing fishing and hunting and the growing packs of humans in search of recreation in the newly formed parks and wilderness preserves of the annexed Southwestern states. Aldo Leopold was tasked with writing the first game and fish handbook for the Forest Service, and developing the first comprehensive management plan for no lesser an attraction than the Grand Canyon. Another of the departmental duties in which Leopold took part was the dogged eradication of the apex predators, which were the bane of local Southwest ranchers. Bears, mountain lions, and wolves were hunted and destroyed on sight, not just for the beef and sheep concerns, but for the sake of game hunters as well. Stone walls may have kept the English country sheep safe enough, but not so in the American West.

In his essay "Thinking Like a Mountain," Leopold details an epiphany that came about as the result of one such wolf extermination that he undertook with companions. They were eating lunch when they saw a she-wolf and some pups downhill from them. They immediately began firing at the wolves, for, as he wrote, *"In those days we had never heard of passing up a chance to kill a wolf."*

He went on: *"We reached the old wolf in time to watch a fierce green fire dying in her eyes. I realized then, and have known ever since, that there was something new to me in those eyes—something known only to her and to the mountain. I was young then, and full of trigger-itch; I thought that because fewer wolves meant more deer, that no wolves would mean hunters' paradise. But after seeing the green fire die, I sensed that neither the wolf nor the mountain agreed with such a view."**

The realization he referred to fully turned his thinking around in a way that came to shape not only the remainder of his life and career but his entire agrarian position that our civilization is still in desperate need of implementing. When he wrote that the mountain wouldn't agree with

---

* Leopold, Aldo. Lines from *Sand County Almanac: And Sketches Here and There*, 121. Oxford University Press, Incorporated, 2020. Reproduced with permission of the Licensor through PLSclear.

the violent, self-centered habits of mankind, what he meant was that by eradicating the wolves in this case, the deer would then be allowed to proliferate beyond the balance that had heretofore been maintained by the natural order of things. One direct result of this surplus deer population would be the denuding of the mountain, when too many deer would eat every leaf and shoot on every plant, from the ground to *"the height of a saddle horn,"* which would result in nothing but, *"in the end, the starved bones of the hoped-for deer herd, dead of its own too-much, bleach with the bones of the dead sage, or molder under the high-lined junipers."*

In witnessing the dying green fire in that she-wolf's eyes, Leopold awoke to the wisdom of "thinking like the mountain." He saw at once how our species is merely one small part of the "great economy" that is all of nature, and the ecological humility that our place in nature subsequently requires. This attitude fell in stark contrast to the much more popular stance that mankind had assumed over the ages, one to which we are yet tenaciously clinging. It has been so powerfully our brand for so long a time that even 2,500-odd years ago, our Greek dramatists recognized the folly therein and gave this singularly human characteristic a cool name: *hubris.*

The essence of the hubris in this case is humankind's inability to comprehend that we do not know and never can know, as Wendell Berry tells it, *"either all the creatures that the Kingdom of God contains or the whole pattern or order by which it contains them."* This was Aldo Leopold's revelation—one that would steer him to introduce more benevolent, eco-conscious policies in the wildlife management of the Southwest. A spiritual shift that eventually, decades later, would see the bear and wolf populations restored to the mountains of New Mexico. His new, clear-eyed principles were founded in a reasoned humility in the face of nature. This set him apart from the totalitarian sensibilities of his peer conservationists, who thought that the natural resources of this planet were to be exploited first and foremost as humankind saw fit.

It has ever been the attitude of us *Homo sapiens* that when we employ our appetites and our technology to take what we like from the earth, if that greed should cause us any sort of problem, why, we'll just use our indefatigable smarts to science us up a solution to that new problem. And if that creates more problems, that's no sweat, because Silicon Valley has a hella slick new algorithm that will steer us above the pesky issues of pollution and the extinction of "unneeded" species. Leopold now understood that the only way to live responsibly, with the values of good citizenship in regard to our planet, our watershed, our neighbors, and ourselves, was to understand our place in that infinite pattern. To humbly acknowledge the inscrutability of Mother Nature's grocery list, and therefore remain ever vigilant about respecting our place upon it.

And that day in the Rebanks household, I seemed to have found the modern equivalent of what Aldo Leopold was searching for.

* * *

Once my thin-blooded, California candy ass had recovered from the conditions that James and Helen considered simply normal, I got a tour of their digs. The majority of the house was a post-and-beam structure that had been retrofitted into a two-story stone barn that had been built on the property in the 1870s. With decorative carvings of faces in the ends of the oak beams, and bespoke touches like a beautifully dovetailed custom surround housing the exhaust hood above the stove, all done by a couple of local joiners, the Rebankses had given themselves the gift of their dream house only a few years earlier.

For his whole life, James had held the stone sheep barn in that special fantasy space that can be so fruitfully decorated by a child's imagining. Improbably, he'd always thought, "How amazing it would be to one day turn that barn into my house," but of course things like that don't happen in reality, because they are neither physically practical nor fiscally responsible. Fortunately for this family, however, they don't need to reside entirely within the walls of reality, because Dad happens to have written some hit books.

This storybook house must powerfully satisfy not only James and Helen and their in-house troupe of wee hired hands, but also generation upon generation of their mildly itinerant ancestors, scratching a posthumous housing itch that likely dates back many centuries. According to James, their sheep have been bred to graze that mountain (hefted to the fell) since at least the first century, when the Vikings were the ones buying packets of crisps at the pub. The Herdwick breed may, in fact, be traceable to the first farmers in the region around 4,500 years ago. So, although James's family has been bouncing around the Matterdale area since 1420, sometimes renting and sometimes owning land and houses, there has never been one long-term family home. Like so many families, then and now, working shoulder-to-the-wheel year in and year out, the Rebanks clan moved from home to home, just keeping a step ahead of the landlord and the taxman.

In much the same way that my acting career affords me a nicer shop of tools than if I were a woodworker only, James's writing success has augmented his intense shepherding life. Despite the prowess he wields at the sheep auction, winning prizes and commanding high prices, it took the extra frosting of a bestselling book to pull off this truly storybook house. On top of the charming construction, the young parents also rigged the farm with a solar panel and lithium battery array for electricity, with a generator for when the occasional backup is needed. Heating is mainly accomplished with burning wood and heating oil. And in the meantime, his flock has also increased. All in all, it's a pretty impressive success story—from the twenty Herdwick ewes with which they started in 2002, they have grown their flock to three hundred good ewes, or as George Clinton calls them, "Mother-sheep." Kids, this joke is from the '70s.

This house required a keen imagination, the zeal of the homesteader, and a healthy dash of whimsy. Some people might call this extravagance irresponsible or stupid. I say it's gorgeous. It's romantic, and brimming with life. Laughter abounds throughout the rooms, and some unhappy caterwauling as well, although thankfully much more of the former. The key to making this playfully conceived house vital instead of a folly is that it is being *used*. Utilized to within an inch of its life. Like the stones in the pasture wall were prized for their utility, everything about this warm and welcoming shelter is being properly exploited, and it was a joy to witness.

Once we had braced ourselves with plenty of stew and a cup of ubiquitous tea (black for me), it was back out into the weather to check on the flocks. We saw the ewes (the ladies), the tup hoggs (the young fellows), and the tups (the patriarchs). I helped James distribute "sheep cake," which sounds really yummy, but don't get excited. It's like large, nutritious kibble for sheep, and nothing like cake whatsoever. I was pissed. The sheep came running from the far corners of the hillside pasture when James called for them, because I guess they also thought there was actual cake. They seemed not as miffed as I was, however, at the bait and switch, and happily munched the nuggets on the ground.

I couldn't help but marvel at the majestic, alpine appearance of these simple creatures, which had been perfectly adapted over the millennia to survive with perfect equanimity in the freezing rains and snow of northern English winters. James and his neighbors were adhering to the tried-and-true agricultural practice of pairing the beast with the place. If your animals are genetically equipped to thrive in their environment from the get-go, well, think about it. Do the math and you'll find they will require much less expense in every direction. If you can stay out of Mother Nature's way as much as possible, year after year it stands to reason that your harvest of her bounty will have a much better chance at consistently high quality.

This method contrasts pretty starkly with the American ideal, not of agri-*culture*, but of agri-*business*. In that methodology, you can generally ignore the nature of the place while proceeding to maximize your output at all costs, including the cost of much lower-quality produce. The reason you needn't worry about the problems nature might hand you (bugs, weeds, depleted soil, malnutrition, etc.) is because any problems can be eradicated through the use of chemicals and machinery.

Of course, these "solutions" invariably create more problems, especially since nothing grows in a vacuum. That's how cancer-causing herbicides like Roundup, from the giant corporation Monsanto, end up in the runoff of every watershed in the country, or entire communities end up with chronic pollution and blight. The "solutions" from agribusiness might kill a weed or even *all* weeds, but the scorecard never ends there.

Like all human problems, the situation is more complicated than just "big farm bad/little farm good," but in the grand scheme of American food production, my attention is consistently drawn to one massive factor: the vast majority of our grain farmers are not actually growing edible food. Instead of working within the parameters of nature (a.k.a. "health") to produce delicious, nutritious food items, all of the corn and

WHERE THE DEER AND THE ANTELOPE PLAY 133

soybeans are destined to become mere ingredients, processed into "food products" in a factory setting.

His adherence to "the old ways" is primarily what drew me to James in the first place. One of the central themes in his writing has to do with recognizing the mistakes we humans have made with regard to farming decisions over the last few generations, and undertaking a program of action to reverse the damage that we have exacted upon our lands, our climate, our animals, and ourselves. Upon nature.

Maybe this is also part of what Wendell meant in his Muir vs. Leopold idea—observing not just what farmers like James were doing to prevent further damage, but what they were doing to reverse the mistakes made in the past, and to restore the harmony that both the people and the land ultimately deserve. That's a hell of a task that will require the efforts (and votes) of many more people than just well-meaning agrarians. Our industrial food system, especially in the US, is an enormous machine in which we have invested decades of wealth and ingenuity, fortifying ourselves in the wrong direction, it turns out. It's a notion that has always fascinated me, ever since I started reading Michael Pollan and Eric Schlosser: We have allowed our food system to be entirely usurped by corporate interests who do not produce our food with *our health* in mind. Think about that. I mean, what is the point of food in the first place? In America, the obfuscation cloaking how our food is produced has reached the point where we have to work *hard* just to discern which food is actually clean, healthy, nutritious, and free of additives, and then pay considerably more to buy it.

By the way, I should point out that the farmers themselves, from large to small, are not the villains here, but simply participants in a deeply flawed system that is perpetuated by faceless corporate entities. Farming successfully on any level is extremely difficult. My very own family members farm corn and soybeans, and they are as hardworking and decent of people as any I have ever met. I have admired my uncles and cousins and their farming households my entire life, for the self-sufficient way that they are able to look at the available options—the fields, the crops, the equipment, the market—and wrestle a profit out of them damn near every year.

On this topic, I usually get in over my head pretty quickly, so I called my friend Mary Berry, lioness daughter of Wendell and Tanya, who has picked up the ball of the family ethos, if you will, and is running like hell for the end zone. In the small town of New Castle, Kentucky, she runs the Berry Center and also sits on the board of the Wendell Berry Farming Program, a relatively young venture in partnership with Vermont's Sterling College, educating young farmers in the ways they might navigate the extremely difficult waters of modern agriculture in this country.

One of the founding principles of the aforementioned Berry ethos was the Burley Tobacco Program, written and legislated into being by Wendell's father, John M. Berry Sr., a farmer and lawyer. The program created a cooperative, which included small, diversified tobacco farmers in the eight-state "Burley Belt." In one of only a few examples of such level dealing in our history, the program took control of production in order to maintain a "parity price," equal for all growers, and eventually applied this parity principle to all of their farming output, ensuring that the farmers had a financial backstop in place. Small-holdings farmers were then able to make farm payments and borrow funds to transition from farm tenancy to ownership. Land and the imperative culture of good land use thus passed fairly seamlessly from generation to generation.

This sensibility makes me long to elect Mary to the highest agricultural office to which we can vault her, as she brings the accumulated wisdom and experience of a few generations of thinking Berrys to bear on the current dilemmas facing farmers. When I asked her about it, she set me straight—that this subject, too, requires a great deal more nuance: "It is important to say that we have given farmers in this country two choices. They can be small and entrepreneurial or large and industrial. There is almost nothing for the middle, where most of our farmers, people who live from farming, are. We are losing these farmers faster than very small farmers or very large ones. In these mid-size farmers lives much of what is left of an agrarian culture. Some farmers have tried, and succeeded, in the world of entrepreneurial farming, but many have failed and it has not built the kind of agricultural community that supports good farming. Entrepreneurial farmers are in direct competition with each other! Many of our farmers have gotten into the grain economy and either failed completely or have kept themselves afloat on debt. Meanwhile, our economy keeps humming along as if the destruction of our land and our people can go on forever. And we will continue to eat!"

I propose that we consider our farmers on a spectrum, let's say, of agrarianism. On one end of the spectrum we have farmers like James, interested in producing the finest foodstuffs that they can, given the soil, the climate, the water, the budget, and their talent. They observe how efficacious or not their efforts are proving, and they adapt accordingly. Variety is one of the keys to this technique, eschewing the corporate monocultures for a revolving set of plants and animals, again, to mimic what was already happening on the land before we showed up with our earth-shaving machinery. It's tough as hell, and in many cases impossible, to farm this way and earn enough profit to keep your bills paid and your family fed, but these farmers do exist.

On the other end of the spectrum is full-speed-ahead robo-farming, in which the farmer is following the instructions of the corporation to produce not food but *commodities* in such a way that the corporation sits poised to make the maximum financial profit. Now, this is the part that has always fascinated me about *us* as a population: This kind of farmer is doing all they can to make their factory quota for the company, of grain, or meat, or what have you, *despite* their soil, climate, water, budget, or talent. It only stands to reason that this methodology is the very definition of unsustainable.

Clearly, this is an oversimplification of an issue that requires as much of my refrain (nuance!) as any other human endeavor, but the broad strokes are hard to refute. The first farmer is doing their best to work *with* nature.

The second farmer is doing their best *despite* nature. In order for the second farmer to prosper, they must *defeat* nature. A great example of this is the factory farming of beef/pork/chicken/eggs/turkey/salmon/etc. The manufacturers of these products have done everything they can to take the process out of nature entirely and hide it in a shed, where every step of the production has been engineered to make a profit; to excel at quantity. I know you're a little bit ahead of me here, but I'll go ahead and ask the obvious question: What of quality? If you're willing to degrade these many lives with impunity—the lives of the animals themselves, the workers "growing" them, the neighbors having to suffer the voluminous poisons being pumped into the ecosystem/watershed, and the humans consuming your products—then what are you about? Can that even be considered farming?

Again, I'm asking this of us. Of you and me, because what I have just described is the way a lot of our food is produced right now, in the system that we all support with our dollars. How did we get here, in both the US and the UK? How can we change our national stance toward agriculture to accommodate more middle-size farmers and less factory farms? How would Aldo Leopold feel about it?

10

MANCHESTER

When I arrived via train back in Manchester after my first few days and nights with the Rebanks family, I began to see the city through new eyes. Barreling through the picturesque white, wintry hills, which were outlined by the very stone walls which I had newly become a master at building ("master" only compared to the other actors, please don't tell James I called myself this, he'll rightly tell you that my side of the wall was rubbish), I began to feel the minor oppression that comes with reentry into the gray urban landscape of England's fifth-largest city. Disembarking into the bustling crowd of Manchester Piccadilly station, I felt a bit melancholy, as though I had been feeding sheep with Peter Pan on the fells of Neverland and now I had to return to the cold, modern world of responsibility, dictated by the machinery of humankind on computers in cubicles in office buildings which loom over the sharp right angles of the streets, sidewalks, and curbs.

Working in Manchester on the Alex Garland show *Devs* was actually not my first sojourn in the historic birthplace of the Industrial Revolution. Five years earlier I had been staying in London with my heroic wife, Megan, as she filmed a television show, and I took the train one day a few hours north to Manchester to see my longtime favorite band. They just happened to be called Wilco, and were fronted by my favorite extreme balls-to-the-wall survivalist-adventurer and yours, too—singer-songwriter-mountaineer Jeff Tweedy.

Back in 2014, I had been obsessed with Wilco for almost two decades, but my friendship with Jeff himself was still new. As a result, I was trembling with the excitement of a kid on Christmas morning, at the prospect of seeing him and them. Living in a swanky hotel in Soho and kicking around London, learning to speak Cockney with the other chimney sweeps, was thrilling enough, but then to have my rock-and-roll mate casually ask if I wanted to come see them in Manchester was far beyond what any boy could be expected to withstand. It was as though I were just chilling with Peter Gabriel and Zadie Smith, maybe heading to the seaside for some proper fish and chips in newspaper, suggesting to him some new djembe beats or telling her some terrific puns I had easily thought up.

When I saw Jeff and the band (recited with ragged fervor: John, Nels, heehee, Glenn, Pat, Mikael, but haha, who's counting?) rock my world that night at Manchester's historic Ritz theatre (now the O_2 Ritz), I had no way of knowing that the city would come to play a substantial role in a future life chapter for me, but it was still thrilling enough.

A couple hours before the show began, Jeff was alone onstage in this hundred-year-old former dance hall with a sprung wooden jitterbug floor, and I was alone in the audience section, watching and hearing him sound-check as the lighting designer ran through his cues. That means that randomly colored and patterned rock-and-roll lights played moodily across, above, and behind Jeff as he noodled a few Neil Young songs out of his booming J-200 guitar, a handsome vintage chap called "Buck."

I've already written about Jeff's cover of "The Losing End"—I featured Jeff in my 2015 book, *Gumption*—but he also played "Pocahontas" and "Thrasher," two great examples of Neil Young's most powerful poetry. I remember these because the chords are quite manageable, which is a profound gift if you're a fan of Neil and you happen to be trying to learn to play the guitar. Both songs feature themes that ring through a lot of the questions that Jeff and I (and George with us, 'member George?) ask of ourselves and of society as we proceed to each hoe our own particular row. The subjects also flow through this book—examining the loss that has accompanied so many of our supposed gains in modern civilization.

"Pocahontas" paints a bleak picture of our historically warlike treatment of Native Americans, complete with teepee murders, cut-down women, and "babies cryin' on the ground." Young juxtaposes this imagery with talk of Hollywood and the Houston Astrodome, two representations of the material excess worshipped by Americans in the 1970s, when the song was written, contrasting the peaceful simplicity of the "aurora borealis" and "paddles cut[ting] the water" with the schlocky, superficial institutions that replaced them.

In "Thrasher," the narrator is a freethinker who awakens to the fact that the people around him have become complacent sheep, lulled into a stupor by the affluence of consumerism. As Aldo Leopold wrote, *"The modern dogma is comfort at any cost."* Having devoted themselves wholly to modern materialism, the narrator's friends have grown calcified in the dissatisfying ruts of their urban lives.

They had the best selection

They were poisoned with protection

There was nothing that they needed

Nothing left to find

They were lost in rock formations

Or became park bench mutations

On the sidewalks and in the stations

They were waiting, waiting

He leaves them behind in an attempt to return to the purer ideals of yesteryear, more in line with the beauty and wisdom of nature's systems. The actual harbinger of the industrial doom in the song is the titular "thrasher," a field grain-harvesting machine and forerunner to the modern grain combine, which is the precise chariot in which corporate agribusiness has lain waste to the grasslands of Aldo Leopold's Midwest.

Writing this, I am reminded of Wendell Berry's essay "Two Economies," a fifteen-page gift of sagacity which posits the "small economies" in our lives, like those of your household; or of Decatur, Illinois; or the nation of Norway; or the "money economy," a.k.a. "Wall Street," against the Great Economy of the universe, that of all creation, which I feel I can safely equate simply with "Nature." With his trademark common sense, Berry points up the futility in concerning ourselves solely with any one or more of these little economies, as though they don't all exist within and as a part of the Great Economy, whether we care to admit it or not. You may have noticed this sense of futility on occasion when you have read or heard in the news that "the economy is doing great," while you look around and see homelessness, sickness, and poverty as ever on the rise.

"The economy" in the news has a lot to do with how the nation's corporations are faring, and little to do with how many salmon are managing to make it back up an Oregon river to their spawning grounds in the face of new dams we have installed. The little money economy that our politicians and bankers openly worship is not the economy about which we should be seeking diagnoses. The Great Economy, in the end, is all that matters.

So perhaps my analogy was inapt, when I wrote that leaving the Rebanks farm and entering Manchester felt like I was leaving the land of play to return to cold, adult responsibility. Because what we have overwhelmingly forgotten as a population is exactly the responsibility of care that each of us owes to the Great Economy, and the lessons in that particular course of education, that had damn better well be grown-up, are much more easily digested on a sheep farm than on the streets of a city.

* * *

Thinking back on all of my trips to the Rebanks farm, as well as what I've been lucky enough to read of his writing, I'm struck by the frank humility with which James writes about the farming efforts made in his neighborhood by the last few generations that turned out to be erroneous in the end. These decisions were not taken lightly, by men and women whom James respected and at whose heels he studied. An important fuel for this catalog of mistakes has been our human propensity for hubris. Feeling the rush of blood and pride when the Industrial Revolution began to turn the objectives of the working class upside down, James's ancestors, along with most of Western civilization, forgot the fealty that we must pay to Mother Nature, deciding instead that mankind could overpower nature with the might of our science and technology.

In the case of the Rebanks farm, for example, natural waterways were straightened into canal-like channels, ostensibly to increase and improve the acreage of the bottomlands, via more efficient drainage. A few generations later, the land was still swampy and relatively unproductive, and a vast swath of biodiversity had disappeared, or at least been greatly diminished, sacrificed in the eradication of the natural creeklike becks. With the loss of the minnows, frogs, and scores of insects that swarmed around a small stream, their predators then also faded away, including entire species of birds and small mammals.

Similarly, the once kaleidoscopic mix of grasses, thistles, and wildflowers in the pastures had long since been supplanted with much more homogenized mono-growth, with the idea that this would be more efficient for the feeding of the grazing ruminants. Again, the insects went away, the birds and bats that ate those insects went away, and the mowing of said mono-crops presented a whole new treachery to species like the curlew, which traditionally nests on the ground in those wild grasses. The curlew, a charismatic relative of the plover and the sandpiper, with a sweet song, all but disappeared in recent decades, though with the kind attentions of farmers like the Rebanks family, they are slowly beginning to mount a comeback.

* * *

This curlew dilemma reminds me of the great spotted owl debate of the 1980s in the Pacific Northwest. The United States Forest Service turned in a logging plan for old-growth forests that would essentially wipe out the entire population of spotted owls, who rely exclusively on that forest for their habitat. In a prolonged battle that grew quite rancorous, a compromise was reached that, of course, favored the money. The number of breeding pairs of these owls has since been drastically reduced, so that the species remains categorized as "threatened" on the endangered species list. Yet again, we humans looked at a vital part of an ecosystem and said, "Sure, we get it, we love the owls. But, money."

The cynical, modern response, or at least the American response, to such an issue is "Who cares? It's an owl, boo-hoo. What's the big deal?"

Ha, you fell into my trap. Because after the dying wolf in the "green fire" incident turned Aldo Leopold's worldview around, he began to see every part of his Wisconsin farm as equally imperative to the overall health of the Great Economy:

"The last word in ignorance is the man who says of an animal or plant, 'What good is it?' If the land mechanism as a whole is good, then every part is good, whether we understand it or not. If the biota, in the course of eons, has built something we like but do not understand, then who but a fool would discard seemingly useless parts? To keep every cog and wheel is the first precaution of intelligent tinkering."

Guess you feel pretty dumb now, huh, Mr. Moneybags Logger Guy?

There is one major cog that we as a people have relegated to the literal dustbin, because we have come to be taught that it's dirty.

Let's talk about soil. Healthy soil. Loamy, moist, cakey soil lousy with fecundity. If we were walking in an ideal field in Leopold's Madison, or Rebanks's Cumbria, I might kneel down and scoop up a teaspoon of the stuff and say to you, augustly, "You know how much microbial life is teeming in this teaspoon of soil? An ass-load." Productive soil will usually contain between one hundred million and one billion bacteria per teaspoon. That's a lot. Like, an ass-load. Perhaps it's easier to picture thus: If you took the bacteria from one acre of good soil and mushed it together like Play-Doh, you could shape it into two good-sized cows.

Here is an amazing description by Wendell Berry, and I'll let you decide who presented the facts more eloquently, me or this august man of letters: "*The soil is the great connector of lives, the source and destination of all. It is the healer and restorer and resurrector, by which disease passes into health, age into youth, death into life. Without proper care for it we can have no community, because without proper care for it we can have no life.*" Okay, I agree, it's a tie. But once more for those in the back row, "*without proper care for [our soil], we can have no life.*"

* * *

Back to the train station in Manchester. And a refresher on some more human nuance. Because Manchester, and what we have done there, and subsequently elsewhere, is also amazing, and damn worthy of celebration. The Industrial Revolution started in Manchester, and for all the badmouthing I do about gross materialism (here comes the nuance), I am simply apeshit about all of the amazing crap we humans have made via the Industrial Revolution! I would have to be a fool not to be enthralled by my affordable blue denim jean-pants, made possible by the sewing machine (awesome) and, oh, sweatshop labor in Asia (shit). I powerfully adore my Ford F-250 diesel Super Duty truck, mainly for hauling massive stacks of entire slabs of tree trunks up and down the West Coast, to be made into furniture and boats and such in my woodshop, thanks to Henry Ford and his factory assembly line system (so dope)! Unfortunately, my truck's emissions are part of the human dipshittery contributing voluminously to climate change (nuance, goddammit!). Also, on top of his amazing contributions to industry, Henry Ford was also a vicious racist and anti-Semite! Son of a bitch!

So, as you can see, our consumption-mad society is a really mixed bag, morality-wise. I find it easy to envision and comprehend the haste with which we as a people turned our gaze from the health of the soil and the Great Economy overall to whatever the manufacturers had created to sell to us. I imagine myself as a youngster in my dad's garden, pulling weeds, and staring again, puzzled, at the kohlrabi (what the F is it anyway?), when the "salespeople" drive up (in this fantasy, they're in a PT Cruiser) and holler, "Hey, Nick, do you want to kneel in the dirt like a hayseed, or do you want to come check out this new little amusement that we're calling DONKEY KONG?" Now, I don't know about you, but I am certainly not man enough to resist a brand-new video game, garden-side or not. Because of how I'm goddamn stupid, you see. And I think you might be, as well! No offense, it's part of our charm. We come by it honest, anyway.

Manchester started things booming with textile machinery, namely the cotton mill, and by 1800, the city was said to be "steam-mill mad." Wool and cotton goods were only the beginning of a true global revolution of industry, at the center of which sat Manchester. Soon, across the early nineteenth century, the city was mass-producing goods of all descriptions. Pretty amazing, right? A source of immense pride, a pinnacle of human achievement, and rightfully s—oh, hang on. Shit. Where was that cotton coming from, in this burgeoning global network? And who was picking it, on the business end of an American bullwhip? Damn it. It's almost as though this insouciant "nuance" permeates every aspect of human endeavor.

One of the absolute stars of the Industrial Revolution was, of course, the choo-choo train—the invention of rail travel. The Manchester Science and Industry Museum, a wonderful establishment housed in a collection of old warehouse buildings, including the original station for the world's oldest surviving passenger railway, had a great deal of proud information surrounding the steam locomotive "Traveling Engine No. 19," more commonly known by her showbiz name, "Rocket." This marvel of engineering was the favored vehicle developed for the nascent Liverpool and Manchester Railway, which was a pretty damn exciting new way to get around. Imagine riding behind a locomotive in a time when the only other forms of conveyance were fueled by either wind or horse. It was sincerely mind-blowing. A local luminary, Dr. James Johnson, was unnerved by "the deafening peal of thunder, the sudden immersion in gloom and the clash of reverberated sounds in confined space," whilst nubile Covent Garden actress Fanny Kemble was awestruck, referring to the locomotives as "tame dragons" and saying, "When I closed my eyes, this sensation of flying was quite delightful, and strange beyond description; yet strange as it was, I had a perfect sense of security, and not the slightest fear." Sounds a lot like the way I felt myself, "riding the tame dragon" to Manchester to catch a Wilco show, although I don't believe I've ever been described as nubile. Ursine? You bet. Nubile? Don't think so.

Before the railways revolutionized freight haulage, when it was time for breeders to sell their flocks and herds at market, previous centuries saw "drovers" literally walking their livestock to the city, which sometimes meant trekking hundreds of miles to claim the best prices. Drovers would hoof it from the highlands of Scotland or the remote Welsh coast all the way to London to sell their beasts. This tradition had its hardships, but it also held certain charms for the people involved. Local customs and idioms were exchanged as the drovers came through, fostering a more well-rounded knowledge of the disparate parts of the island. Breeders were able to learn from one another, what was and wasn't working with their breeds, thus improving the overall quality of their stock, with a proper sense of community. James told me that sometimes the drovers would catch a ride back to the farm, leaving their dogs on their own, because those sheepdogs were so smart that they would find their own way home, pub by pub. Not only was this amazing, but the pub owners would recognize these dogs, and feed them, adding their fodder to the drovers' tabs for when they next returned.

This is charming as hell, and it's just one tiny detail of all that is lost when we mechanize *any* process that used to rely on the knowledge and skill of human hands (or feet). When expansive fields of grain on the American prairie are farmed entirely by machine, in a way that never once requires the farmer to insert their hand into the soil to assess its health, we lose perhaps the most precious aspect of having farmers among us. That is the responsibility that small farmers shoulder in monitoring and maintaining the health of their little patch of our ecosystem, not just for the health of the agrarian world but for the health of their own plot and their own family.

"That sounds just lovely, Nick, what a romantic notion for this storybook farmer you have dreamt up. But, um, money."

In my woodshop, I revel in the constant rewards I reap from learning the "old ways" of shaping wood with tools. In some sects of fine woodworking, the more mastery one gains, the less one requires electricity to power one's tools—said masters are able to rely upon the finesse achievable not only with chisel and handsaw, but with balance, leverage, and accumulated wisdom as well.

As an example of this, I offer for your consideration the heroic dovetail joint. In a nutshell, dovetails are a method by which two pieces of wood may be joined together, puzzle-like, with interlocking angled fingers called pins and tails. This treatment is often found in the construction of drawer boxes in fine furniture. Traditionally, the dovetails can be cut and excavated using just a couple of simple hand tools, like a chisel, a mallet, and a dovetail saw. Free-handing this process is indeed a mark of mastery, and it requires many hours of practice, which includes the ruination of a lot of boards. The nice part is you can put on some Nick Cave or some Patty Griffin and savor the sounds and smells of cutting joinery the same way woodworkers have been doing it for centuries.

Now, if you're trying to build, say, a chest of drawers with sixteen dovetails apiece in each of five drawers, plus another twenty dovetails in the carcase, or body of the piece, for a total of one hundred dovetails, you're looking at a considerable commitment of billable time, which you have undoubtedly underbid in the price you gave your client. So you get out your woodworking textbooks or you jump on YouTube and find a few different ways to supposedly speed up the process by involving your band saw or table saw, and you spend a bunch of time dialing in the processes and jigs necessary to that "improvement." Whether you actually save time in the long run is always questionable. But wait, there is indeed more.

When you're looking for quick dovetail helpers, you can actually blow right past the saw-based tricks and into the realm of the router guide. Without getting too technical, this is basically a metal template that attaches to your board, allowing a spinning router bit (like a very large dental tool) to be guided along and in and out of what looks like a series of teeth, so that the spinning cutter bit simply removes all the necessary wood and creates the dovetails very quickly. The router motor can vary in size, but joinery bits are best housed in a motor about as large as a medium coffee can. Once you have the knack of this, your dovetails can be cut much more quickly than they can with only hand tools (unless you're Christian Becksvoort, the modern master of the Shaker style—if dovetails were in the Olympics, he'd have several gold medals).

The trade-off, as you may have guessed, is that a router motor doesn't just resemble a dental rotary tool, it actually sounds like a giant tooth drill. Between the motor and the noise of the bit cutting greedily into the wood, it's a veritable assault on the ears that, even with ear protection, makes me grit my teeth. The razor-sharp dovetail bit, usually between a pencil eraser and the tip of your pinky finger in size, is spinning at around twenty-four thousand revolutions per minute, or as the young people say, "hella fast," or as their even younger counterparts DM each other, "fast af." This speed also makes this one of the most treacherous tools in the shop. But, money.

In so many ways that are referred to as "progress," we happily leave behind such an incredible wealth of accrued human knowledge. I know that for myself, I have learned (again and again, because I am stupid and stubborn) that I would rather work in the old ways. Don't get me wrong, I drive a modern vehicle, I use a smartphone, I even plug a probe thermometer into the pork butt I'm smoking, but wherever and whenever I can, I indulge in the traditional ways that my ancestors might recognize. The thermometer might be fancy and newfangled, but the eight pounds of smoked pork over an oak and hickory charcoal fire is downright eldritch.

In fact, this brings to mind the great quote from Jonas Salk: *Our greatest responsibility is to be good ancestors.* To me, this means that I want to leave, as my message to the coming generations, furniture that can be translated as, "Knew the wood, knew the tools, knew the tree." This would be the type of message I would prefer, as opposed to the swollen landfills full of disposable but cute athletic shoes and plastic everythings.

With my trademark oversimplification, I'll now swing back to James and his family, and many of the farmers with small holdings that I know, who honestly aren't all that different from fine woodworkers. Fewer router-cut dovetails and less factory livestock mean fewer dollars or pounds, but they make up for it in other ways. I mean, come on; farmers, like schoolteachers, should be treasured and protected vastly more than they currently are, as they are the ones who treasure and protect the growing crops that will sustain us going forward. We should be subsidizing small farmers, and with funds from Homeland Security, because it is those farmers who guard our first and last best defense. Reward the families who bolster the health of our soil, our watersheds, and our communities. It makes little sense that almost anywhere in America you can find yourself driving past factory farms, which you can smell for many miles before they rear into sight. That the people engaged in that depravity should be able to earn as good a living as a farmer doing their best to cultivate healthy meat, dairy, and produce in step with Mother Nature is a pretty damning blight on our society, and it requires some pretty thick blinders to miss. But, money.

11

QUEEN OF THE BELTIES

My second trip to Racy Ghyll, the Rebanks farmstead, came a few weeks after the first, in early February of 2019, and not a moment too soon. I had been shooting my sci-fi show *Devs* on a huge soundstage in Manchester, which housed the full-size, futuristic research facility at the center of the show's narrative, a building called Devs (for "development"). In the middle of the set's ultramodern expanses of glass and steel floated a breathtaking sculpture that resembled, to my way of thinking, a robot-spaceship-jellyfish. Meticulously assembled from thousands of tiny mirrors, rods, plates, and circuits, this hypnotizing chandelier-like construction was the quantum computer hanging at the core of the building. Our scenes, which revolved around this shiny foreign object, were as coldly dramatic and alienating as the freezing snowstorms that had moved into Manchester. The production was taking very good care of me, but my hotel fare just couldn't hold a candle to Mrs. Rebanks's homegrown, grass-fed beef roast.

I arrived early on a Saturday and was treated to fresh eggs from their own laying hens. Let's slow down here and give this occasion its appropriate weight, because there is nothing I love more than eggs. As is the custom on well-appointed farms in the know, the dozen-or-so Rebanks hens have a coop that sits on wheels so that they can be trolleyed about, then relegated to a temporarily fenced-in feeding area while they pick the delicious bugs and beetles out of the grasses and the cow and sheep dung—or "muck" as they call it there in Matterdale—then repay the section with an even spreading of their own chicken poop, which is full of nitrogen, potassium, phosphorous, and calcium. Rich also in organic matter loaded with micro- and macronutrients, chicken manure is actually considered a "soil amendment."

Let's hit pause real quick to talk about the Terry Gilliam's–*Brazil* level of dystopian shit-show that is modern retail labeling language, specifically regarding food. Much has been made of the chicanery surrounding the terminology that starts out earnestly enough, your "organic" or your "all-natural," and is then quickly and summarily co-opted by corporate interests who lobby the FDA to considerably loosen just what can legally be described as such. For example, right now there are different sets of rules for labels that read *Organic, Certified Organic,* or *Certified 100% Organic.* What this makes immediately clear to me is that the governmental body tasked with overseeing the quality and nutritional health of the food we're being sold is full of shit. Companies can legally follow the USDA rules and still market highly processed foods as "organic." Just think about the fact that your food product can qualify as either "organic" or "100% organic." I mean. I don't know about you, but I would prefer that the purveyors of fine comestibles, foodstuffs that are the main currency of health, not only to our physical bodies and those of our families but to the natural ecosystem as well, not to mention the foundation of our values, be made to tell the goddamn truth. Ah, yes, but money.

Similarly, taking a stroll through the egg section at my local Whole Foods (a.k.a. Whole Paycheck), I can read a litany of "sincerely" printed carton-talk: *Free-Range, Cage-Free, Pasture-Raised, Alfresco* (I shit you not), *Certified Humane, Animal Welfare Approved,* and of course, our old friend *Organic.* A couple of these terms are official USDA-speak, but they all refer to the tradition of producers and retailers nickel-and-diming how they can legally describe their wares. *Free-Range* conjures an image of chickens merrily clucking about the hooves of herds of deer and antelope playing at home, on the range, but all the qualification requires is that your chicken shed have a little door out of which the hens might or might not even roam, buffalo or no. *Certified Humane* and *Animal Welfare Approved* are the labels to look for—they are endorsed by the ASPCA and the Center for Food Safety, among other animal welfare groups, and they connote the conditions most resembling a healthy and happy, rotationally grazed flock, and are therefore the hardest phrases to find in the store.

No matter what the brand of eggs may be, however, I have never seen a store-bought yolk that could hold a candle to the rich, yellow-orange vibrancy of homegrown eggs. At the table of Helen Rebanks I was served a soft-boiled egg in an egg cup, coupled with some home-made bread slices, toasted. Under the generous tutelage of the Rebanks kids, I gingerly tapped the top of my egg with a tiny egg spoon, then removed the top of the shell. I proceeded to scoop out the gelatinous egg and spread it on a piece of crunchy toast, which really made for a most agreeable egg-delivery system. Taken as a whole with a cup of black tea, this was a surprisingly rich repast, and when held against it in my memory, even my most *Alfresco* of *Pasture-Raised* store eggs comes across as awfully pale and bland.

Aldo Leopold wrote, *"There are two spiritual dangers in not owning a farm. One is the danger of supposing that breakfast comes from the grocery, and the other that heat comes from the furnace."* This can be broadly applied to so much of modern consumerism and our ignorance to the provenance of every single commodity that crosses our thresholds. The vast majority of us couldn't even identify the source of the life-giving water we drink every day, beyond a shrug and "The city? Pipes it in from . . . a river?," let alone where and how our eggs were produced. But I think the point is simple and powerful: When production is limited and local, when people pay attention to the quality and health of their eggs, or cucumbers, or beef, or you name it, the end result is better for everybody involved. Every member of the community is part of the ecosystem.

(I take a deep breath.) Let's talk about beef. In recent years, an enormous misconception has taken powerful root, that the *"climate impact of meat is enormous—roughly equivalent to all the driving and flying of every car, truck and plane in the world,"* according to a statement from Greenpeace. This is just a gobsmackingly ignorant statement, lacking any nuance or context whatsoever, and it reflects a pervasive, reactionary attitude that we can quickly debunk. In a nutshell, I'll lean on a phrase that I learned from Diana Rodgers and Robb Wolf and their excellent book and documentary called *Sacred Cow*. The phrase is simply, *"It's not the cow, it's the how."* Cramming thousands of cows, pigs, and chickens into feedlots and confinements has a lot in common with planting monocultures across the Midwest. It's an abomination of nature, creating a rampant breeding ground for deadly bacteria that must be fended off with copious dosing of antibiotics. Our meat production needs to spread the animals out. We need more farmers engaging in rotational and mob grazing, and if that means less unclean, unsafe meat, then so be it. The current system is simply unsustainable. We need to hold the USDA accountable for the safety of the products we can buy but also for the methods by which they are allowed to be manufactured.

Anybody who wants to argue that the meat *industry* is terrible in many ways, I will be right there with you. "Goddamn right!" is something you might hear me yell. But again, this conversation requires nuance, people. The words *meat* and *industry* should simply never be found within spittin' distance of one another. During the pandemic, a rash of COVID-19 cases in our nation's meatpacking plants caused some shutdowns and made the news because the conditions were so dangerously inhuman for the plant employees, yet they weren't allowed to shut down or take the necessary CDC-recommended precautions due to the demands of the industry. Now, I don't know about you, but when I think about delicious meat, I don't then want to be given to understand that it has been "packed" in a "plant." It doesn't speak well of the end product, nor the life of the animal that has led up to its being processed in a plant, like any other processed food.

"*I dislike the thought that some animal has been made miserable to feed me. If I am going to eat meat, I want it to be from an animal that has lived a pleasant, uncrowded life outdoors, on bountiful pasture, with good water nearby and trees for shade.*" Wendell Berry wrote this in 2010, and when he puts it that way, it seems strange that it would have to be said. The problem is that the producers of the overwhelming majority of the meat available in the United States today have paid very good money for regulations that look the other way. Once again, instead of working toward producing meat that is *healthy* for the consumer, the animal, and the environment, the corporate mindset works in the other direction—toward exactly how much *ill* they can get away with. For example, a recent *Mother Jones* article entitled "There Is Poop in Basically All Hamburger Meat" . . . well, no more sentence required, really. Because, money.

I read arguments that this factory-style farming is the only way to supply the dietary needs of our country, not to mention the rest of the planet, even just accommodating the voracious appetites of the fast-food industry alone. To which I reply, yes, exactly right. By insisting that we can only maintain the current level of output by serving ourselves unhealthy meat and produce full of chemical preservatives, hormones, and antibiotics, all allowed with a minimum of oversight concerning the safety and hygiene of the stuff, you are proving the point that this *industry* of food is perfectly unsustainable.

PS: I am not judging here. I will scarf down any of this garbage as quickly and happily as the next donkey. I am fully aware of the diabolically cynical recipes involved in so many "tasty" food items, with colors and flavors and textures literally developed in a laboratory, not to sustain us so much as to trick us into craving and thus buying more of it. Can't eat just one, buddy. I know all this, and I can still be fully on board to hit a drive-thru, and this is what angers me. Our human ability to be manipulated by calculating bad actors in the consumer sphere.

This blind loyalty to our triggered taste buds reminds me of the effects of nicotine upon me during my years as a heavy smoker. When smoking was banned in Los Angeles bars in 1998, I was ready to fistfight anyone who thought they could tell me where or when I could or couldn't smoke my lung darts. Years later, once I had quit smoking, I couldn't believe the brainwashing effect that nicotine had had on me, and the way that I was basically prepared to get legitimately violent in order to maintain my steady supply of it, via smoking. I can bring a decent amount of common sense to bear in almost any circumstance, but the way that nicotine caused my body's perceived need to overpower my normal perspicacity was truly disturbing. That being the case, nicotine is astonishingly not classified as a controlled substance. It's merely a stimulant, as though a pack of smokes is no different from a six-pack of cola.

And this isn't new, not at all. When it comes to beef, our capitalist food system has a disturbingly consistent track record of turning a blind eye to matters of health in exchange for dollars. As Leopold would have it, this means they're turning a blind eye to nature. I mean, there is literally shit in the meat, but also I'm saying that this circumstance, like the processed chicken and the ground beef, is full of crap. The white guys with the money figured out how to turn corn into beef, as well as like 85 percent of the rest of the stuff at the grocery store, including the packaging. A lot of what they make is very bad for us. Think of high-fructose corn syrup, for example. Nobody is saying no to these corporate interests, and so now we have chicken factories and cattle feedlots and hog-raising outfits that are so overcrowded that they have created literal lakes of shit. We're in trouble, and the root of the problem might just be our willingness to ignore Aldo Leopold:

"*All ethics so far evolved rest upon a single premise: that the individual is a member of a community of interdependent parts. The land ethic simply enlarges the boundaries of the community to include soils, waters, plants and animals, or collectively the land.*" I mean, I'm just an actor who likes to smoke a brisket and write a book once in a while, but even I can see that the condition of American so-called agriculture is pretty embarrassing in light of this statement.

* * *

I had finished my egg, tea, and toast, and we had taken a brisk February morning tour of the Herdwick flock and fed them out a breakfast of sheep cake, when James announced that we were going to Scotland. I was a little surprised, as I had only just arrived, and was by then happily swinging large bales of hay out of a small stone barn (c. 1860) onto the quad bike to haul around to the few disparate pastures for the further nourishment of the sheep. James said not to worry, we were going to see a lady about a cow.

During my last trip to Racy Ghyll, we had set out first thing to visit the sheep barn and check in on James's Belted Galloway heifer, who had just calved that morning for the first time. Everything was in order; mother Jamevie and calf Lily were healthy, although Mum still had some of her birthing equipment hanging out of her loading dock in back. James said they call it "cleansing," when the afterbirth sac is evacuated, only this one was apparently hung up, only partly released. James tried to give it a gentle tug, but for some reason Jamevie didn't care for this ex–rugby player tugging at her nether goods, so she took a swing at him with her head. He's nimble and managed to dodge, and he said he'd check it again later—it has to fall out or be removed to prevent any infection from traveling back into the cow's baby-maker.

Belted Galloways are sometimes called "Oreo cows" because they are solid black with a wide belt of white around their middle, resembling the popular cookies, and they originally hail from the southwestern region of Scotland known as Dumfries and Galloway, which is slightly confusing, like calling my home state Illinois and Wisconsin. I don't much care for the Oreo term either and am trying to reverse the trend by instead calling chocolate biscuits sandwiching white filling "Belted Galloway cookies." In an effort to diversify his farm's grazing profile, James had begun to build a small herd of "Belties" to dovetail into his pasturing schedule, adding their masticating and manure contributions to the overall mix. Their hoof-treads are also remarkably effective at aerating the soil wherever they roam, which I'm told is powerfully beneficial to the health of the microorganisms doing all the work down there. When the time would come to harvest a cow or two for beef, this handsome and hardy breed was also known to yield the most delicious of steaks and roasts.

It was with this nascent herd in mind that we drove a couple of hours into Scotland to meet with the venerable Anne Bell of Clifton Farm in Dumfries and Galloway. Her reputation preceded our visit, as James explained that she and her late husband, Alastair, had built up what was considered by many to be the cream of Galloway herds. This was borne out when we arrived and she immediately invited us in for tea and cakes and we could scarcely find a place to sit down, so festooned was the ground floor with prize ribbons and silver-cup trophies from the Royal Highland Show and other agricultural shows. Anne, who now ran the farm herself with the intermittent assistance of her daughter and grandchildren, was petite and snugly appointed in her coat and wellies as she led us out to the barns to tour her herd, but her disposition and the set of her jaw made it perfectly clear that she ran this farm with skill and determination.

We trudged up the lane to the craggy granite hill section of her two hundred acres, where we met a smattering of heifers with varying ages and degrees of desirable attributes, which were then casually discussed in detail by her and James, peppered by the occasional smart-ass comment from yours truly. I learned what gorse looks like, that its yellow flowers come in the winter, and that these Belties are prized for their ability to graze on almost anything green, including tough, thorny weeds and thistles (the national flower of Scotland). They merely require a diet of garbage plants, water, and time to create the most succulent marbled beef one could hope to pull off the grill.

Anne then walked us down to the bottom of the farm and toward a small, oddly shaped, furry mountain, which turned out to be her prize bull, Clifton Hercules. When properly addressed, or when you want to scold them, pedigree livestock have two names: the farm name first, then their given name. It has been said that the bull is half the herd, so a great deal of emphasis is placed upon the quality of his genetics, since he will ideally sire every calf born of your cows. To acknowledge this male power, bulls often bear evocative names, like Maestro, Maximus, or Hercules, and this guy earned every bit of that moniker. James had earlier turned me on to a bit of British slang that I believe is more sports related, but still, I went out on a limb and asked him, "Would Hercules be an example of what you meant by 'an absolute unit'?" James shut his eyes and nodded solemnly.

The bull's immense size, excellent proportions, and perfect belt (wide, straight, consistent white belts are preferred) commanded top dollar around the globe for a "straw" of his semen. Anne said with no small amount of pride that Hercules had children in dozens of countries, on nine or ten of the continents. Dazed into submission by her bull, we allowed ourselves to be led back to the barns where "negotiations" were about to commence.

I had been through some of this livestock boot camp with James when he introduced me to his prize Herdwicks, including rams, or "tups," that would respectively give Hercules a run for his money. Solid, trucklike beasts, with names like, well, the Beast. And King Kong. And Jedi. These lads were a few absolute units as well, which was apparent

even to my green eye. It was like looking at a girls' PE class and picking
out the obvious one who could throw a touchdown pass. It's in the proportions, and their carriage, plus there's just that X factor. They knew
they were the best. James is obsessed with this side of animal husbandry,
with the breeding of champions—it requires discernment in determin-
ing which animals will pay off and which are not good investments. A
couple of times a year the livestock is shown at the local show, and people can recognize who has a talent for this work and who doesn't, and
that's one way to generate income. People came to understand that
James's Herdwicks and Anne's Belties were masterfully curated, and so
they would queue up to pay extra for an animal or some semen to get
some of that refined bloodline worked back into their own flock or herd.

This quality in both Anne, a weathered champion with the trophy
collection to prove it, and James, newer to the game but not quite green
either, bearing an intrepid confidence, then made for me a most riveting
session of cat and mouse in the main barn. Anne would only offer a
couple of select animals to James for sale, and James would chew on that
information, maybe asking a question about parentage, or politely pointing out some less-than-ideal attribute or other on the cow in question.
He would also perform "questions" to me (which he had previously
warned me would happen), to soften his own criticisms. "I like her quite
a bit, but what do you think, Nick? How do you like her belt, is it too
thin? Hmm, maybe you're right. You're a tough customer." I would nod
sagely and perhaps offer an "Mmm. Quite." Then James would say, "You
know, I don't think I would like this heifer named Daisy, Anne, but I *would*
go for her sister, called Rose, did you say?," to which Anne replied every
time that Rose, or whatever other choice he preferred, was not for sale.

This went on for quite some time, as there were several iterations of
cows on offer versus cows James actually wanted to purchase. Finally

Anne invited us back inside for a cup of tea and a bowl of roborative roasted red pepper and tomato soup fueled with a low fire of spice. (*Roborative* is an excellent word that I picked up in Patrick O'Brian's seafaring novels about Captain Jack Aubrey and his good friend Stephen Maturin, usually employed to describe strong coffee on board whichever of Her Majesty's ships they happened to be presently employed upon. I was later dismayed, however, to see that the word is not listed in the Merriam-Webster dictionary, when I wanted to substantiate its addition to my arsenal of good adjectives. I did subsequently find it on Wiktionary.org, where it is defined as "giving strength; invigorating," so I'm going to toss it around with impunity, and I hope you will as well so that we can one day see it recognized as legitimate by those snobs over at Merriam-Webster.) Homemade from her own garden produce and herbs, that soup was an absolutely perfect repast after standing in a cold barn, shifting our feet and blinking at award-winning cows.

Outside the window from Anne's kitchen table, a large bush was teeming with small, lively birds. I asked what they were, and Anne told me right to my face that they were tits. I looked carefully into her eye, and then the eye of James after her. Nobody so much as flinched. This was the flashiest display of the grim mirth of the Northerner I had witnessed since the last time I read *Hedda Gabler*. Surely they were having me on.

"What's that one?" I asked.

"Blue tit," answered Anne.

I nodded and grimaced slightly, waiting for Anne to break the tension and mock me for the soft American I was, but I found no glimmer of humor there in her countenance. I turned to James for some help. He would not meet my gaze. I set my jaw.

"And that one?"

"Coal tit."

Goddammit, woman. Just what was she playing at? Was this part of the cow negotiation? James loudly sipped his tea and pretended to look at Twitter on his phone. I steadied my breathing in preparation for my final salvo.

"What about those?" I queried quietly, pointing at a jaunty, stupid trio of slightly larger birds. I thought that I had sufficiently readied myself to withstand any possible third answer in the hallowed comedy tradition of three rounds of question-and-answer patter. I had not.

"Those," she said, "are great tits."

At this, my famously stoic face began to tremble. Or no, it was deeper than that. It began to quake. Tears filled my eyes and I excused myself to use the restroom. I slipped out of the house and ran down to the pasture of Hercules, where I explained to him what had just happened, absolute unit to absolute unit, and, just like his matriarch, Anne, Queen of the Belties, he stared at me with a deadpan so unyielding that I paid him three turnips for the lesson. These cattle folk are so dry, they don't just make you wait for the cathartic release of the laugh from a joke—"wait for it"—the best of them actually just never laugh at all. The absolute pinnacle of impassively droll.

Class at Mrs. Bell's schoolhouse was not quite over, however. James was ready to hit the road for home, but regarding the cow-shopping he merely agreed amicably to "sleep on it." I didn't actually register much of the final exchanges between the three of us, as I had been fully kneecapped by Anne's wicked sense of humor. I was waiting in the car in a bit of a daze, actually, burping up warm remembrances of roasted red pepper and cumin.

The next day, James was jigging about the kitchen with delight, as he took in an email from Anne. It seems he had played the situation flawlessly, despite my mild puzzlement with the posturing and you-drive-a-hard-bargain-ing that went on in the barn. What James had apparently conveyed to Anne with great success was that he indeed had a discerning eye as a man of livestock. The animals she had offered were not her best, but many buyers would still have bit with enthusiasm, jumping at the chance to own any representative sliver of her farm's award-winning pedigree. Not only did James impress her with his forbearance, but he then doubled down on his eye for quality with the choices he proposed she sell him instead. Hence the unspoken conversation between them was about what characteristics made her cows exceptional, without their coming out and explicitly saying it.

By asserting "This one is worth your asking price, but that one is not," he had also given Anne the reassurance that her precious bloodline would be safe in the hands of a canny, responsible breeder—the many years of hard work and sacrifice by her and her family would be valued and protected by this judicious young shepherd. She congratulated him in the email, then offered up for purchase a couple of the jewels that had not been on the table yesterday.

As of this writing, the Rebanks herd has blossomed to eleven members, and James and his family quite enjoy the ladies scattered hither and yon in their hillside pastures, rotationally grazing in the most ideal method for producing beef and healthy pastures simultaneously. Here are farmers who have managed to withstand the typically American temptation to "go big." They have both succeeded, James and Anne, at producing the finest Belted Galloway beef cows, but they have not then allowed greed (a.k.a. the American Way) to deflate the pleasure of their success, by hungrily looking at next year's ledger with an eye toward "maximizing profits." Their excellence is achieved by understanding the balance of the size of their herds on the acres available, under the expert scrutiny of a master of the Beltie.

12

MINOOKA MADISON

When I look at Madison, Wisconsin, on a map, I sometimes see a bow tie, or an orchid, or the Bat Signal, or like an underneath view of legs in underpants, depending upon how many beers I've had. The peculiar shape is created by the layout of the charming capital city on an isthmus, a strip of land that lies between two lakes—Mendota to the north, and Monona to the south. Not only is the stately domed capitol building centered on this land bridge, but a good deal of the University of Wisconsin at Madison is situated along the northern edge of the bow tie on the shores of Lake Mendota. I grew up a couple hours south of there, and as far back as I can remember, any time Madison was mentioned it carried with it the weight of history and charisma.

One of the best parts of my job as a humorist has been touring the English-speaking parts of our planet, spreading mirth as best I can. This includes my performing in, at last count, forty-seven of our fifty United

States. I have yet to rock the socks off of the citizens of Mississippi, Idaho, and Hawaii, but fret not, y'all, or aloha, and/or whatever one says in Boise to express neighborly affection; I will get there. Often I'll have visited a state because one of their universities will have invited me to perform for their students who like to hear about woodworking, and this has been a great way to discern where it is that "my people" reside. Even in places with more openly "conservative" politics (which is a polite term for discriminatory culture, as in "We would prefer you take your rainbow ass elsewhere as we are conserving a Christian™, white ethno-state hereabouts"), the open-minded thinkers and the nonconformists and the lovers of decency come out for a laugh and a think at content like my song about Brett Kavanaugh entitled "I Like Beer."

Actually, the national embarrassment that is Brett Kavanaugh is a great example of how we dumb Americans can be so staunchly divided on a given point. A guy with a long résumé of extremely partisan GOP dirty chores is suddenly forwarded out of nowhere as Trump's pick to replace Justice Anthony Kennedy, who is just as unexpectedly stepping down. Just before this nomination, in 2017, Brett was on the receiving end of a mysterious, massive financial windfall, coincidentally just like he was right before his *last* federal nomination to the DC court of appeals in 2006. Huge red flags were left waving in the breeze as the spotlight suddenly shifted very dramatically.

Salient information was presented (and how many cases of this have we witnessed in recent years?) that this person exhibited a pattern of the worst sort of entitled, wealthy, white male toxicity in the form of sexual harassment/assault. Brett-bro was being vetted for a seat on the nation's highest court, a posting that is laughably supposed to be marked by august jurisprudence and impartiality. We are looking for persons of impeccable character, who can maintain impassive neutrality.

Unfortunately for the already considerably compromised Brett, some perfectly credible allegations were then leveled against him by Christine Blasey Ford about how he sexually assaulted her at a party. Other women came forward. Brett's groomers weaponized these allegations as powerfully as they could, to distract the public from the rest of Kavanaugh's unanswered questions and moments of perjury, as the hearings then became some of the most embarrassing political theatre that we have witnessed in this country, including a truly histrionic performance by Lindsay Graham that narrowly missed winning him the Tony that year.

Kavanaugh proceeded to bluster, sob, and mewl his way through misdirection after obfuscation about his problems with alcohol and impossible sources of income, and some sort of racket involving expensive tickets for the Washington Nationals baseball games and so forth. By the way, as much of a clown as this guy is, alcoholism is no laughing matter, and instead of enabling his weakness, his party should have been sending him to the sort of facility where such a sickness could be addressed. The point is, when this person loudly brayed his tomato-faced fulminations to a country asking him and itself if this is the stripe of integrity (or lack thereof) that we would like presiding over our most supremely important court cases, he wasn't presenting evidence, or passionately refuting accusations with logic and truth. Instead his defense sounded a lot like this: "*I like beer!*"

Gritting my teeth and stepping past the disgust and betrayal that all actual beer lovers felt in that moment (don't try to pin this on us, frat boy; most of us are able to handle plenty of suds without needing to force your idea of penis fun on innocent victims), I arrived at the crux: Of the people paying attention to this travesty, the majority in credible polling *rejected* the prospect of his approval, because we understood that he is ultimately not morally good. He and his supposedly religious party ironically stand in the way of our nation's spiritual progress, in every way except the accumulation of failures. "But they won," you might say, to which I would rebut that such a victory is the worst type of moral failure on all of our parts.

Here is a tough fact: According to an NPR/Marist poll at the end of the hearings, a majority of Republicans (54 percent) said they thought he should be approved *whether Ford's allegations were true or not.* I suppose I shouldn't be surprised by this, coming from a party that slavishly loved their double-impeached, alleged rapist in the White House. If Kavanaugh was innocent of the allegations leveled against him, crimes both financial and sexual, all they needed to do was exhibit a defense comprised of evidence and testimony. The Republicans chose not to do that, and they weren't able to prove anything about the man's character, leaving massive questions about his integrity, which, again, is why the majority of Americans think he's a shit-bag. If it cries like a dick and quacks like a dick . . .

One of the heroes you might recall from part 1 of this book, Olympian Jeff Tweedy, was performing a solo show in Portland, Oregon, at the same time that these beer-tear hearings were occurring, and a member of the crowd began to randomly shout "Kavanaugh!" every few minutes. Finally exasperated, Jeff stopped playing and said, "Okay, what? What about Kavanaugh? I take it you're in favor?"

"Yeahhh!" shouted the drunken genius in reply.

"Okay," said Jeff, "what's your favorite ruling?"

This elicited a devastating explosion of laughter from the audience, which was already wondering who was the dumbshit who had paid to see a high-end music show and then brought the selfsame show to a halt to service his own emotional needs. What a perfect example of a political mindset that merely wants to loutishly and lazily assert its place, backed by no reason or ideology other than they want their worldview to remain unbothered.

There are people who want things to stay the way they are, or be "conserved," and then there are people who understand that "the way things are" is actually quite shitty for a lot of our fellow Americans, so they are interested in our social construct's "progressing" to the long-dreamed-of point where the promises of the Constitution can be kept for all Americans. Right or left or in between, our positions have all resulted from the cumulative work of human history, which is a many-tentacled beast, but I don't think the two sides are at all even, and that is why I think that the white supremacist foundation of the right will never prevail.

I'll reiterate, we're all flawed. Any group of humans numbering two or more will always require emotional maintenance and empathetic compromise in a program that must never end. As we people grow and change, so evolve the systems of nature in her unfathomable routes of commerce that we can never fully comprehend. As Rachel Carson sagaciously details in her seminal *Silent Spring*, we humans, with our swollen egos, are stupid enough to poison an entire lake with insecticide to eradicate, say, one species of gnat. We are then utterly dismayed when several unforeseen additional species disappear because we couldn't have predicted how the plankton would accumulate the initially dilute poison, and then the fish that eat the plankton would compound the accumulation, and then the birds that eat those fish would be even more acutely poisoned until they entirely vanished from the lake in but a few years' time.

It is inherent in human nature to destroy, with ever-burgeoning ease, everything we touch. It's truly what we're best at. The examples are un-ending. How many mountains have we destroyed in mountaintop-removal mining? How many old-growth forest biospheres have we laid waste to for the two-by-fours within? How many species of organism have we eradicated through our carelessness without even being aware we were doing it? How many human cultures with their millennia of wisdom and human ingenuity have we flushed away in the name of commerce, through slavery and American genocide? We are prone to rush into things, because money, and we have adopted the de facto motto "Better to ask for forgiveness than permission. Because, money."

As I have repeatedly said, we are complicated. All such conversations require some degree of simplification, which can excise a great deal of the very nuance I'm asking us not to cut out. However, here is a moral rule of thumb that I feel pretty secure about: Don't wish pain on others.

The political tribe to which I subscribe (a fluctuating notion at best) is going to be the one that strives continually toward an actual democracy, while doing its best to ensure every citizen has state-funded health care. There are many more issues at hand, but let's focus on this one for now. Those of us who have been labeled cucks, snowflakes, libtards, social justice warriors, and more recently, radical left, socialists, Hollywood elites, and pedophiles, have generally come under this barrage of name-calling because of our endeavors to see one form of empathy or another delivered to some group that is being victimized in some way. Are we flawed? Certainly. Do some professions of extreme ideologies get a bit carried away? Hell yes, they do. But at the heart of these efforts is one form of compassion or another, and that is compassion for everyone. That's the deal, that's what Jesus taught. Even if you're a shit-spewing asshole, the liberals want a government that guarantees your life and health. Full stop.

The Republicans, the Trump supporters, the white supremacists, the

Proud Boys (saddest gang name ever coined, hard to say out loud without a single, cinematic tear rolling down the *right* cheek), the militias, the religious right, have grown exceptionally open about their desire to see the liberals suffer pain, violence, or death. Their coffee cups, T-shirts, bumper stickers, and social media are festooned with slogans about killing journalists, *"fuck your feelings,"* but the one that always stuck with me was the prevalence of Republicans declaring their love of "liberal tears." I mean, just stop and think about that: right-wing voices delighted in seeing "liberals triggered" by the discriminating, bullying, cheating, or otherwise evil actions of the right. I want to belong to the community of people who feel the opposite of that. It is deeply infuriating behavior, and the worst side of human nature. To delight in your opponent's tears is low and shameful.

We should all be well aware of the laundry list, or rather, butcher's bill, tallying the victims of mass shootings and violent attacks on non-violent protests, like several instances of psychopaths driving their vehicles into, injuring, and killing pedestrians at protest marches; police murder and brutality against Black people; and so forth. The vast umbrella that shields this shameful sect of our population is the low, glowing, ever-smoldering fire of hate. Yes, the ku klux cops and movie-theatre-mosque-school-church-Pulse-nightclub shooters are obvious firebrands or erupting volcanoes of this hate, but the molten lava that remains red-hot beneath the surface of civility is the seething hatred and resentment of the losers, sipping their bitter cups of liberal tears.

I don't mean losers as in Trump's fabricated and oft-cited *"haters and losers."* I mean literal losers, of many contests, across history. The largest example, methinks, would be the losers of the American Civil War. Let's remember that racists, not just in the South, but all over the country, sincerely believe that for biological reasons, or religious reasons, or any other batshit crazy reasons, white people deserve to dominate the rest of the people without white skin, as well as the entirety of nature's creation. The good news is that they are repeatedly shown to be wrong, which has allowed our civilization to slowly and painstakingly evolve, chalking up consistent victories over the centuries in all sorts of human rights. The bad news is that we have a long way to go before everybody is receiving the same number of baloney slices on their sandwich, as it were.

As I write this, the losers of the 2020 presidential election are erupting shoots of malfeasant lava all over the goddamn place, outlawing the teaching of honest American racism in schools, passing absolutely bonkers voter suppression laws, and so forth and so on. I suspect that instead of liberal tears, the cups of these losers are actually filled with warm schadenfreude, and the sad folks who sip from them don't understand that "*whatsoever you do to the least of your brothers and sisters, you do unto me,*" to coin a phrase.

The thing is, all of our relationships are inescapably intertwined. The passage of commerce of all sorts, colored by affection, is what makes it all go 'round, from person to person, but also between us and every aspect of nature. We must respect our position, our rank, in the Great Economy. Appropriately scaling our consumption to the economy of Mother Nature all over the globe is a difficult row to hoe, but we have done an amazing job so far, all things considered, in that we have not only survived, but we have flourished as a species. Things have gone so well, in fact, that a large number of Americans are able to live in relative comfort, lulled into paying little attention to the way our country is being run. I get this. I have, in the past, been in touch with the part of me that thinks, "I have a car, I have a job, I have a roof over my head, I can buy at least some delicious garbage from a fast-food drive-thru . . . why pay attention to anything else?" It's easy to mindlessly indulge in this indifference to the machinations of our government until suddenly they affect us. All can be fine and dandy in our small town until the factory hog lot out by the creek completely poisons the local groundwater, and you need to quickly recall what being part of a community means.

The luxury of this American mindlessness is an important condition to recognize and address, if we hope to continue our evolution toward equal human rights. Of course I'm racist. We're all racist, we exist in a world, a framework, that was constructed by, and for the benefit of, white people, particularly wealthy white people. Let's start by owning that. To deny it is a violent sort of ignorance. If our entire infrastructure is largely racist, then let us turn our attention to educating ourselves about that history, and then instituting programs by which reparations can be exacted. It's really not that complicated: We fucked up. We did a bad. The bad we did pervades our entire society, this is undeniable. If we are ever going to be able to hold our heads up as *actually patriotic* citizens, then we have to take the first step of admitting we have a problem. Admission is such a relief, by the way! It will ultimately feel great, I promise. Until then, Americans' denial of our racist past and present is like a kid who just gloriously shit the bed standing before his parents covered in slick, fragrant evidence, claiming that he in fact has never even had a meal.

In the same way, let's own the ways in which we have treated the earth with violence. Let's admit the wounds that we have caused, so that we might proceed to live on in continued comfort but without wounding her. We know now that the whole of creation is one infinite metabolism, and so our every action is inseparable from the economy of the world, and thus chemicals that we dump in the ocean, or bury, inevitably end up back in our drinking water, the food we eat, and the air we breathe.

All of these notions, therefore, are inextricably connected. The establishment of our national parks, for example, and our disregard for the Indigenous tribes who once lived in them. Raising good beef or producing clean, healthy eggs. Distributing the wealth of our land and our people. All of these are steeped in white privilege. If every living creature is a cog or a wheel in Aldo Leopold's vernacular, then it's easy to relate our poor treatment of the Midwestern topsoil to our unfair treatment of non-white citizens to the jaw-dropping amount of plastic we have dumped in our oceans. Looking straight-on at the full report card of the human race, I'd say we are still very much doing a bad.

Therefore the conversations I want to be part of, and the debates I want to engender when I tour, simply examine where we American dipshits need to be applying our focus, for the common good. When I was touring Australia in 2019, I merely mentioned Kavanaugh disparagingly, if that's not redundant to say, and the place went wild with hooting and booing. I'll reiterate that this happened specifically in Perth, Australia, and then I said it again the next night in Adelaide, and they were angrily ballyhooing even louder than in Perth. Everywhere, including a couple of conservative cities on the other side of the world, people knew that Brett Kavanaugh was not selected in service of the common good. Look at the racial makeup of the current Supreme Court—seven out of nine justices are whiteys, five men and two women. Plus one Black man and one Latinx woman. Does this mix sound like it was selected for the common good?

* * *

Let's take the tour back to Madison. I want to establish for you the heroic qualities of this groovy, Midwestern center of learning.

When I first began touring, I had a pretty simple rider for my backstage needs. A little meat, a little cheese, and two beers for after the show, because after rocking the worlds of a couple thousand college kids with some slow-paced talk of smoked pork shoulders and chisel-sharpening etiquette, I'd usually be so juiced on adrenaline that a couple of beers would just bring me back to equilibrium so that I could get to sleep and travel the next day and do it all over again. This system worked fine at regular, hard-ticket theatres, but I was quickly dismayed to learn that colleges could not legally procure alcohol for me, since some of the students working the venues were not yet twenty-one. What could be more counterintuitive than a college saying, "Um, that's a no-go on the beer"? This was really a bummer, because it kind of took the wind out of the sails of the whole "college show" feeling. There was no place I wanted a beer *more* after a show than a college, out of a powerful nostalgia for my own hedonistic youth. Nonetheless, I just learned to deal with it and find a couple beers usually once I arrived at my hotel for the night, which wasn't nearly as romantic.

This is not to say that the occasional university didn't step up to that plate and deliver, like the time that Iowa State students tailgated in the parking lot to prepare for my show, and the smell of their grills drew me from the backstage door, floating along a trail of scent like a cartoon wolf, to a redoubtable group of fans serving amazing cheddar burgers, who may or may not have slipped me a couple of local brews for my postgame reverie. To this day, I cannot drive through Ames, Iowa, without taking a knee and offering my devout thanks to her citizenry.

Several years past, I was invited to perform my show *American Ham* at the University of Wisconsin at Madison, and I was thrilled. They have a gorgeous and stately auditorium directly connected to the German beer hall and restaurant called Der Rathskeller at the student union.

Outside the beer hall is a terrace upon which one can recline with one's beer and bask in the breezy pleasures of Lake Mendota. Had I attended that estimable school, I fear that I would have seen fit to extend my education to twelve or perhaps thirty years so that I might continue sitting upon that glorious terrace with a schnitzel and a Patrick O'Brian novel.

My parents drove up from Minooka to see the show, which made it even more momentous, and the crowd was damn boisterous, and generous with their tolerance of my clumsy stylings. Sometimes I would engage the audience in a Q & A after my ninety-minute show had ended, if it seemed like everybody was game to keep the fun happening. This night, the Q & A was probably the best one in which I have ever participated. Between the audience questions and my smart-ass rejoinders, we really had some powerful laughs, and I came to understand that these were especially my people. I don't know why—maybe it was the cheese curds, maybe we were righting the karmic imbalance of then-governor Scott Walker embarrassing America's Dairyland mere blocks away—but I was really reveling in simpatico that night.

Of course, as at all colleges, some square administrator type had told me upon arrival that they couldn't provide me with beer after the show, as per my rider. I sadly said that I understood. So imagine how utterly bowled over I was when I finally stepped offstage and a magnificent young lady handed me a plate with two fat bratwursts upon it, and a tall, curvaceous, twenty-four-ounce glass of frosty, refreshing Hefeweizen, that substantial, delectable lemonade of beers. After consuming their sausages that tasted of sweet labor and slow dancing and washing them down with an intoxicating glass of German jolly-juice, I knew that I had found a golden hub of curiosity and learning. At long last, I understood the feeling of wonder and relief that travelers must have experienced upon arriving at Rivendell, the Elvish sanctuary in *The Lord of the Rings*.

This was the very college where John Muir had received his learning, speaking of wizards. His tenure as a student predated the construction of Der Rathskeller by some decades, but it's nearly certain that the two of us tinkled upon one of the same stately maple trees near the capitol. Muir launched his legendary trajectory from this neck of the woods, and the school would also produce other luminaries who would prove very instrumental in my life, like Frank Lloyd Wright and Tom Wopat. But perhaps the magic was most substantiated there when in 1933 a young employee of the US Forest Service was appointed the new professor of game management in the Agricultural Economics Department, and Aldo Leopold came to Madison to cement his legend in the pages of the soil of Wisconsin.

13

LABOR

If a man loves the labour of his trade,
apart from any question of success or fame,
the gods have called him.

—Robert Louis Stevenson

Back among the lakes of Cumbria in the year 2019, James laughed at me. We were laboriously transforming a large hill of cut log sections into a massive stack of split firewood with the aid of a crappy little electric wood splitter. It was a second-rate, partly plastic affair that required the kneeling operator to sort of clamp/ brace it with their legs when the log section was placed in the business spot, and the motorized sliding wedge did its cleaving. We took turns running the splitter or bounding about (in an enthusiastic but middle-aged way), fetching the logs to the operator, then tossing the splits onto the mountain of splintered firewood. It was hard, warming work in a chilly barn that required a few repeatable tasks—the kind of drudgery that most sane humans abhor—and James thought it was funny because on the contrary I was as happy, as they say, as a pig in shit.

I had been back to the Rebanks farm, Racy Ghyll, a few more times since they adopted me, in winter and summer, and if only the commute from Los Angeles were slightly more manageable, I'd have been back even more. For some reason, experiencing a smart, talented, good-hearted family as they have a respectable go at running a healthy, biodiverse farm even while they rear young, respectable citizens, and also Tom, gives me exactly the thrill that Disneyland wishes they could sell to their park-goers.

"It's pretty lucky that you enjoy the bits most people avoid," James said as we coaxed and cajoled and bullied the splitter into continuing our clumsy, wrestling firewood dance. His comment cut to the heart of the intense pleasure I have always derived from doing good, hard work, especially in collaboration with others. No task brings that emotion to the surface more than cutting and splitting firewood. Throughout my youth, I spent many frosty weekends with my dad, cutting up deadfall trees in the woods on the family farm, then splitting those trees into the firewood that we relied on to heat our big, old farmhouse through the winter, via two woodstoves.

Of course, at the time I was most certainly *not* as happy as that aforementioned pig to be made to work in the snowy woods instead of getting to watch Saturday morning cartoons. But even back then, at age ten or twelve, I got it. I understood that our household was on a tight budget, so gleaning this firewood (which was free) with the sweat of our labor (also free) allowed us to stretch Mom and Dad's modest incomes (as nurse and schoolteacher, respectively) farther. A not insubstantial amount of my childhood was spent piling firewood into massive, neat, and sturdy stacks, which carried with it a degree of collaborative

importance to the family's well-being, and the resultant flush of satisfaction. It was like if I was in charge of filling the thirty-one-gallon gas tank
on the Suburban for a road trip, but I could only accomplish it one ounce
at a time, with a spoon. As Dad then drove us all on our way in this
hypothetical and we passed a sign that read, "Welcome to Michigan," I
would look out the window and nod to myself, thinking, "We did this."

Similarly, thanks to several recent frigid nights spent at Racy
Ghyll, I also had a personal stake in this firewood James and I were
processing—back in the dead of winter, I had relied heavily upon the
previous year's firewood batch to keep me toasty through the night out
in the guest apartment attached to their sheep barn. That sounds rustic
and a bit rough, and frankly I wish it were more so, to up the "bucolic
idyll" factor even higher—"Guests may throw down a bedroll amongst
the hay bales, just be sure to stay out of reach of any munching Herdwicks come morning." This labor I was performing with James carried
a solid weight—we weren't two guys working hard for a cash wage. We
were creating affection, via warmth, for all who would benefit from
the fires this wood would fuel. Our good labor would directly propagate
life, with no middleman or -woman.

We two have shared a good deal of discourse about the lessons
handed down to us from our fathers concerning good labor. Good work.
In a rural setting, there's no end to the good one can do with some
know-how, a few tools, and some productive labor (or "graft," across the
pond), which hopefully means some extra hands. Some of it will lead
directly to income for the farm or family, but some of it will earn a different kind of recompense, lucre that can only be cashed in in the form
of birdsong, honeycomb, fresh leeks, or a pint jar of lilacs. A largemouth
bass. A stack of cured white oak planks. In other words, the physical and
spiritual health of our bodies and also of our environs can pay out great

dividends indeed, without sending anybody a check. This stripe of labor is beautiful in the eyes of the Great Economy, but it is not the labor being referred to in our small money economy, when the bankers talk about the "labor class." The corporate definition of labor paints a more dehumanizing picture that is concerned with the health of the laborer and their workplace only insofar as they affect the bottom line. To the corporation, "labor" is a binary line item in a profit report that demands just as little or as much dignity as other items, like "gasoline," "Post-it Notes," and "mayonnaise."

This is a substantial problem. How can we expect anyone to pay attention to our relationship with labor upon the land when our military-industrial complex won't even value the human being to start with? Aldo Leopold wrote, *"Civilization has so cluttered this elemental man-earth relationship with gadgets and middlemen, that awareness of it is growing dim. We fancy that industry supports us, forgetting what supports industry."*

The vast majority of our population is never required to think about how we're doing as stewards of the land that supports all of us, a blissful ignorance which is turning out to be a dearly purchased luxury. Think about all the necessities in our lives that we purchase from corporations: electricity, steaks, gas heat, sausages, most of our groceries, ribs, pharmaceuticals, bacon, clothing, pork chops, vehicles, ground beef, and so forth. It's easier to think of what items we *don't* get from corporations, which brings to mind the local farmer's market, my raw wood materials for Offerman Woodshop, some hand-tools, and little else. When we give our money to corporations, in most of our situations (especially for urban and suburban dwellers), we are also handing them our agency—implying a tacit agreement that they will be producing and sending us our electricity/breakfast cereal/diapers in a way that is respectful of other humans, but also the environment. The resources required, and the mode of transport or delivery, the packaging involved, and so on, comprise a long list of responsibilities that we are trusting our corporations to honor. I doubt that anyone reading this would be so naïve as to think that the majority of these companies are doing a good job with those responsibilities.

Because in many cases they don't *have* to do a good job. The ever-strengthening choke hold that corporations and their lobbyists have on our regulatory agencies generally works in favor of the polluter, and you know how we humans behave. If nobody tells us we have to clean up our rooms or do the dishes? Well, according to the American money economy (not to mention the last Republican president), you're a "sucker" if you follow a rule nobody is making you obey.

Take for example the case of some factory hog facilities in Illinois that were found guilty in recent years of egregious local water pollution in which streams were so drowned and blackened by sewage overflow that all life was snuffed out. That means hundreds of thousands of fish and mussels (and of course, the teeming microbial life that supports all the rest) in *hundreds of miles* of waterways. The culprits were a handful of facilities generally referred to as "hog confinements." I mean, do we need any more persuasion than that term alone as to the morality of this practice? Raising animals for meat in cold, industrial buildings known as "confinements" is pretty hard to defend with a straight face, but rest assured, these "farmers" do.

Most of Illinois's CAFOs (Concentrated Animal Feeding Operations, per the state's moniker) house at least five thousand head of hogs at a given time. In cages, basically, in gigantic sheds. In terms of the *balance* of nature, of the Great Economy, it's not difficult to step back and see the central problem: When we grow animals like we're pumping out Twinkies™ in a factory, those teeming herds produce way too much digestive waste for the comparatively tiny acreage they inhabit. CAFOs are literally and extremely full of shit. This is obviously disgusting, but also dangerous from a hygienic point of view. These confinements are but one example of the proliferation of monocultures, which have taken over American agriculture. Whether it's with foul, fish, beast, or grain, when we exclude any and all variety from our farming produce, we supply an open invitation to Mother Nature to discipline us by sending any number of plagues to wipe out the harvest. Viral enemies, insects, weather-based disasters like drought or flood—you name it.

The way we relegate ourselves to this very vulnerable position is by trying to avoid as much labor as possible. We do everything we can to increase a farm's output far beyond a scale that is manageable to humans or the nature we inhabit, by moving the miracle of life from out of doors inside to highly engineered meat factories. The articles I read about those criminally shitty pig confinements in Illinois boasted that it was producers "like these" that accounted for Illinois's being the fourth-largest pork-producing state in the nation. As though quantity is what you're shooting for when it comes to producing food. Because, money.

When I first started Offerman Woodshop twenty years ago, my business manager kept haranguing me to choose one of my furniture pieces to put into production, ideally a piece he could get placed in the *SkyMall* magazine, which was a thing that used to exist on commercial airplanes, kids, because otherwise all I was getting out of the shop was the small trickle of profit that came with each commission and a veritable river of satisfaction. I patiently explained to him time and again that mass-producing a wooden item, say, a wastepaper basket, would be perfectly counterintuitive to the purpose of the shop. The personal *labor* involved in the crafting of a table or chair or canoe was the whole handmade point.

When Aldo Leopold assumed his new position at the University of

Wisconsin at Madison in 1933 he was also placed in charge of the school's arboretum, where he was able to perpetuate the obsession that had held him in its sway since he was a child on the shores of the Mississippi: lovingly observing and cataloging the trees, plants, birds, and animals in a given watershed. Besides simply maintaining a healthy census, this practice also helped him to determine how these nonhuman neighbors were faring in the wake of the local weather and on the receiving end of the activities of the men and women dwelling amongst them. This discipline spellbound his attention so fully that he sought to continue the practice on his own time with the help of his formidable bride, Estella, and their five erudite children on a worn-out Sauk County farm that they purchased in 1935.

The family fixed up an old shack on the property that had once housed chickens, and made of it their rustic paradise, to which they escaped whenever possible. With the help of the kids and countless collaborators and volunteers over the years, the Leopold platoon planted thousands upon thousands of native wildflowers, shrubs, and grasses that had previously been eradicated from the area in favor of more "profitable" plants and methods. The prairies and forests of their farm began to hum with a renewed variety of insect and bird life, and the long job of replenishing the once-healthy topsoil that had been despoiled and eroded was begun. As a land steward, Leopold had no equal, as is well chronicled in his masterwork, *A Sand County Almanac*. The reason for this was that he made stewardship itself his objective. This flew in direct contrast to American agribusiness, which then and even exponentially more so now, held itself apart from nature. It attempted, and yet still attempts, to solve every man-made problem with another man-made problem. It somehow thought that it could prosper by violently overpowering nature, instead of working in concert with her. Wendell Berry wrote, "*The clear tendency of industrial agriculture has been to destroy any living thing that cannot be sold*," and the Leopolds were devoted to the opposite extreme, armed with Aldo's cautionary knowledge of the mountain without the wolf, and the spent, lifeless condition of their farm's soil when they had first arrived.

I had no idea that I would be writing this chapter when Mr. Rebanks chased me away from my tea and biscuits back out into the Racy Ghyll meadow. We were planting oak saplings all over the rolling hills, strategically located to provide strips of woodland that related to the waterways, or becks. We had a system down between the two of us—a quick spade, insert tiny root-ball end of two-foot spindly trunk, install biodegradable green protective sleeve to keep nibbling sheep and deer from hurting our feelings, tramp the dirt down, repeat. James had me running back and forth to the pile of saplings and green tubes, and the faster I would go, the farther ahead of me he would stay. Typically American, I wondered why were we working so fast, when we might slow down a tad and take in this beautiful weather and scenery.

The answer was simply that the more we got done, the healthier the farm became. I was a tourist, looking for a pleasant lollygag, but James and his family were not messing around. They loved this land, and they loved their place upon it, or even within it, and the more they hustled, the more they were repaid with treasures galore: tadpoles, nesting birds that had been absent for decades, grasses and wild leaves that had once been declared "garbage" but were now redeemed. These activities, remarkably like the Wisconsin-based efforts of the Leopold family eighty-five years earlier, are how the Rebanks team fill in gaps between other farming responsibilities. I was but one of dozens of volunteers across the year, and we planted not only trees but myriad scattered wildflowers and grasses as well, again, trying to bring the pastures back to the ancient

robust fecundity they once knew before us dummies showed up to "improve" the land.

The parallels between the Leopolds and the Rebankses don't end there, either. Aldo Leopold's kids would later talk about how they craved their visits to "the Shack," where they vowed to bring only the items that were absolutely necessary: a guitar, a gun, a picnic basket, and a dog. Sure sounds like a good time to me. I've also seen footage in which the family is employing carpenter's tools to repair and expand their humble shed, nearly doubling the square footage. Leopold's daughter Luna remarked, years later, that their time there was a study in *"how one can find absolute happiness with the least amount of stuff."* This phrase absolutely lit me up, because it's exactly what I have always said about my own family's annual fishing trip to a cabin in Minnesota. I guess I should say "almost exactly," because my own list of "stuff" usually adds the words *beer, grill,* and *pinochle deck* as well.

Speaking of card games, one of the most delightful evenings (for me) at the Rebanks house was attempting to teach James and his two daughters how to play Liverpool rummy, which is the traditional barn burner of the Offerman household. It's great fun but has several rules, and each hand adds another card and grows progressively harder, so after they put up with me for a few hands, we quit and turned to their two traditional household pastimes: a dance competition and a form of charades.

The dancing incorporated a game on the Wii console that was played by mimicking the animated dancers on the telly whilst holding a game controller in the right hand. The whole family were very enthusiastic dancers whose moves exhibited talent and panache, so one was required to dive right in and give it a proper go if one hoped at all to succeed, no inhibitions allowed. Fortunately, making a fool of myself is what I do for a living; in fact, I was classically trained to excel at opportunities just like this one, so I was able to relish my go and show those shepherds just how magnificently a clown can fall upon his face.

These examples of amusements are imperative, I think, to the Leopold sensibility. Firstly, they require a minimum of consumer goods. Yes, the Wii game console and television violate that notion, but they were not necessary. They were merely embellishments to what would have been a perfectly achievable good time without them. Kick-ass dance moves are better ideally with music, but as music is easily had in this modern era, shaking one's booty is a human art form that can be employed at any time, almost anywhere. Second, the pastimes required the participant to check their ego at the door. The group presented no danger of judgment or ridicule, but only a collective support; a tacit agreement that delight and mirth were the pursuits at hand. Third, it goes almost without saying, but all three of the discussed arenas—the Leopolds' Shack, my family's fishing cabin, and the Rebankses' house—were also readily supplied with books. Everybody was reading something at some point, and sometimes writing, and also drawing and painting.

All of which is to remind myself (and you, should you care to hear it) that life can be incredibly rich and rewarding without involving modern distractions and consumer goods. I might even argue that the well-curated lifestyle of the Luddite is *more* edifying because it lacks the disappointment of empty accomplishments. A simple example would be the time I spent two solid weeks defeating a video game, versus when I occupied a couple of weeks building a coffee table from a gorgeous slab of California claro walnut. Both activities produced plenty of dopamine in my body, causing me to feel mounting pleasure as I completed more and more levels of the ultimate task, but as you might have guessed, when the video game was finished, and I had won the ultimate victory therein, vanquishing all of the "bosses" on every level, I suffered an immediate emotional crash. The utter meaninglessness of my "achieve-ment" washed over me like a brisk, salty Hebridean wave. Of course, when the table was finished, I sat next to it and set my beer upon it, and felt the substantial comfort that accompanies making something of good use out of raw materials. To assiduously simplify the matter, as is my wont, I firmly believe that Mother Nature would vastly prefer us to be making tables and singing songs rather than playing video games. In part 3 of this book, we'll similarly compare the exploration of a trail on foot with traversing it under the power of a gas engine.

What I am talking about here is the importance of the *right kind* of labor. What Wendell Berry and my dad call "good work." Some of what I have above described falls into the trite category of "labors of love," but I disregard that phrase in this context, because I think that, to an extent, the Leopolds and the Rebankses (and sometimes the Offermans) have learned that if you play your cards right, then damn near all of your ef-forts come from a place of affection. We must understand that we are not passive passengers on this mother ship Earth, but instead we must *participate* in the journey, whether that means grabbing an oar and help-ing to row, or feeding the crew, or holystoning the decks. Only then will we be able to help steer this venerable vessel away from the shopping mall/Amazon.com and toward the woods and the meadow and the beck.

What Aldo Leopold and all of the clear-eyed agrarians who came after him want us to see, I think, more than anything else, is that the labor and attention of a human have very specific limits of scale. This means that we need many more good stewards of the land responsible for smaller parcels, so that our society's much-diluted attention can be brought back up to the full strength that farm families like the Rebankses pay to her. We have tried focusing solely upon the quantity of dollars that might be wrung out of a given piece of territory, and discovered it to be an empty and destructive task, excepting that a very few people make some money, and that, only temporarily. Having recognized the failure in that pursuit, on behalf of the people, the animal life, the plant life, the soil, air, and water, I guess put simply: All of creation, let us be discerning and farseeing. Let's tax the few who have amassed billions of dollars from the exploitation of the Great Economy, and apply that communal wealth to the mending of our errant industrial methods.

14

THE LAND ETHIC

August 28, 2019, found me back at the Rebanks farm once more. Since I had last seen the gang, the traveling circus of my work had taken me home to Los Angeles, then touring as a braying humorist all over America, Australia, and New Zealand, and now back to the vibrant green of England's Lake District and Scotland to the north. I had just visited the wonderfully uneventful Scottish island of Islay for a few days to film a new commercial campaign for Lagavulin single-malt Scotch whisky in and around its picturesque distillery on the island. I had then filmed a few more days of commercials in Glasgow, including one that featured me on horseback, dressed as the famous anti-Semite Mel Gibson when he was dressed as the famous anti-English William Wallace from *Braveheart*, elocuting in a passionate Scottish brogue that I fear was possibly even worse than Gibson's accent in the film. But boy howdy, was I having fun.

The morning before shooting the *Braveheart* scene found me curled up in the fetal position, lying naked in the tall, wet grass of a Glasgow park (have we talked about midges?). While there were times in the past that would have perhaps seen me behave thusly due to some degree of inebriation, this time I'm pleased to say that it was just another commercial scene, this one set at the dawn of time, and thankfully MOS (that's fancy film talk, meaning "mit out Scottish"). Between the chilly morning dew and the horseback hollering, a light cold had taken root in my nose and throat, so by the next night I had fully lost my voice. Unfortunately, I was also scheduled to perform my comedy show that night, including seven songs, for a sold-out house of twenty-five hundred souls at Glasgow's O$_2$ Academy theatre.

James and Helen Rebanks came to the show, and, thanks to copious amounts of tea, honey, lemon, and powerful lozenges (plus a wee dram of Scotch or two), I managed to croak out the ninety minutes of material intelligibly enough that many patrons stayed for the whole show. Well, maybe not "many," but several anyway, and the Rebankses were among the tolerators, because they have very good manners. I'm sincerely grateful that I was able to successfully communicate my material and get a few laughs, because so far in our relationship, the two of them had exclusively been brandishing heroics hither and yon and repeatedly knocking me on my ass with their stamina and competence, as I merely skittered after them, giggling and trying to catch my breath. "How old is this stone shed?" "What is this fluffy puff of heaven? A Yorkshire pudding? Um, okay. It's like a popover!" (I burst into tears.) "Floss [the sheepdog] is kissing me!" "How can you two possibly get this much done?" And so forth. And although they had been *lightly* familiar with some of my acting work before we met, this performance was the first time since I had presumed myself a new member of their family that I could show them what *my deal* was.

I said, "Oh, you're raising four kids and two hundred fifty sheep and some cows and a couple ponies and many chickens and stewarding your land as best you can with an eye toward her continued health for yourselves but also for generations to come, all whilst penning bestselling, award-winning books? That's all you have to show for your efforts? Well, sorry to shame you right out of the gate, but I *wrote this lyric*, so . . . *Some folks live a fancy life in homes of glass and steel, / Some find satisfaction in a yurt. / Some believe monogamy is the only love that's real, / Some are less persnickety where they squirt.*"

Thank you, reader. I can hear the slow, heartfelt clap of approbation you are augustly performing in appreciation. I needed my new mom and dad to understand firsthand that I *also* had a contribution to make to the overall advancement of our species. Was my A/B rhyme scheme remotely commensurate with the agricultural output of their grassy holdings? Only you, the reader, can be the judge of that, but before you reckon the final tally please give me another quick once-over to be sure you didn't miss any of my subtler puns, and don't forget I cultivate a terrific moustache. Please clap.

As luck would have it, they very much agreed with the tone and point of view of my show, and I was most gratified to hear about it over breakfast the next morning, because I had fallen for them, hard, and it's common knowledge in showbiz that when your new squeeze comes to your show and you're not good? Or they are somehow inexplicably fans of Brett Kavanaugh? They quickly become your *former* squeeze. We had gotten in quite late post-show after driving ninety minutes home to Racy Ghyll, and slept in 'til a luxurious six thirty the next morning. Once my head shrank back down to its normal extra-large size after being swollen by their praise, James and Helen proceeded to regale me with tales of a nighttime event on the farm that I had just missed a few nights earlier, called Bats & Brownies.

A nifty naturalist duo (Heather and Cain) called Wild Intrigue out of Northumberland came out to the farm after dark and gave a talk about the several local bat species to an appreciative audience of visitors. They discussed how the bats live, what with their flying and locating their insect prey using sonar and such, as the attendees munched on Helen's scrumptious baked goods. That sounded well worth the price of admission already, but then they handed out special bat-detecting head-phones that allowed one to comprehend the usually hypersonic squeaks and clicks that the bats use to locate their prey. The healthy pastures at Racy Ghyll attracted a smorgasbord of insects, which in turn attracted a diverse array of bat types, so the attendees basically got to experience the Glastonbury music festival of bat jams out in the meadow.

I was sore to have missed this event, but evidently I was blessed with the "luck of the humorist" (which is a thing I just now made up), because Wild Intrigue was coming back in a couple days to do another cool nature powwow, this one entitled Moths & Muffins. I had to run around and do a couple of comedy performances in Manchester and Leeds, but both cities were near enough that I was able to get back to the farm for life-giving injections of both sleep and sheep, and more importantly, that meant I was present on the morning of moths. The naturalists had set out "light traps" the previous evening, which were basically tented buckets that attracted a considerable collection of moths at night, using as bait only a small illuminated light. Getting any group of curious peo-ple together to satisfy a hunger for learning is fortifying to begin with, but then you throw in some homemade muffins (thanks to Helen and often one of the kids) and some tea or coffee, and it becomes about as ideal a Saturday morning as this moth fan can imagine. Cain and Heather gingerly removed the moths from the enclosure one at a time and placed them in small, clear containers so that they could be passed around and handled without doing any damage to the moths themselves. What our investigation uncovered may surprise you.

Moths, as majority members of the order Lepidoptera, are at a severe aesthetic disadvantage when held in comparison to their sunnier cousins, the butterflies, or so I thought. I mean, if this were Butterflies & Beignets, Bagels, or Burritos, I'm immediately envisioning a much larger turnout, on the strength of both the beloved butterfly and its delicious accompaniments. But, holy promethea, were we in for a surprise. The wide range of sizes, shapes, and colorations of this batch of moths produced a hilarious orchestration of oohs, aahs, and "Well, I'll be jiggereds" as we held each precious specimen up to the light. Even just a sampling of their names, like burnished brass, dingy skipper, elephant hawk moth, painted lady, peach blossom, and garden tiger, will no doubt illuminate visions of unexpected wonder in your mind's eye. Each miniature glider had a set of wings emblazoned with a work of art that bore closer and closer degrees of inspection.

Heather and Cain spoke knowledgeably about the moths and their importance to the ecosystem of the farm, and they answered our many questions with patience and smarts. Once we had exhausted our collective curiosity, the moths were freed, unharmed, into the woods. The twenty or so paying guests said their thanks and went on their merry, more-educated-than-when-they-arrived way, and I showered the Rebankses and the Wild Intriguers with praise, delighted like a kid who has just been given his first balloon. Being the sort of clown I am, I immediately began pitching further sessions to the gang—you know,

Otters & Omelettes, Crows & Croissants, and so forth. I can't tell you how much joy it brought me months later when they announced a new "mini exped" based upon one of my silly pitches, and I only hope that I can get there in time to experience Frogs & Flapjacks. In any case, my lawyers are in talks with the family to be sure I am properly compensated for my intellectual property. "Proper compensation," in truth, for people who say things like "proper compensation," would closely resemble a swift kick in the ass.

Come spring, according to James's Twitter feed, the frogs arrived in full force, and not by chance. For some years now, James had been undertaking the project of rewilding his acreage, or striving to return it to an older way of farming that walked more comfortably hand in hand with nature. One prime example of his efforts was the "re-wiggling" of that aforementioned stream in the valley bottom that had been straightened into more of a canal a few generations back, with an eye toward more efficient drainage and improved bottomlands. Mother Nature had already spent nigh on an eternity laying out the day-to-day operations of the valley's metabolism, so of course the human dabbling was doomed to fall short of her system.

One reason that the canal version was visibly worse than the snaking-beck version was because in a straight waterway, one loses any variety in topography. The curves and turns are where soil and gravel accumulate when deposited by the current, creating a variety of water features like ripples, rapids, and quiet eddies. A couple of small ponds and marshy areas were also sculpted back into the bottoms. Each of these areas promotes different sorts of aquatic and water-adjacent life, and so the Rebanks family quickly saw the return of so many signs of life that accompany a healthy stream: frogs and their tadpoles, fish, insect life, waterfowl, and a complement of other birds attracted by the new bugs and creek life.

These re-wiggling, rejuvenating actions are not undertaken to se-cure a "profit" in the contemporary, small-economy sense of the word, because the outcome cannot be reduced to a simple cause and effect. In fact, on paper, the labor involved would register as quite the opposite of profit, but it is a sound investment nonetheless when looking at the ac-counts of the Great Economy. It is part of James's attempt to pull one foot out of the dance of modern commerce and transplant it instead where his forefathers once danced in step with the seasons and a much more ancient farming tradition, choreographed with the music of the solstice, played upon the instruments of fertility. Some of these ancestral footprints are lost, but some remain easy to discern, because they have never faded—they demarcate paths that have never ceased to be used over the centuries.

In the Lake District county of Cumbria, in the valley of Matterdale (which coincides with the parish of Matterdale), into which is nestled the farm Racy Ghyll, the private landholdings and villages fit into the valleys like the pieces of a most picturesque jigsaw puzzle, segments often lined by stacked stone walls or hedgerows. Above these individual parcels, however, loom the lofty heights of the fells, or mountainous hills that are historically regarded as the "common." Each of the twelve or so families that farm this little dale is able to access the shared com-munal hills above, and about ten of the families drive their respective sheep herds up to the altitudinous peaks to spend April to October of each year thriving. By the way, *drive* in this instance means "to compel forward," on foot, through the village, through ancient stone gates, and on up the fells, as opposed to the American connotation of *drive*, in which our sheep are loaded into Cadillac Escalades for the commute, allowing for a swing through the Starbucks drive-thru.

Fascinatingly, like salmon instinctively returning upriver to their annual spawning beds, each sheep flock has over the centuries come to know its particular section of the common, which is known as being "hefted" to the land. The discrete flocks are amazingly able to graze and wander and cohabitate across the entire season with little to no supervision. The Herdwick breed that is James's specialty is especially suited to this rugged lifestyle, and everything about their well-being is unquestionably best served by allowing them to simply thrive in nature. To put it in more mercenary terms, their *monetary value* is maximized by leaving them alone to participate in the Great Economy as they evolved to do.

I grew up on the prairies of Illinois, known as "the Prairie State," for crying out loud, so to stride across the windswept, blustery heights of the fell with James and countenance these noble creatures made me truly feel like I was in a work of fantasy. Here was a pocket of Western civilization where the agricultural interests had not looked at the commodity of sheep and said, "Okay, this is fine, but how can we engineer *more* profit out of these beauties? We are humankind, so surely we can confine these critters (I mean, walking up this hill here is hard) and pump them full of some industrial corn-based wonder juice or other and leverage more wool and more meat out of them?" Thankfully the shepherds of Matterdale have not yet succumbed to the siren song of American-style "bigger and better" farming, but the resistance requires constant vigilance, for the wolves of capitalism are ever at the door.

Standing atop this fell, commanding a breathtaking view for many miles around, I couldn't help but think of the base similarities between the Rebankses and my farming family, the qualities that had originally drawn me to the work of Wendell Berry and subsequently so many others, including Aldo Leopold and one James Rebanks. The common meats on our tables were humility and a penchant for good, quality, hard work. One of the most rightly venerated essays in Leopold's *A Sand County Almanac* is entitled "The Land Ethic," in which he asserts: *"I have purposely presented the land ethic as a product of social evolution. Because nothing so important as an ethic is ever written . . . it evolved in the minds of a thinking community."* There on the fells of Matterdale was a rich, long-established example of just such a thinking community, where lives of value were being lived, but from which nobody was getting rich. There have certainly been disagreements, and perpetual negotiations are required, as is true of any group of humans agreeing to cooperate for the good of all, but by and large, it's hard to imagine an economy like this existing for long in America.

They do exist, in varied, sporadic instances—community-supported agriculture programs (CSAs) are common across the country, as well as various local co-ops and small farming collectives, reminiscent of the Burley Tobacco Program penned by John Berry Sr., father of Wendell, grandfather of Mary. Although their patriarch's legislation is no more, the Berrys have more recently founded a beef and veal operation called Our Home Place Meat, which is based on the same Burley principles that kept a healthy, small-farm economy alive and well in Kentucky much longer than in other places in this country. The farms participating in the collective raise the cleanest, rotation-grazed cattle that they are then able to sell at a fair price through the program. By guaranteeing a fair price to the farmers, the organization is able to ease the normal pressure they experience, participating in the boom and bust commodity market. Mary says they are making good farming pay. "We are not expecting farmers to do it all: grow it, market it, deliver it. And the product is exceptional. Daddy says that we are allowing people who buy our meat to 'eat with a clear conscience.' Our Home Place Meat is putting something between the farmer and the marketplace to move product and set a fair price. We make a commitment to our farmers in January of every year and then we live up to it. The farmers in our program can count on making a certain amount every year."

I applaud and support their efforts, and not just because I have robustly enjoyed their exceptional Rose Veal. Thanks to the internet and the extravagance of modern shipping practices, I have been able to partake of the offerings of other cooperative ranch and farm outfits in Northern California, Arkansas, and Washington/Oregon. The thing that all of these movements have in common is that they're built from scratch, from the ground up, which reassures me with regard to the inexhaustible pluck of our good farming neighbors. However, it also begs the question, how can we also support farming efforts that are good for the people and the land from the top down? Can we not produce healthy meat, dairy, eggs, fruit, and produce for the whole community without needing to ship it in from Chile?

This takes me back to the Civilian Conservation Corps, which I talked about in part 1. In 1933 Leopold actually got an entire ninety-thousand-acre watershed to agree on an experimental collaboration, in league with the US Soil Conservation Service and the University of Wisconsin. With the added elbow grease of CCC workers, hundreds of farmers in Coon Valley, Wisconsin, worked with scientists specializing in agriculture, forestry, and wildlife to develop agrarian methods of crop rotation, erosion protection, fertilization, strip cropping, and terracing. This revolutionary research had a profound effect on the quality of farming in the Midwest—that is, for the families that adopted the practices. Unfortunately, industrial farming motored into the scene over the next couple decades, took a brief look at the moderation required by these methods of conservation, and said decisively, "Fuck that noise."

As James wrote in *The Shepherd's Life*, "*Later I would understand that modern people the world over are obsessed with the importance of 'going somewhere' and 'doing something with your life.' The implication is an idea I have come to hate, that staying local and doing physical work doesn't count for much.*" I've said it before, but the cancer of consumerism is so insidious and pervasive that by now in 2021 the actual act of *shopping* is considered a legitimate pastime. The sensibility named in James's quote is at the heart of the disregard we have developed for rural spaces, especially the vast agricultural spaces that, according to the corporate interests, are good for nothing unless you count sheep grazing. Yawn. That's so boring, counting sheep is actually a trope for how to put oneself to sleep!

The effect of consumerism on us is, by now, that the vast majority of our population is simply unable to fathom the fidelity that James is talking about. Some of us garden, or perhaps keep bird feeders, but that is the extent of our direct communing with the Great Economy, and even so, we are considered the outliers. By and large, the ecological citizenship to which James and Leopold refer does not appear on the arbitrary list of choices for things with which a modern American might concern themselves. Once again, we are coddled by the false sense of security that our representation will see to it that our local resources are dispensed with everybody's best interests at heart.

When Aldo Leopold wrote, "*A land ethic, then, reflects the existence of an ecological conscience—and this in turn reflects a conviction of individual responsibility for the health of the land. Health is the capacity of the land for self-renewal. Conservation is our effort to understand and preserve this capacity,*" he was really giving us Americans a lot more credit than we have proven to be due. How often do we think about our "individual responsibility for the health of the land"? That term *ecological conscience* also kicks me right in the beanbag.

I think my donkey-size awareness of this moral deficit is a big part of why I so enjoy working alongside people like my mom and dad, my aunts and uncles, and the Rebanks family. I know that I can't wrap my head around the whole complex dilemma, but they have a little bigger and better grasp than I do, so helping them has to be adding succor in the right direction. It's a hell of a mess, our modern sense of conservation in America, thanks in no small part to the corporate interests that pay a lot of very good money to keep adding to the mess with impunity while seducing us into looking in another direction.

To my way of thinking, visionaries like Aldo Leopold have made clear for us what it will take to maintain the health of our community, meaning the land and every one of its multitudinous citizens, including us. It comes down to our conscience. Our *values,* a term so cheapened by modern political discourse that it's almost laughable. Where I come from, values still exist, and they're based not on skin color, or religion, or sexual orientation, but solely on decency. I was taught to examine my actions and see if they can be reconciled with my sense of decency when held up against it. I'm pleased to report that many (eleven) times I was in fact able to reconcile my actions (at the time of this writing) with what my parents taught me!* But here in America, our Supreme Court has decided that corporations must be treated as having the same rights as individual citizens, and I wonder about that. Did the corporations' parents teach them about decency, and if so, do they hold each of their corporate actions up against that ruler of moral values to see if it is reconciled positively? Do they maintain a "conviction of individual responsibility for the health of the land"? How stupid are we?

---

*Editor's note: Dutton™ is not accountable for any statements of moral or criminal culpability or lack thereof on the part of the author.

PART III

15

THE NUTMEG

Parts 1 and 2 of this book were mainly focused on my 2019 trips to Glacier National Park and to my friends the Rebankses' Lake District farm in northwestern England. Those varied and robust life chapters took place in what now seems like an innocent fairy tale: life before the COVID-19 pandemic. We thought things were rough then, and they were to an extent, as we attempted to navigate the national and global repercussions of having elected one of the most embarrassing possible humans to the highest office in America. Thanks to the unregulated channels of social media and the leering propagandists of Fox News, Infowars, One America News Network, and their septic ilk, misinformation was at such an all-time high that we were facing millions of otherwise competent-seeming citizens holding up wet bags of shit, screaming that it was chocolate ice cream.

We had climate change, we had Black people being murdered by police officers, we had our usual national menu of violence against women, we had all kinds of discrimination happening, and if you're still here with me for part 3, then you know the list: all the societal evils that blossom at the bottom of the barrel in a population and fester and spread the cankers of hate and fear and greed. The qualities in humanity against which some of us strive to *progress,* and thereby improve, in the hopes that one day nobody will have to endure being systemically shat upon. Accordingly, and accurately, this relative stance causes us to be labeled "progressives," but it doesn't stop at that, apparently. We are also radical, socialist, communist, Marxist, leftist libtards whom our detractors love to see cry. So that was all going on.

Then the pandemic hit, officially shutting America (mostly) down in March of 2020. My bride, Megan, and I purchased some surplus toilet paper and hot sauce, which was arithmetically sound, and stayed home along with the rest of the citizenry who were lucky enough to be able to do so. We watched the news quite a bit and did our best to deal with the weird half-depression that came with the stasis of a lockdown. I was supposed to have worked on another television series and also tour more of England and several other European cities as a humorist. All canceled, obviously.

As I mentioned earlier, good, hard work is the daily bread that I have come to prefer in life, mainly because I have learned that idleness is not healthy for me. In hindsight, I wish I would have had the clarity to declare, "Well, looks like we're sitting on our asses for several months. In that case, I am going to build a boat." Instead, Megan and I, along with most folks, had a general feeling of unease about traversing the world in any way unless absolutely necessary. We endeavored to be as cautious as possible, going out for groceries (mainly more sriracha and TP) every one or two weeks while adhering as best we could to every protocol (the science ones, not the dingdong president's insane bleach suggestions). I smoked a lot of meat on my Hasty Bake charcoal grill/smoker, and Megan became obsessed with baking and cooking. I actually lost quite a bit of weight during this period. Oh, did I say "weight"? I meant "thinness." We were doing our best to cope, along with everybody else on the planet, with the usual metabolism of our lives being so upended.

In our house, good ideas generally come from Megan's quarter. Ideation is a strong skill of hers—cooking up a scheme or caper or even just a single hijink, at which point my abilities are then brought to bear, such as long-distance driving, dog wrangling, carrying luggage, and road trip cooler strategies. She gets us somewhere amazing, and I start a campfire there. At some point a month or two into lockdown, Megan had the great idea to get some sort of RV or camping trailer, in which we might travel across the country so as to spend Thanksgiving with my family in Illinois. Like I said, she is amazing at ideas.

She had heard from a friend about these nifty-as-hell new collaborations between Mercedes Sprinter vans and Airstream, which were basically like very small campers with all the engine and chassis quality of a Mercedes, but then outfitted with the deluxe fit and finish of an Airstream trailer, which sounded perfect for us. The Sprinter van has become very popular on film sets in recent years for traveling people to and fro from base camp to set, or taking a director with a handful of producers and crew out on location scouts. It has all the latest vehicular amenities plus a ton of standing headroom. We set off for the Airstream dealership to check one out, and found a few different models nestled in the middle of a parking lot otherwise festooned with those classic aluminum Airstream trailers.

They looked pretty bitchin' from the outside, but in a matter of minutes, squeezing into the back living area, we discovered that these clever rigs were just a tad snug for a couple of softening old vaudeville hoofers looking to take their ease in the autumn of their years. The vans were really impressive, and tantalizing to imagine traveling and sleeping in, but just a tad claustrophobic to us. Don't get me wrong, being able to fry up a couple eggs while sitting on the can is an *astonishing* attribute for any living space, let alone one that gets eighteen miles to the gallon (twenty-one highway), but perhaps it's a game best played by younger initiates than us.

The day was not remotely lost, however, because the idea factory who wears my ring suggested that we just have a peek inside one of the full-size Airstreams, you know, just to check it out, even though these were clearly way too cumbersome for us to consider. We looked at a few fetching models, with evocative names like the Flying Cloud, Bambi, the International, the Caravel, and so forth, and we giggled and ogled all of the nifty built-in conveniences that have been perfected over the last several decades. Then we sat on the groovy bench/couch in the lounge of one model as the breeze blew through the screened windows, carrying upon it visions of redwood forests and crashing surf, the highways of America, Roger Miller's "King of the Road" on the radio, and I mean, what can I say? We left having purchased a brand-new thirty-foot Globetrotter, unexpectedly excited in anticipation of our unforeseen new lives as 'Streamers.

I wish that I had been able to be of more service at this juncture to my partner, but unfortunately for her efforts, I had a book to be working on (this very one! Trippy!). This left Megan on her own to research and select locations at which to stay overnight on our trip, a somewhat frustrating endeavor. Normally, I take pride in being a comfort to my wife, and pitching in with both shoulders when she asks me to lend her assistance of any type, so I was acutely pained to be unavailable and a useless deadbeat to her as I immersed myself in writing about George Saunders and Jeff Tweedy and such. As I was to later realize, she was able to learn a great deal about locations called RV parks—establishments that were specifically outfitted to accommodate rigs like our Globetrotter.

Megan set straight to work outfitting the Nutmeg (of Consolation), as we called her, employing her usual aplomb for interior design, meaning rugs and throw pillows and linens—I mean, friends, when she puts sheets and also the sheety-like bags that go over the pillows on a bed, it feels so amazing to slide into that I often laugh out loud with pleasure. Not that we had actually gotten to the outfitting yet. We have no place to park a thirty-foot trailer at our home, so I intended to retrieve her from the dealer about a week before our departure, and roll the dice parking her on the street. Until then, my bride took over the garage floor with a dazzling array of fabrics, cookware, utensils, and just good flavor, like literally, as in jars and bags of spices and grocery items for the galley. It looked amazing, like some kind of vision board from one of those fancy design magazines, except with even cooler choices. I'm not exaggerating when I say she's out of my league. If anything, she *owns* my league, and I'm just in to pinch-hit off the bench, getting the signal to bunt.

The day finally arrived for me to bring the Nutmeg home from the Airstream spawning grounds, and so that I could comfortably haul our new four-ton baby, I had traded in my sensible Audi Q5 for a much brawnier Ford Expedition (V6, 400 HP). As a kid in Illinois, I had been trained to operate the necessary trucks and tractors so that I could be called upon to haul another wagon out to the field, in case all of the actual able hands were unavailable. I had also hauled trailers working on a construction crew as a teenager, which means that I could maneuver a trailer forward and un-forward after I'd had a couple beers, because this was in the eighties when one was required to drink a beer before getting behind the wheel of a work truck. This is all to say that I knew my way around the peculiarities of hauling a trailer. So long as you pay attention and make nice, wide turns, driving it down the road is not a huge deal—you quickly realize that you have to drive modestly. And the fact that the eight-foot-wide vehicle combination appears to take up the entire lane from dotted line to dotted line? Well, I believe that is the problem of the other drivers.

I live on a cul-de-sac and I knew that was going to be a problem, even during the short time we'd have the Nutmeg at our home. First, would I be able to turn my rig around, with twenty feet of Ford and thirty of Airstream behind me? That adds up to somewhere between forty and sixty feet! Then, presuming I could get it turned around to head back out the way I came in, how in the Wide, Wide World of Sports was I going to decently back an eight-foot-by-thirty-foot rectangle into the side of a circular cul-de-sac? I guess before I go on any further, I had better introduce you to Adam.

Adam and his wife, Sandy, are a type of neighbor that we often refer to as "Norman Rockwellian." They would make great horror characters, because they are so terrific and nice and supportive that there must be some terrifying secret being kept in the basement. *Something is up. Nobody is that cool.* In this day and age when the social norm is to behave in quite the opposite fashion of their unflagging generosity, we really won the neighbor lottery with these two. Part of Adam's incredible powers has to do specifically with our shared interests, which also happen to mostly be subjects that are very helpful around a domicile. He likes woodworking, carpentry, home construction in general, so also plumbing, electrical, masonry, etc., for all of which he collects and maintains the necessary tools and fasteners. He keeps an immaculately organized garage. History also fascinates him, and he likes Scotch. So, come on. He's like a superhero called *THE NEIGHBOR.*

Of course, I had discussed my plan with him for driving the Airstream home and attempting to park it. Wouldn't you know it, when I first arrived there with the Nutmeg, he had coned off the spots by our house that I was hoping to occupy for the next week as we loaded her up for our Thanksgiving road trip. As it turned out, I was in fact able to turn our travel train around successfully, taking it *very* carefully, and so now we had arrived at the moment of truth: backing into the spot.

The basic rule for backing up a towed trailer is this: If you want the ass of the trailer to go right, steer the ass of your vehicle left, and vice versa. Once you can get on top of this weird push-me-pull-you feeling, the rest comes pretty easily. As I prepared to give it my first attempt, I had a devastating realization: With the normal SUV side mirrors on the Expedition, I was 100 percent unable to see around the sides of the Nutmeg, rendering me completely blind in terms of being able to essentially parallel park. This looked like a job for *THE NEIGHBOR!* Adam nimbly landed from leaping over a tall building, and with his aid I was able to smoothly snug our Airstream into her berth in a mere twenty-seven tries. Phew!

Via a couple of adapters, I was able to plug the 50-amp electrical cable into an exterior 110-volt outlet on my garage that was close enough to the street to be accessible. We turned on the Globetrotter's lights, and I carried Megan gingerly up the little steps and across the threshold, and Lord, it was fine. She spent the next few days installing the garage's worth of accessories, filling up the refrigerator and freezer, and making this beautiful land-ship into our home. The majesty of her talents was being made fully manifest in this aluminum lozenge that a few months earlier we never would have dreamed we'd own. But the pandemic changed a lot of priorities for a lot of people, and this was no exception. I turned down some nice acting jobs to take this trip, which Megan had now fleshed out to a couple of months, with several stops throughout the Southwest. In many ways, the world felt strangely "on pause," and there would (hopefully) be more acting jobs later. She had put into this vehicle and this journey a veritable ass-load of extremely hard work and affection, and, donkey that I am, I still knew better than to miss it.

While she was working the interior up into the 2020 love-nest equivalent of the bottle from *I Dream of Jeannie*, I was finally able to pull my head out of my exit and begin my contribution. I first dove into the manual and learned all about the Ford Expedition and its tow package, and really all the newfangled systems you can get in your car nowadays. I still feel like I'm in *Battlestar Galactica* if a vehicle just has power windows, so this bonkers luxury wagon, which legitimately has the capability to both heat and cool the two front captain's chairs, while they also operate as *massage chairs*, is, pardon my French, fucking *stupéfiant*.

I dug out the spare tire and the fast, furious jack system which seems to get increasingly adorable as the years go by, which is perhaps not the ideal adjective I want describing my safety equipment. I changed a tire for Megan recently on her Audi, and that model currently comes with a compact, deflated, folded spare and tiny compressor that you have to plug into the twelve-volt outlet in the car to then inflate this spare while making a *very bad* noise, like if a mosquito and a trim router had a baby that could *really* sing. As the spare inflates, it unfolds and suddenly *pops* open through a couple of tiers of openness, which scared the pants off of me on behalf of anybody who has to countenance this action for the first time on a dark road some night. The engineering is neato, but I'm not sure I want to trust the whole finicky process over the clumsiness of carrying a slightly larger, already inflated spare.

I digress, apparently. It's a moot argument these days, anyway, since the percentage of times an ill-prepared person will get a flat where they're out of cell range or the reach of some help like AAA or a tow service is pretty infinitesimal. I just happen to love changing tires. It is an unexpected problem that I can tangibly solve with the tools to hand, and that makes me feel great when it happens. Let me put it this way: I'd rather be faced with changing a flat tire than be asked to download yet another "convenient new app" so that I can try and fail to view some video content or other through a website that has *boxx* in the name.

Once I had a firm enough grip on the Expedition's bells and whistles, I turned my attention to the Airstream, the Nutmeg herself, which is a damn impressive tub full of engineering accomplishments. I learned all about the trailer itself, including the brakes and the signal lights that plug into the Ford so that all of my driving maneuvers, like braking and turn signals, are communicated by the lights on the hindquarters of the Airstream. I learned about the onboard water system that supplies a kitchen sink, a bathroom sink, a shower, a toilet, and even a little outdoor shower rig, should things get that groovy somewhere outside of Barstow. I learned about the *black water* (toilet) tank, including how and when to properly empty it out at the appropriate facilities, and also details that wouldn't have occurred to me, like how to make all of this plumbing operate successfully even if you're staying where the weather is below freezing.

I learned about the propane stove, oven, hot water heater, and furnace, which are fueled by a couple of seven-gallon tanks that ride on the tongue of the trailer. Depending on the temperature outside, the furnace sometimes works in tandem with an electric heat pump on the roof, in a unit that also houses the air conditioner. There are two good-size TVs, a stereo speaker system, and a pretty decent refrigerator and freezer. Throw in a bunch of LED lights throughout the joint, and there were more than enough details to keep this prospective 'Streamer occupied.

The Globetrotter's electrical system is a little complicated, especially if your tool specialty happens to reside in woodworking, like that of your humble correspondent. Thanks to my handy dad, I am competent with the basics of plumbing and electricity, but as soon as things get more complex than, say, switching out an outlet box, I like to consult a more knowledgeable technician. If the problem is straightforward, like my plugging a Skil saw into a house circuit without realizing that Megan is also running a hollow chisel mortiser on the same line, and we blow the breaker—I can usually parse the issue, reset the breaker, and find another circuit for my sawing needs.

The system in the Nutmeg is a whole other animal. It's a pretty deluxe version, as RV electrical systems go, as it needs to juice the rooftop heat pump/air conditioner, the refrigerator/freezer, and a microwave(!), all on top of the basic lighting and entertainment needs. In ideal settings (nice RV parks), we just park in our allocated spot and plug a massive fifty-amp cable into a convenient fifty-amp outlet, and then simply fire up the whole casino with the clack of a big, satisfying switch. Neat, clean, no muss, no fuss, right? Sure, in the *ideal* case. Less-than-ideal cases involve parks that only have thirty-amp outlets available (which means I can't blow-dry my hair and microwave my lasagna at the same time), or when you want to camp in places with few to no electrical hookups, like "the wilderness," for example, and you have to then judiciously depend upon the *backup system,* which is battery powered.

Nestled on the tongue of the trailer between the front wall of the camper and the standing aluminum compartment that houses your two propane tanks is a lidded metal box housing two vehicle batteries. These maintain a punch of twelve volts, and they are trickle-charged whenever your fifty-amp rig is plugged into power. On top of that, the cable that plugs into the vehicle (the Expedition in my case) also diverts a trickle of juice to the batteries. This is pretty amazing, if for no other reason than it allows you to fill your fridge and freezer with weeks' worth of groceries while the Airstream is conveniently parked in front of your house, plugged into a mere 110-volt outlet, and then the batteries keep them running cold as you unplug from the DC power and head out onto the road for all-day drives. It is a perfect system.

Whoops. It was not a perfect system, again largely thanks to my ignorance. Basically, the outlet on the house was not supplying quite enough amperage to keep things fully running, with the main draw being the fridge. So, unbeknownst to this donkey, the electrical system was sipping off of the batteries for just a little help day in and day out across the week, slowly draining them, until I finally noticed it the night before we were scheduled to leave. Inside the trailer is a nifty little panel that displays the fluid levels in the water and waste tanks, and also tells me the current voltage of my batteries. Ideally, it's going to read between 12 and 13 volts. As Megan and I were buttoning things up to get on the road the next morning, I checked the meter and it said the batteries were down to 9.5, then 9.1, at which point everything basically shut down, meaning *all of our refrigerated food was about to be ruined*. This obviously sucked very much, especially since we were both exhausted from all the hustle in prepping things for the last week. I did what you do when the power goes out: I got ice, and transferred everything into four large coolers, and we hit the hay, bone-tired, but thrilled to begin our adventure the next day.

I got up bright and early, raring to go, and all I had to do was— Whoops . . . shit. And I mean, oh, shit. I mean, you have gotta be kidding me. The drained batteries had caused a whole new dilemma, one I hadn't even had a moment to consider. Basically, a trailer rests upon three points of contact: the wheels on each side, and the hitch up front, supported by the tow vehicle. When one disconnects a trailer from said tow vehicle, the third point of the triangle is removed and must be replaced by some sort of support leg. All of the trailers I had operated in my younger days had just such an accessory that would swing down into place, and they were pretty slick. Imagine this very heavy trailer, carrying a tractor, or tons of lumber, or a thirty-foot aluminum camper, and you need to release it from the hitch. The swinging leg system works like this: You pop the lock on the ball hitch, loosening the connection. You then swing the leg down and lock it into the upright position. You then crank the top turn-handle, which lowers the foot (which sometimes has a small wheel on it so the trailer can be manually push-rolled around on the wheels), until the leg takes the levered weight of the trailer. You keep cranking and the leg continues to extend, now lifting the weight up until the front hitch rises clear of the ball, and the tow vehicle can be driven forward, free and clear of the trailer.

This system requires a bit of muscle and familiarity with leverage and simple machines, but it's tried-and-true, and, as with changing a tire, I have always loved it because I know how to accomplish the heavy, potentially dangerous work it does. This work is also imperative to a successful journey/project/workday, because it's the crux of the trailer's job. You have to be able to hook up and also consciously uncouple from the trailer again and again, in many different circumstances. If you can't find a level spot upon which to park your trailer, you need to securely block the wheels to prevent a runaway Nutmeg. If you know the ins and outs of the hardware and implements involved, you can pull off this trick in the dark or in the rain, or both.

Now, if you'll indulge me in a little curmudgeon time, the "improved" system on the Nutmeg is a sizzling example of "improving" our technology and our gear right past the point of goodness and firmly into the realm of in-one's-own-foot-shooting, as I discovered the next morning when I bounded, bright-eyed and bushy-tailed, out to the street to hook up the Expedition to the Nutmeg and launch Megan and myself (and our charismatic poodle, Clover) upon our epic adventure. I backed the Ford into a close proximity for hitching, a process made infinitely easier with the advent of reverse-view cameras in vehicles, allowing me to single-handedly back up to the hitch with perfect accuracy. I hopped out of the driver's seat and skipped back to the trailer's "third leg," which in the case of our Airstream was not a swinging manual affair, but instead a luxurious fixed leg that was raised and lowered by a hydraulic motor, making the process easy as pie.

Here's the "oh, shit" part. The hydraulic motor is powered by the Airstream's electrical system. The Airstream's electrical system that was now stone dead. If I couldn't raise or lower the leg, I couldn't hitch up for the trip. Okay. Okay, part of being dependable in such situations is being able to adapt and improvise in the face of adversity. I had weathered scenarios like this before, and lived to tell the tale, so I was not panicking, but I was definitely offering the newfangled and dead "luxury leg" some rather choice epithets in praise of its sheer crapulence.

Now, one reason I didn't panic is because I have been down this road before. For example, I had read that when an outboard motor won't start electrically on a boat, you can pop off the hood and there will be a pull-rope starter option there for just such a dilemma. So, you have to examine the problem from every perspective—maybe if I couldn't raise the trailer hitch higher I could make the ball hitch on the Ford go lower. I thought about rounding up all the neighbor kids and telling them to put stones in their pockets and then pile onto the tailgate. I also knew I could go down at least five or six inches if I let the air out of the back tires.

Then, hang on! I remembered—beneath a pop-out cap on top of the leg assembly was a nut on the end of a shaft, and that nut had been engineered in that spot precisely to save my dumb ass in this very moment. I retrieved the nut-cranking wrench that came with the kit of sundry items that a very supportive "Camper Daddy" had talked me through when we bought this beauty, and I was all set to get back in business.

Whoops. The aluminum propane cabinet was snugged right up against the back of the leg top, meaning that any wrench-turning one might enact to manually spin the emergency nut would bang prohibitively into the cabinet. Okay, now maybe I began to feel some panic, and sweat began rolling down my unfortunately hairy torso. I had just commenced with formulating the explanations I would try to plead to Megan, and then started to think about which neighborhood I should move to when she invariably dumped this sorry excuse for a husband, when a heroic shadow fell across my impotent wrench. It was *THE NEIGHBOR*!

Among his many laudable attributes, Adam maintains the sort of domestic garage that would make the Craftsman tool people's hats fly off. Every necessary tool is represented, many dating back to his dad before him, beautifully organized and maintained. One particularly admirable aspect is his penchant for going the extra mile to seek out tools of quality that are manufactured in the USA. An enthusiast after my own heart, he updates me regularly when he discovers new sources of "buying local," which works for table saws just like it works for beef and eggs. By and large, when any tool production moves overseas, the quality goes down so that somebody's wallet can get fatter, which is why I want to be like *THE NEIGHBOR* and buy American whenever I can.

He also has shelves and shelves of fasteners and washers and gaskets, assorted rolls of tape, plumber's strap, angle iron, and mending plates, beneath rafters bristling with stores of PVC pipe and conduit and scrap wood trim. But the most important element in his garage is its *life*. He is not a mere hobbyist or collector—in the decade or so that I've known him, he has built two different exterior decks and assorted gardening stations, fixed his roof, and completely remodeled his kitchen. He is a superhero exactly because he scrutinizes and maintains the readiness of his garage for just such a moment as had befallen me.

The fire of delight that illuminated him when I explained the situation was that of a Thoroughbred who is finally about to be set free to do what he was born to do—run. His first pitch, and it was a good one, was to chock the appropriate five-eighths-inch socket into a beefy hammer drill, notch it onto the nut, and use its powerful motor to spin the leg shaft. The only problem was that the torque required to raise and lower the eight-thousand-pound trailer only by turning this diminutive nut was considerably more muscle than even a hammer drill could provide. If we ever did deduce how to successfully turn this nut, it was going to be an arduous job for the turner.

THE NEIGHBOR was waylaid by this setback for all of ten seconds.

"Hang on," he said as he jogged into his Lair of Sufficiency (garage), clanged a few things around, and came jogging back. He held in his hand a twelve-inch steel extender shaft, the end of which would receive the five-eighths-inch socket, effectively sticking straight up off of the leg shaft another foot, and the other end of the extender rod received the original cranking wrench, now raised above the impedimentary propane cabinet, allowing the wrench to rotate with impunity! *THE NEIGHBOR* had done it again!

Now all that remained was for me to crank that extended wrench rig around and around for way too many revolutions to get the Nutmeg's tongue high enough so that I could back the Expedition's ball hitch beneath the trailer's connector. I'm not going to equivocate here—this exertion was goddamn hard. It required the engagement of my full body to juxtapose my weight against the lateral pushing and pulling of the crank, but it was working, and that meant that I would get to stay married, so I heaved away like I've never heaved before. Despite all the trials and tribulations of the last day, we were ready to go.

* * *

Epilogue: The first time I stopped to refill my propane tanks in Arizona, I discovered that the aluminum propane cabinet was pretty easily removable by unfastening one large interior nut, which would have allowed the cranking wrench to clear just fine. Please don't tell Adam or Megan!

16

VIRGIN FLIGHT

Aaaand, we're off! Finally on the road by lunchtime after losing most of the morning to the laborious trailer-leg issue and other last-minute items, I was sopping with sweat, engaging in some deep breathing to ready myself for the next nine or ten hours on the road. I was in a state of emotional and physical exhaustion with which I imagine the parents of young children must be well acquainted. Fighting some sort of truly existential battle, emerging victorious but just barely, then picking oneself up and starting a full day in that state of both triumph and fatigue.

After the hustle and fret around the dire circumstances of the hitch difficulty, followed up by a bout of exercise that I would liken to pulling a vehicle up a hill toward oneself by means of a rope which one grasps, hand over hand, and heaves and tugs in a stance that can just barely be maintained in terms of stamina and balance, I was feeling quite spent.

Performing *just within* the limits of one's strength capability for twenty
or thirty minutes, say, will leave even the most enduring of mules ready
for a nap. This is hardly the time you want to get on the road, but as any
self-respecting jackass will tell you, I was going to be goddamned if I was
going to be defeated on day one of our love trip by a *hardware problem.*
This degree of stubbornness has served me exceptionally well in my life,
excepting the time I tried wrestling a California-king-size mattress up a
staircase for an hour and herniated a disc in my spine. But guess what?
That mattress is upstairs getting slept on regularly, so *who's the stupid one
now,* mattress?

Since one of the characteristics of Los Angeles that best defines her
is her traffic (the way stink defines a skunk), driving away from the city
always evokes a pure and lovely feeling, getting out into the open desert
and feeling the wind in your hair, even if it's the sedate version, where
we just kick the AC up to 4 or maybe 4.5. As we barreled eastward in
our thirteen to fourteen thousand pounds of elephantine rig, once you've
added the SUV and the Nutmeg together, I was, as I said, awash with
emotion. Physical depletion would have to be dealt with later, certainly,
but for the moment what I mainly felt was elation.

Megan and I had both been dealing with our own personal flavors
of depression. I have previously asserted, in this book and elsewhere,
that my general happiness depends upon my ability to accomplish good,
productive work that does somebody some good. Whether it's as an actor
or writer or woodworker or son or husband or neighbor, I have had very
good luck over the last few decades in almost always having been able
to be of good use to someone. Having the vocational side of this personal
economy stripped away from me, then, was quite alienating and left me
feeling useless and adrift. When the pandemic began, all forms of work
(well, with the exception of writing this book) instantly disappeared, but

I'm grateful that I was still needed by Megan to fill my role as spouse, or I would have been truly in peril.

Now eight months had passed, and we were breaking out of the co-cooned malaise that had clouded our household for too long. I sat up tall in my massage parlor of a seat; placed my hands in the neighborhood of "ten and two"; checked the Ford's gauges; checked the extended side mirrors that I had purchased the day before and installed; gazed briefly at the most beautiful woman I had had the fortune to come across and our magnificent little pup, Clover, who in all sincerity ran our household; then cast my gaze forward, permitted myself a modest smile, and proceeded to "keep 'er 'tween the ditches" for another four hundred miles.

Besides the triumphant travel mates in the passenger seat, there was another reason for the elation I was feeling, and for once, it wasn't meat-based. The sensation was not dissimilar to the way that riding a bicycle never fails to make me feel twelve years old again, wind whipping through my hair (apparently that's my thing. Now I'm trying to remember if I ever felt pleasure without a top-breeze), as though I'm out of school and getting away with something. In this case, the (eventual) success of the morning, specifically with regard to "making the equipment work," combined with the now (so far) successful operation of said equipment, brought me straight back to the times as a teenager that I was entrusted by my dad or my uncles on the farm to transport or operate heavy, expensive equipment, or coax an older-model tractor or pickup truck into starting up and behaving amiably until the work was done.

Over the years since then, I put in a lot of hard work, and I mean grueling physical labor, as a carpenter, and as a theatre actor (carrying the good-looking people on- and offstage), and then as a woodworker, before my dream of success as an actor really took root in my mid- to late thirties. After that, things began to change in profound ways for me, pretty much all for the good, but still, it's complicated. For example, when I suddenly had juicy acting jobs for most of the year, that really cut down on my time in my woodshop. So, my dream was finally coming true as an actor, but my beloved second vocation was being diminished. Practically speaking, I was also working jobs that required a lot less physical labor than when I was at the shop three weeks out of every month. That meant my hands grew softer, and my diet also had to be streamlined since I wasn't burning as many calories slinging slabs of trees around the out-feed table.

The irony is not lost on me that even as I was becoming well known to television audiences as a fictional edifice of masculinity and physical fortitude named Ron Swanson, in real life I was growing softer by the day, metamorphosing from rough laborer into artist. It's not a big deal to me either way, as I was previously happy at the woodshop, and I'm happy now in front of the camera, but it is a life shift of which I remain aware, partly because I enjoy returning to the shop when I have time between artist gigs.

With that in mind, everything about this journey was reawakening the dauntless explorer in me—the part of me that was always the guy enlisted to drive moving trucks for friends from Champaign-Urbana to Chicago, to New York City or Los Angeles, as well as up and down the coast of California. It felt amazing, and I never would have had the wherewithal to make it manifest if Megan hadn't cooked the whole thing up. The big, fat life lesson in this for me is that *things can go too well*. I had happily settled into the extreme comfort of high-end acting jobs, and it was going well enough that I could pretty much fill the calendar. Sounds amazing, right? What's the problem?

A little idiom I like to call "too much of a good thing." Megan and I come from places that have actual weather and four full seasons of it, to boot—Oklahoma for her, Illinois for me—and so one thing we both dislike about Southern California is that the weather is way too nice, way too often. For one thing, it means your ecosystem is usually choked with drought, but just spiritually the famous sunshine day in and day out is *too much of a good thing*. I love a well-marbled cowboy steak, medium rare, off the (cast-iron pan on the) grill, but I don't want that for dinner every night, because then it's no longer special.

I had stumbled my way into a life where I was getting the acting-job equivalents of California sunshine and nightly steak for dinner, which I think would have taken me way too long to realize had we not been brought up short by the COVID-19 pandemic. Even so, it took my magnificent life-curator bride to kick me solidly in the behind and plunk that behind into this diamond-studded massage chair of a driver's seat. We were about to spend a couple of months on the road together, a choice that had no motive beyond sharing a romantic adventure and getting to see her people in Oklahoma and mine in Illinois, which immediately brings to mind the Aldo Leopold family's ethos of exploring their land around their shack for reasons of agrarian fidelity and familial love, fully in the knowledge that they wouldn't be getting paid for it.

So, here we were, thanks to my childhood training, the loving support of our neighbors, and the astonishing ability my wife has for picking things out. It had been some years, but I was deeply grateful to realize that I was, once again, intrepid. Our ship's crew was depending on qualities in me that hadn't been tested for a while, and by Hermes, god of the road, that's a feeling that will keep me young.

* * *

In the last few weeks and months, as I mentioned, yet another area of expertise in which Megan had been matriculating was the ins and outs of RV parks. Our first destination was a gorgeous establishment called Catalpa Canyon in Cottonwood, Arizona. Megan had meticulously researched the place and secured us one of their "newer" spaces, with what was truly a spectacular view. We had received a "welcome email" from the park office, with instructions for arrival and whatnot, although I hadn't looked too closely at the fine print beyond "pick up your welcome packet at the guard house and proceed to your assigned space, and sweet Danny Trejo, have you kids picked an absolute doozy of a site."

Cut to: Totally forgetting about the time change to the Mountain time zone, we rolled up to the guard shack at about midnight. Once we flagged down the excellent on-duty Dana Carvey character who eventually came coasting silently along in a golf cart, we were duly informed by him—let's call him "Merv"—that we were intensely shit out of luck.

Lesson 1: The better RV parks have "quiet hours," usually from like ten p.m. to seven a.m. or so. This makes a ton of sense, because you're basically a temporary village of sometimes dozens of vehicles, all parked within yards of each other, often equipped with an assortment of caterwauling children and their bicycles, scooters, water cannons, video games, and so on. All things of which I'm generally in favor, but then we all want to get to sleep at some point as well.

Lesson 2: "Quiet hours" means you can't drive your thick-ass Ford Expedition with a turbo V6 pulling a thicker-ass Airstream Globetrotter into the park, where, even if you're heavily experienced and smooth as butter, getting parked and set up is still a rigmarole that involves some inescapable noise.

Lesson 3: Read the goddamn welcome email. If we had done so in this case, we would have known that if we didn't get settled in by ten p.m., we would be shunted over to a side parking lot *with no hookups.*

This would come to be key terminology in our lives as 'Streamers; in fact it was the first thing one asked of a prospective campsite: "Do you have full hookups?" What is meant by this term? "Full hookups" indicates that your site has the previously discussed outlet for your fifty-amp or thirty-amp electrical connection, it features a hose spigot with fresh water which you may attach to your onboard water system, and it has a three-inch drain plug in the ground to which you can attach your "black water" sewage drainpipe, also commonly referred to as your "stinky slinky." Sometimes your site will also have a coaxial cable connection to hook your trailer up to cable TV. Usually these amenities are grouped together, close to each other, and when everything clicks into place and works properly, it can feel pretty dreamy. You park your Nutmeg, and within ten to fifteen minutes it can be a fully functioning, cozy little land submarine.

On that first night, however, I'll repeat, we had no hookups. We might as well have been in any parking lot anywhere, for all the good this place was doing us. Oh, and it was *cold*. It was November 15 and we were in the high desert, closer in feel to Flagstaff than Phoenix, so it was in the ballpark of thirty-six degrees outside. And let me now also remind you that we had no goddamn electrical power. Ha ha! What a dependable captain I was turning out to be. The trickle charge from the Expedition to the Airstream batteries while we drove was not nearly enough to overcome the severe depletion I had laid on the system while it was parked at our house. At least we had a propane furnace.

Lesson 4: Whoops. Know your systems. Maybe you're savvy to these things, and you were already saying, "Why don't you just fire up the propane heater?" I thought the same thing, pal, okay, and once again the answer to the question is "death by technology update." If it had been just a propane furnace that had a pilot light I could even light manually, we would have been golden. But no, it's a way more deluxe modern appliance hooked up to an electric thermostat and electric starting mechanism, which unfortunately requires *electricity*.

Lesson 5: When you have no electricity and it's night in the desert, look up. Holy Gila monster, the Milky Way was like a vast, psychedelic puddle of sparkling galactic vomit, to make a figure of speech. It was truly overwhelming, and we stood chest to chest and looked up and held our amazing dog and then we slow danced. I can't recall if one of us played a song on our phone or if the music was just in our heads. Either way, we had gone through a hell of a lot to get to this pitch-black, freezing parking lot where we were, by God, still in love.

So that was the situation. We ate some cold pasta that Megan had prepared for the drive, and Clover had her dinner. A proper scout, I usually have a few choices for you should you be looking for a flashlight, and Megan had some very cute little battery-powered globe lamps. Using these, we got situated and climbed into bed as soon as we could, which, thanks to Megan's talent for draping sleeping quarters in the finest linens stuffed with the most magically warm goose feathers, was toasty and cozy as hell.

When we awoke the next morning, it was still hilariously freezing, and we were like a couple of little icicles tucked under the covers. We sprang into action, buttoned up the Nutmeg, and rolled into the park proper, catching Merv just as his overnight shift was ending. He gave us our welcome packet and a map, directing us to our long-awaited little slice of heaven, an RV site that we like to call C-48. As we wended our way through the park, passing all manner of Recreational Vehicles, Megan began to suspect something was off. She didn't recall the site number being so high as 48. We continued to pass different groupings of sites with varying situations vis-à-vis the vista, but all looking at something marvelous across the expansive Arizona desert.

It was around then that the road began to wind downhill and curve into a sort of canyon, but really it was more of a ditch. There was a distinct feeling that we had passed through the "good" spots and zipped right past the "okay" spots because now we had clearly arrived at the "shitty" spots. We found our number, and this site was of a style that I would come to relish, known as a "pull-through." This means it was a strip of land big enough to accommodate all RVs and trailers, with a little yard to spare, and each end of the site was bordered by road, allowing the renter to drive into the site, park, recreate, then, once they had done their worst, to drive right out again, never being required to back that son of a bitch into a tight spot between other RVs.

So, I actually drove around the loop of road a couple of times to eyeball my final approach, as this was my very first landing of the Nutmeg in the wild. Once I had gotten my dander properly up, I slowly rolled us into place and threw the Ford into park. Megan was on the phone, but I hardly noticed as I sprang into action, engaging our nifty Airstream-shaped mirth delivery system! I hooked up all the hookups, which was a bit fraught, since they were located almost directly beneath the pop-out bedroom of our next-door neighbors. It then began to occur to me that this rather intimate proximity to them was not ideal at all, and as I circumnavigated the trailer, I clocked some more details: We were parked in a tight corner of the lowest end of the property, and our views were basically of the other trailer homes in what appeared to be a not-very-attractive neighborhood. I unfolded her little two-step staircase and climbed it to enter the Nutmeg and begin unfastening all of the items lashed down for travel.

Okay, here's a difference between Megan and me. People like these, right? Differences? When we're traveling, in any capacity, and we have accomplished all the required legs of the excursion, meaning the drive is over, or the train journey with required taxis on either end has ended, or let's just say: pack—car to the airport—check in—go through security—flight—invariable Dallas layover—impossibly long tram ride—connecting second flight—baggage claim—car to hotel—check in—get safely to hotel room with luggage accounted for. Okay? When all of these steps have been achieved, and we are legitimately exhausted, I don't care if there are no linens on the hotel room bed, or the bathroom is gross, or the window is shattered and rain is blowing straight into the room—I have finished traveling. Whatever the problem is *will be fine*. We're done with the airport, we're done carrying bags, we've achieved the *planned itinerary*. One upper corner of the bedroom is filled with hornets? Not ideal, but not a deal-breaker. You don't bother them, they won't bother you, I will sleep just fine. Time for a beer.

Because she is a domesticated, civilized person, this is not the case with Megan. When something is wrong with our room, she rightly *spots* it, first of all, as I have already begun to lightly snore on the bed, and she then takes the immediate, appropriate action, for which I always initially damn her but finally thank her. I mean, come on! If she weren't so right about these hotel iniquities, I could be tipsy and drowsing by now. Why did I have to marry such a quality person?

Just then, Megan stepped up and into the Nutmeg with a full head of steam, and a spirit fit to bursting with both piss and vinegar. It finally began to dawn on me that we had been given the wrong spot right about when she said, "They gave us the wrong spot!"

She was waiting for "the guy" to call her back, and she was really upset.

In terms of keeping things fresh, one of our main techniques as a couple is when either of us has the opportunity to plan something as a treat or surprise for the other, we give it everything we have. Megan, as a truly sophisticated picker-outer-of-shit, is especially great in this arena, which means that she spends a lot of time doing a lot of research and legwork into any place we will be staying. If we were taking a trip to London, she would canvass friends and coworkers to learn which was the freshest, most flavorsome of the Kit Kemp hotel family, then she would glean all the atmosphere she could online, and learn which category of suite was best suited to our peculiar tastes, but *then* she would get somebody on the phone and grill them about which of the five suites had the best idiosyncratic details—a weird, cool balcony, a real antique stone fireplace, a house elf (!).

So, of course, she had trained the crosshairs of her considerable acumen onto the category of RV park spots. As she explained to me, waiting for "the guy" to call, the websites for these places were generally very thin. Perhaps this is because many of these places established their particular panache (or lack thereof) before the internet took over, so whereas we're used to seeing way too many pictures of any given location, the RV parks thrive in something of a shroud of mystery. As Megan pointed out, there is often literally one photo on a given website, perhaps of a tree, or a colorful rocky vista. For that reason, she had spent the duration of many phone calls trying to suss out the ideal spot for two lovebirds and their magnificent poodle.

When "the guy"—let's call him Gary—when Gary finally called back, he and Megan figured out that she had indeed reserved for us a spot called K-4, which, when we later went and looked at it, was nothing short of glorious. The problem was, Gary explained, that a few months ago she had reserved the spot for three nights here in November, but since then, another camper, with "member status," had wanted K-4 for two weeks, and since they were members, they automatically were given priority treatment.

Megan had Gary on speakerphone, and at this last assertion we just looked at each other in disbelief, jaws agape. It turns out this campground, Catalpa Canyon, was an Almost Heaven resort, meaning it was one of 178 such campgrounds dotted around the US of A where you could get similarly shafted in a cheery tone. Megan collected herself and asked him if that was standard business practice, specifically that the company wouldn't honor a reservation if a "bigger fish" came along. And if so, why wouldn't they at least contact us to let us know of the situation?

Gary, confusingly, could not have been happier to explain that, oh, yes, now he understood our befuddlement—what we had failed to do, in the weird, apparently unprecedented case that we wanted our *reservation* to actually *hold our space in reserve,* was to pay an extra $75 holding fee on top of the deposit we had been happy to pay. I guess we didn't know about that "extra deposit on top of the deposit" practice? Or we apparently should have just become members, which costs (I just looked it up) $615 annually for *one of five zones,* meaning you can rest assured that your reservation will be honored in the appropriate fifth of our nation. Oh, sorry, did you want to actually *travel* when you, um, travel? Extra zones can be unlocked for $65 a pop. This is simply a different method by which they would receive extra money from us, and only then would we have been treated with what we have come to understand in most American business dealings as "decency."

This strangely chipper guy really did seem to feel for us, because we were clearly just rank greenhorns, entirely out of our depths in terms of RV park street smarts. He told Megan then and there that he would refund our money and he even recommended another nearby campground that would likely have a nicer spot for us. Megan gave me a skeptical look, because it seemed that at some point one of Gary's coworkers might have written him a note that said he was talking to a reasonably popular television comedy legend, and that's when he turned his "friendly" dial up to 11.

I unhooked our hookups and we drove away.

Lesson 6: When it comes to navigating RV parks and their gatekeepers, there is a substantial culture of unwritten laws of the jungle, and these customs can only be mastered by loading up your Nutmeg and charging straight into the heart of darkness.

17

ANGEL FIRE

Sure enough, we safely moved fifteen minutes down the Verde River, from Catalpa Canyon RV and Camping Resort to Verde Ranch RV Resort. Megan had called ahead on the brief drive and secured us a space, which I went and confirmed inside the office/gift shop once we rolled in. Two very nice ladies and I, all of us in masks, managed an affable transaction using my credit card and copious applications of hand sanitizer. One of them had spoken to Megan on the phone some minutes earlier, and they had correctly determined that the place for us was down by the river under some giant, broad-leafed cottonwood trees, where there were several available spots.

A word on personal preferences. In this particular case right here, I couldn't for the life of me comprehend why the first spots to be snatched up wouldn't be the ones down by the river, under the shady deciduous trees. The majority of the other lots were then, by default, up a slope and out in the blazing sunshine, and they were pretty much all taken. I know I just spent some considerable page space describing the way in which my smart wife and myself were proven to be dumb and uninitiated in the ways of the camper mafia, so maybe you're thinking, "Down by the river is great, if you like mosquitoes, dumbass," or something in that range. That did not prove to be the case. Our spot was without a blood-sucker in sight, and frankly just plain wonderful once I had successfully backed into it on my third try.

This, thankfully, always happens to us. We are not beach people, and we don't crave the sun in any locale. Instead, because we miss the drama of the varied weather systems under which we were raised, we love to go stay at ocean-side resorts during the off-season. This works out great, because everything is cheaper and less crowded, and if our luck holds, we might even get to enjoy some rain. Perhaps this condition, meaning our proclivity for selecting the "alternate choice," had some-thing to do with what makes us artists. We're the strange kids who like to sit in the back of the school bus and make up a secret language.

Whatever the case, it had certainly landed us in a sweet spot (378!) with full hookups that felt like the most soothing of salves upon the wounds of the previous twelve hours. We set up camp and spent the next couple nights in relative bliss, answering Clover's bidding and exploring our first RV camp.

What a difference was made by the merest shift in attitude from the first, exclusive park, wielding unwritten rules that had completely rained on our parade (or, I guess, given our preference, shone clear weather down on our parade?) to this second campground, where the administration simply treated us like neighbors and dealt with us squarely, invoking no bonus fees. As a well-off, middle-aged, straight, white couple in America, I can't imagine anyone ever withstanding the painful discrimination and suffering that we had just experienced and living to tell the tale.

After our success beneath the cottonwoods, we got back on the road and pointed the Expedition northeast, hoping to travel eight hours and then some to the mountains above Taos, New Mexico. We were feeling free and optimistic once more, having stumbled and regained our 'Streamer feet. Megan had wisely phoned ahead to confirm our upcoming park reservations, and sure enough, this next one, called Angel Fire RV Resort, had done the exact same thing as the first place—a longer reservation had arrived, so they shoved us to a new space, presumably in the basement or out behind the tannery. The woman on the phone assured Megan that our new spot was virtually as good as the old spot, and Megan had their site map up on her smartphone and was apparently pacified by the woman for the moment. The Angel Fire manager also openly admitted that, yes, for a $50 fee, they would have locked our "reservation" in place.

We drove through Albuquerque and on to Santa Fe, where we stopped at a charming little chocolate house called Kakawa. This was not a cute little bonbon shop—it was hard-core. Their passion, they say, is authentic and historic "drinking-chocolate elixirs." These include traditional elixirs from pre-Columbian, Mesoamerican, Mayan, and Aztec cultures; some elixirs from seventeenth-century Europe; plus some from colonial America and colonial Mexico, and I'll tell you what—their top-drawer hot chocolate beverages were so delicious and invigorating and innovative and irresistible that we went out of our way to get back there two more times before leaving New Mexico. Blended with powerful cacao and chili powders, theirs was the perfect roborative beverage to power us up the last couple hours of our wintry drive in the high desert.

When we arrived at Angel Fire, it was after quiet time again, but they luckily allowed late-night entry. I snagged our welcome packet hanging from the guardhouse doorknob and we silently rolled into the expansive field of RV sites, but something was off. As we drove along, navigating by the site map I had just acquired, the moon was bright enough for us to look all around us in disbelief. We sallied forth, farther and farther into the park, until finally in the farthest corner we saw the large RV that had taken our reserved spot, and *no other campers.* We had been bumped from our spot in an RV park in which we were the only occupied spot. Oh, sweet Gaia, how we laughed. We did hoot and holler as we rolled to our newly secured spot, a few down the row from what was apparently the unquestionably greatest spot in the state of New Mexico. Hot damn, but these RV people were strange.

The next morning we awoke to an inch or so of light powder covering everything. As I walked an uncertain Clover around the almost entirely empty park, my education in 'Streamer life proceeded apace. This was a very nice, almost brand-new facility, evidenced by its version of the building I would come to learn is a staple of RV parks—the shower/laundry house. The one at Angel Fire was really nice—the bathrooms were spacious, and there were a few very nice stone-tiled showers, each in its own private room. The laundry facilities were clean and brand-new, and there was a fire pit behind the building with all-weather furniture and a robust gas fire going, which was pretty extravagant in the light twenty-eight-degree snowfall.

One gratifying part about living in the Airstream is the ability to haul your domestic comforts anywhere you can park that thing. This sometimes feels thrilling, as to a child, like when you are out in the woods all day and return home dirty and tired, and you can take a hot shower in the diminutive but totally functioning shower. Or when you're road-tripping and you pull into a gas station to fill up but the bathroom situation looks pretty skeevy, especially during COVID, and you can just pop in the back and use the bathroom that you happen to be hauling around with you. That said, it's also pretty cramped in there, which is sometimes fun and sometimes less than. That made these shower buildings pretty golden, especially when there was nobody else around. 'Streaming is a blast, but it's also nice to be able to scrub off all of the algae without making your wife listen to the scraping.

On our way back, a couple new camper units had arrived, one of which was a gigantic motor home, and the other was a fellow Airstream—a newish-looking Flying Cloud. It was funny, the way we humans operate—just seeing the same brand of trailer made me feel an immediate esprit de corps with the owner, despite not even having seen them.

Megan and I enjoyed a cozy breakfast with a dazzling view of the snow-blanketed mountains before I disconnected the Ford from the Nutmeg so that we could head down to Taos and walk around. When we got there, only a handful of lonely tourists like us were wandering about, looking in shop windows. Everything was effectively shut down due to the pandemic, which was honestly a comfort to see. One of the strangest, most depressing things about the whole COVID situation was that certain sections of the country, depending upon their political leanings, of all things, were choosing to eschew the advice of medical experts when it came to safety protocols around the virus. It just doesn't make any sense, even as I sit here typing it. The same antimask Republican regions have been assigning the same asinine politicization to the vaccine, now that we have it, and it's just a real head-scratcher. Impoverished nations around the globe would give anything they could for the miraculous relief of this medical achievement, and here these neighbors of ours are pooh-poohing the shot, like it's a haircut they would rather skip.

"I'm not sure, should I do bangs? Or are they a liberal hoax?"

New Mexico is a blue state these days, thank goodness, so common sense is *generally* on display. Let's save any further scrutiny of this topic for our arrival in Texas, shall we?

Our wandering brought us around the charming, dusty plaza, past historic adobe hotels, Native art galleries, and groovy-but-shuttered outdoor adventure outfitters to a nice little park area, which included, nestled between some cute Little League diamonds and a basketball court beneath some welcome shade trees, a small graveyard. Our attention was drawn to an interior grave site surrounded by an old cast-iron fence, which we saw held the remains of famed mountain man Kit Carson and his third wife, Josefa.

I didn't know a lot about Carson beyond the general legend surrounding him as a Southwestern-flavored Daniel Boone or Davy Crockett type, and the sign at the park's entrance did little to disabuse me of that idea. It read: *Kit Carson—Scout—Citizen—Soldier—"He Led The Way."* This caught my interest, since there's such a strong Native American presence in Taos, and after the reading I had done surrounding the treatment of the Indigenous tribes farther north, I made a mental note to read up a little more on old Christopher Houston "Kit" Carson.

We cruised back up the hill to the small mountain village of Angel Fire, which was reportedly named centuries ago when the local elders of the Moache Ute tribe noticed mysterious flames of orange and red flickering in the early morning sky. The swing they took at naming it was "Fire of the Gods," which Franciscan monks later misnamed, or "reinterpreted," as "the Place of the Fire of the Angel." Well done, padre.

Back in the Nutmeg in time for lunch, I was bursting with anticipation for my afternoon. For the first time on our Airstream trip, I would get to hit the trail for a substantial hike. Megan loves to hike as well, but not necessarily in the winter when there was a cozy new Airstream to enjoy, so she was planning to stay home with Clover and cook. Besides, as in any relationship, but especially in one that's currently occupying a mere 240 square feet, it's good to spend some time apart once in a while (whether your husband is astonishingly gassy or no).

Just a mile up the road from the RV park was the trailhead for the Elliot Barker Trail, and when I arrived, I was tickled to see a sign declaring that the forest this handsome trail traced its way through was in fact Carson National Forest, as in Kit Carson. That guy got around.

I have since done some reading on Mr. Carson, and discovered him to be one of the most complicated characters I've come across yet in my reading for this book. By this I mean he was a rock-star-level national hero in his day, thanks to his rugged feats as a wilderness guide, hunter/ trapper, and soldier, especially given that he only stood five foot one inch tall. In sensational dime novels and unauthorized biographies of the day, his exploits were greatly exaggerated, although they certainly didn't need to be embellished to be hugely impressive. Carson was instrumental in helping the burgeoning United States explore, map, and ultimately conquer what would become the southwestern quarter of the country.

The complications arise in that verb *conquer*. I am given pause when I consider that much of what was considered his heroic service entailed brutally and viciously killing Native Americans or the Mexican military. He was often billed as the great "Indian fighter," but descriptions of his heated actions are shocking, chock-full of homicidal mutilations and murders that, at this far remove from those days of harsh survival, seem like details from a horror script.

It goes back to that sense of "heroism" and "patriotism" that we softies discussed in part 1. These terms generally referred to acts of violence in the service of one's own family or tribe or state or nation. In the 1830s Kit Carson even had his own run-ins with the very Blackfeet we were learning about up in Glacier National Park. Carson and his fellow "Indian fighters" treated these braves as less than human. According to historian David Roberts, *"It was taken for granted that the Blackfeet were bad Indians; to shoot them whenever he could was a mountain man's instinct and duty."* Many Indigenous tribes were considered "bad Indians," which simply meant that they fought back against the white people who were *invading and usurping* their lands. The Apache, Kiowa, Navajo, Crow, and many more were considered pests deserving of eradication, on the same level as the apex predators, the wolf, bear, and mountain lion. It was considered heroic to wipe these human beings out like vermin, employing the bloody techniques of the psychopath, like scalping, burning, and execution.

About eighty years after Carson's string of "heroic feats," in the spring of 1912, a young forester named Aldo Leopold was named supervisor of the million-or-so-acre Carson National Forest, in which I was trudging, and it was there in the mountains of New Mexico that his own adherence to the "manifest destiny" of pest extermination would lead him to shoot and kill a certain she-wolf—an act that came with repercussions which would change the way he saw nature forevermore.

The nuances coloring the lives of both Carson and Leopold are just as prevalent today, except that we can benefit from observing the mistakes that they both made in their exceptional but humanly flawed careers. To my way of thinking, this is what is meant by the term *woke.* *Woke* is very much in the news right now, just as *politically correct* was there in recent decades. Both terms refer to an open-minded understanding of the causes and victims of discrimination, usually focused upon, you know, the oppressed, be that women, or people of color, or

WHERE THE DEER AND THE ANTELOPE PLAY 247

LGBTQ folk. You name it. For example, to acknowledge and speak out against voter suppression in a state like Georgia would be considered "woke." To oppose such acknowledgment, and deny the attempts at curtailing voting rights and instead insist that those speakers should "shut their pie-holes," would be "anti-woke," or "Republican."

I am so grateful that a percentage of our population *is* woke, and always has been, because that is the contingent that recognizes our human flaws and the subsequent flaws that have been built into the organizational structures of our civilization. The pain and systemic disadvantages caused by these flaws are as plain as the noses on our Caucasian faces, and by Bing Crosby's vibrato, I would certainly hope that we Americans as a people would not choose to sleep through the struggle of our brothers and sisters, but indeed remain woke to it and face it head-on until it has been corrected.

Facts are facts, and the right-wing propaganda machine cannot ultimately change that. They *are* sadly able to influence their viewers, because there is certainly a contingency of people who would like to not be bothered, to remain asleep. It's *absolutely* a pain in the butt to have to deal with healing the wounds of slavery that we have inflicted upon our population. It's a total pain in the ass to have to acknowledge and deal with the massive sins of Native American genocide. But, friends? Those total bummers are obviously nothing when compared with living as the victims of slavery and genocide, and all the other ills that some number of us have inflicted upon some others. I guess being "woke" means that one has enough integrity as a citizen, a neighbor, and a human to cop to these sins. I want to be awake. It's undeniable that we Americans fucked up in the ways that we did. Undeniable. So we can strive to be "woke" about it and face it head-on, or we can go on Fox News and beg the audience to let us remain asleep in our fluffy beds that we have so thoroughly shat.

* * *

There's a little game I play with myself when I'm out in a remote area, far from civilization: I pretend I've traveled back through time to the era when Europeans first explored this terrain, and I try to imagine the harsh details of the expedition—I'm on horseback, I'm either freezing or sweating my balls off, any number of bugs is driving me insane, I haven't had a latte for months, etc. Then, at some point, contact is made with the people who already inhabit the region. The Indigenous people are referred to as a "tribe," and the invading Europeans-cum-Americans are called "explorers," because the histories have been written by us explorers. But truthfully, from the point of view of the people upon whose lands we are trespassing, we have been insidious thieves and marauders.

Had we been honest in our dealings, the conversation might have gone something like, "Hello, we are white people. Very nice natural resources you have here. Do you mind if we have this? [*gestures all around*] Yes? Um, okay. Are you sure? Because these here thunder-sticks are what we call guns, and these little letter-T things are called crosses, and when we combine these guns and crosses, we are able to excuse any and all depravity required of us when it comes to taking what we want by force. You want to sleep on it, maybe? We'll be back soon and we can teach you about *paperwork*."

Some Indigenous tribes tried to play ball and were viciously double-crossed. Some tried to fight back and were brutalized, raped, and pillaged. Village after village was reduced to ashes. From sea to shining sea. Ultimately, what the European colonists did to the inhabitants of North America, specifically with regard to the United States, was we *conquered* them. We killed them better than they killed us, so we got to keep all their shit. That made us *heroes* and that made them *losers*.

Now, having arrived at this trail by traveling in an expedition of my own—my Ford Expedition, that is, in which my very chair would give me a back rub in case I wasn't feeling as happy as possible—I was reveling in the crisp silence of the mountain winter, further insulated by the groves of pine trees, but absent the usual whispered susurrations of the breeze through the aspen leaves, because the leaves had long since fallen. I pictured a Kit Carson scouting party, perhaps one of the celebrated journeys on which he guided US topographical engineer John C. Frémont, making their way through these woods. I wondered if they flew any kind of flag or banner, to communicate to the local tribes to what nation they owed their fealty.

I thought about such parties from other settings in other times, like medieval England, or feudal Japan, and how it was necessary, when riding or marching outside of one's home territory, to clearly display your band's colors or coat of arms, so that other parties one ran across could know from a distance whether you were friend or foe, and I realized that Kit Carson's tribe would need no such accessory, because soon enough everyone came to understand that simply the white skin of their faces would serve as a more terrifying flag than any Jolly Roger ever by a pirate flown. I suppose that some type of emblem existed, though, to send a signal ahead of your party and let the home team know what sort of business you intended.

The reign of terror represented by Carson and his contemporaries reminded me of the groups in our country who have continued to use tactics of violence and intimidation to achieve their supremacist ends. To make sure that all the dollars we acquired via Manifest Destiny are going to remain firmly ensconced in our *Dukes of Hazzard* wallets. The Ku Klux Klan, the Oath Keepers, and the Proud Boys have long and successful records of flying their flags, burning their crosses, and wielding their tiki torches to communicate that they are prepared to inflict violence upon anyone who would like to improve our civilization's mechanisms on behalf of the disadvantaged.

Shortly before we left on this 'Streamin' trip, our nation elected a new president in Joe Biden, and soundly rejected the former guy, to the tune of seven or eight million votes. This despite the "patriotic" social clubs, I mean militias, in the news leading up to the election, wherein we were treated to a strange phenomenon: flotillas of fiberglass boats and parades of pickup trucks flying no fewer than two or three Trump/Confederate flags per watercraft or vehicle. The slice of right-wing folks in boats (a group of lemmings is known as a "slice") was perhaps best known for literally slamming into each other and *sinking* several of their boats on Lake Travis, begging the question of whether their vision was hampered by the flags themselves or by their even more occlusive social blinders?

This notion struck me for the clear lineage of intention, tracing back to the dubious origins of our country. What other "movement" goes out of its way to clog street traffic, burn expensive fuel, send its hard-earned American dollars to China in exchange for some Trump flags, and sink its sixteen-foot plastic boats, all in the service of hoping that the rest of us won't look for any nuance in the national conversation? The blind passion one could feel emanating from these boat and truck maneuvers felt like the noises that blare from bleachers full of bovine, braying hometown fans, drunkenly disparaging the visiting team. I have been in those bleachers, with beer and the screaming that vents so much of life's frustration. It's sometimes not pretty, but that is a sociological function of sports—to purge the humors of violence at an athletic contest so that we don't come to blows waiting in line at the DMV. I don't, however, want to work our democracy like we work sports. We shouldn't want to elect our leaders on the basis that they're our home team. The people we elect to represent *all* of us should be selected soberly, by rational consideration, not Friday night bloviating.

The second RV park we'd just left in Arizona, the nice one with the cottonwood trees, had a little group of six or seven mobile homes that had created a little circular mini-camp. They were all modest camper models, each with a Trump flag and an American flag, and sections of plastic picket fence and Christmas lights (sorry, I'm a member of the radical Hollywood elite, so—*holiday* lights) demarcating the borders of their, what? Cult village? It was scary, to be honest. No matter what those people were telling themselves about their stance and their values, for those of us opposed to that candidate and what has slavishly become his party, their flag was little different from a Klan hood. We can't be expected to think that it represents good people who want the best for our country, when you have told us yourselves that you want to see us liberals crying in pain.

I should mention that later in life, Kit Carson actually became more "woke" with the local tribes; in fact he was selected as a federal Indian agent to act as go-between with the Moache Ute people, Jicarilla Apache, and Taos Pueblo in a sizable area of the northern New Mexico Territory. Incongruously, the duties asked of this famous "Indian fighter" were to *"prevent conflict as far as possible, to persuade the Indians to submit to the government's will, and to solve problems arising from contact between Indians and whites."*

He also commanded a regiment of one thousand New Mexican volunteers against Confederate forces at the Battle of Valverde during the Civil War in 1862, which is unquestionably the move of a good guy. So nuance rears its head in the final reckoning of Kit Carson, who killed Natives because he thought it was right, then protected other Natives because he thought *that* was the way to be. One thing's for sure: 160 or so years ago, life was tough in Taos for a pimp.

After I'd slaked my thirst that day for trees and snow (and Clif bars and coffee) and sky, I hauled my cold nose, hands, and feet down from my seven or eight miles of hiking in the mountains and arrived back at the toasty Nutmeg, the inside of which smelled so good it about knocked me down. Megan had been whipping up a new pasta recipe, orecchiette with sausage, and it once again reinforced one of the greatest things about cold weather: The longer you stay out in the cold, the more delicious and rewarding are the hot food and drink when you finally make it back inside.

18

THANKSGIVING

I want to mention another type of flag that consumed the narrative in 2020: the protective face mask. Unlike the red MAGA hat, which is an overt symbol of cruelty, face masks are actually flags of empathy and affection—symbols of inclusion and solidarity, announcing, "We're all in this (pandemic) together." When I see a Trump hat or flag, on the other hand, the message I receive, as a person opposed to his racism, misogyny, flagrant lifelong dishonesty, titanic narcissism, I mean, you name it—his utter lack of decency across the board—the message I receive from that symbol on your head, chest, or lawn is that you condone those qualities. "He is my guy, and if you don't like my pussy-grabbing president, then Fuck You." You are sending a message of *exclusion*.

Those of us who wear face masks to substantially help prevent the transmission of the deadly COVID-19 virus during a pandemic that to date has cost over six hundred thousand American lives are sending a different message. The mask-flag doesn't bear an actual, literal slogan or any message other than a powerful and figurative "I love you." It states, "I admit to our collective human fallibility, and so I submit to the advice of the world's leading doctors and epidemiologists who say that, while we don't know everything about this pernicious virus and its variants, we do know that wearing a mask definitely helps to hinder its spreading." Masks signal a tacit agreement to behave in the best way we can for the common good, selfishly for our own health, but also for the well-being of our loved ones, our neighbors, and everyone else, which is one of the basic tenets of Christianity to which I seldom see Republicans adhere. As the King James Bible has it: "*Therefore all things whatsoever ye would that men should do to you, do ye even so to them, bitch.*" That's from memory, but I think I'm in the ballpark. When viewed in this way, the super-spreader public rallies that Trump held can be viewed as precisely anti-Christian, or in the modern parlance, "evil af."

This was on my mind as we pulled into a charming, funky RV park in Oklahoma City called Twin Fountains RV Resort, which was packed to capacity. We were lucky enough (thanks to Megan's competence and persistence) to have landed one of the last couple available spots. This was Megan's hometown, and she had some substantial business to which she needed to attend, so we had arranged to "kennel" the Nutmeg and stay in a hotel for the few nights we'd be there. A couple years earlier, we had been bedside with Megan's beautiful, heroic mother, Martha, when she peacefully passed on at age ninety-seven, and the time had come for Megan, an only child, to divest herself of her mom's house and what belongings yet remained after a few previous sorting sessions.

Megan's folks had moved into this house in 1964, when Megan was but a tiny bunny rabbit of six years old. Megan then spent the remainder of her formative school years living in the house until she left after high school to attend Northwestern University in Evanston, just north of

Chicago. Her dad, Carter Jr., was a tragically afflicted alcoholic, and a lot of dramatic problems plagued their house as a result, both before and after Martha divorced him in the 1980s. He and his abusive behavior came and went over the years until his death from cancer in 1992, but Megan's mother stoically remained at the picturesque Nichols Hills address for the last fifty-two years of her life, bolstering Megan's studies and then her subsequent acting career with unwavering support. She was also a beloved fixture in the lives of her friends and neighbors, and a second mother to Megan's inner circle of friends.

That is all to say, there was an enormous amount of emotional history wrapped up in this location, and we thought it advisable to tackle the arrangements from the luxury of a nice hotel room.

Oklahoma City was a welcoming place to adopt as my second hometown, and after eating at Johnnie's for twenty-one years now and counting, I feel a loyalty to it. To the city, and to Johnnie's as well. I also heard a rumor that they're bringing the Charcoal Oven back, and if that turns out to be true, you can sign my interested ass up for some more Theta Burgers and Megan will have two Chick-a-doodle-doos, please and thank you. Partly thanks to her mom's work as de facto den mother, Megan has maintained a group of tight friends there since they were all in about first grade, so it's usually with some or all of them that we venture out to these eateries, and when we want a meal that doesn't contain the word *frankfurter*, we head to the friendliest fine dining in town, a spot called the Metro Wine Bar & Bistro. It's not the greatest name, now that I see it typed, but the warmth of the folks taking your order more than makes up for it.

We've never been sure over the years about the politics of the Oklahoma circle, but we have generally assumed they vote Republican, since Oklahoma skews in that direction. Most of these friends are also pretty well-off, and we have been flabbergasted in the Trump years to discover the large swath of wealthy people who have held their noses and un-equivocally voted for an alleged rapist, simply because he makes them money. Apparently this is a default setting in families where affluence is a birthright to be perpetuated, and so the continuing renewal of the family fortune is the top priority. It's a slippery slope we're navigating when we can overlook the ever-swelling number and immoral brand of violations and criminal behavior on the part of the former president and his minions, shrugging at the news to say, "But, our money."

Sarah Kendzior, a sharp St. Louis journalist who tells it like it is, has written, "*When wealth is passed off as merit, bad luck is seen as bad character. This is how ideologues justify punishing the sick and the poor. But poverty is neither a crime nor a character flaw. Stigmatize those who let people die, not those who struggle to live.*" This is a framing with which I have had to come to terms over the last twenty years or so, during which I saw my own fortunes sizably expand. Making the leap from hand-to-mouth carpenter and aspiring actor to fully employed and well-compensated guy with a beard and an Airstream has provided me with an ongoing education, wherein I am now given access to the tables of "the elite," all while continuing to see the same working-class donkey I've always seen in the mirror, albeit spitting out a fancier toothpaste.

So, I don't know for whom they voted, but affection-wise, the Oklahoma friends are golden. They are generous and intelligent and funny. I genuinely enjoy spending time with them, and after two decades of holidays and other visits, they might as well be family. When we saw them on this trip, everybody was wearing masks and talking about how strange/dumb it was that many people weren't, because their chosen channels of misinformation were telling them not to. During a deadly viral pandemic.

In red-state towns like this, both in Oklahoma and in those we'd later visit in Texas, I kept seeing this puzzle: I'd arrive at a restaurant to pick up the order of breakfast tacos I had called in. Outside the establishment would be a sign requiring all who entered to be masked. The employees, both in the front of house and in the kitchen, would also be masked, but the places were otherwise packed—every table full—with carefree revelers and diners, wearing no masks, as they were eating and drinking. It was illogical, counterintuitive, and just plain stupid. The few times this happened, I just stepped right back outside and finished my transaction out of doors, baffled at the willing ignorance of the human animal, and angry that those people got to enjoy their delicious food with their friends at a direct cost to the rest of us, who were behaving responsibly by making the sacrifices suggested by the CDC and the World Health Organization.

Yes, the odds of contracting COVID-19 were relatively low, so why not roll the dice and go laugh and feast in a restaurant with friends? I hear that. That exact circumstance was one that made lockdown such a severe drag, but I think that if you could ask the *millions* of dead people worldwide and their families if it would have been worth it not to sit and laugh in a restaurant, they would probably say that yes, it would have been worth it *not* to sit and laugh. Right?

When Megan and I had hatched this Thanksgiving plan, I texted my family in Minooka and asked if they would be able to quarantine at home previous to our visit, and/or if we could arrange for them to be tested a couple days before our arrival. I wasn't totally surprised to hear that most of the adults were still going to their jobs, albeit masked, and the kids were sometimes in school, or engaging in extracurriculars with or without masks. My three siblings and their families all live within one—that's right, count 'em, one—block of my mom and dad, which means that they were all in a sort of unofficial pod together, given baby-sitting and shared chores, although frighteningly the group could have been infected from any of several directions at the drop of a hat. My family are as good a bunch of citizens as you could hope to come across, and the fact that their circumstances kept them thus vulnerable, along with the lion's share of our population, while our government was not only fumbling the ball but seeing how far they could shove the ball up each other's asses is powerfully infuriating. At the time, I was relatively unaware of the full situation, due to a reticence on everybody's part to discuss these domestic details. Fear was in the air, and nobody wanted to admit the ways in which we all might be unprotected, even as the leader of the free world was on television asking one of his doctors if maybe the answer to treating the virus was to inject bleach into our bodies, or perhaps shine an ultraviolet light inside there?

I'll remind you that in the middle of 2020, the initial, overarching message was that the virus was especially dangerous to people over sixty years of age, and sure enough, there were tragedies galore being reported in which the virus had been brought home by unwitting family members which then sent their aging parents to the hospital and worse. In Los Angeles, we took that warning to heart, and went out of our way to obey every strict protocol around sanitizing groceries, intense social distancing, and of course, mask wearing, but again, we have no children and we live in a very blue city where goods and services abound. We were able to get tested by a few different means, while in small-town Illinois there was one testing choice available at the local clinic, requiring a wait of hours just for the test, and then a few days' wait time for results. This was obviously inconvenient, and the lag time rendered the accuracy of the outcome relatively useless. Vice President Mike Pence, unmasked, the supposed leader of a COVID-19 virus "task force," made an utterly shameful showing of telling us in his creepy monotone that everything was in hand, while the virus raged across the country.

Because things sounded this iffy around the safety capabilities in our hometown, we decided to err on the side of caution. Since it was forecast to be below freezing in Illinois that weekend, Megan and I left the Nutmeg safe and sound at the RV park in Oklahoma and hauled ass in the Ford the eleven hours up Interstates 44 and 55 to Minooka. My brother and dad had arranged standing propane heaters around the backyard, so every household could group in seats under their own heater, and they also lit a nice bonfire in a pit. Mom put out blankets, and all in all, it was a pretty fun and cozy solution. In the same way that they turned childhood power outages into fun-time candlelit adventures, our parents had made a fine batch of lemonade from this particularly dark batch of lemons. For dinner, everybody ordered their own individual (delicious!) pizzas from the local spot with the uninspired name Pizza For U (at least do 4 U and steal a little mojo from Prince) so that we were all set up to rock a full-on party in the backyard, despite the extreme cold and the lack of physical proximity. Actually, though, on second thought, maybe *I Would Die 4 U* is not the sentiment we want to be invoking in this particular context.

This get-together was the initial impetus for the whole trip and purchasing the Airstream in the first place, and we had pulled it off! In the middle of a really weird, dystopian-flavored stay-at-home order, we had transported an adorable poodle two thousand miles across the country. We had hauled our shiny silver love nest up some mountains that John Muir had celebrated, down an original trail or two troublingly cleared of "savages" by Kit Carson and thereafter further cleared of wolves and bears by Aldo Leopold, over the Oklahoma roads paved with cattle, oil, and familial acrimony, on up to the sleepy little Midwestern village of my youth. The sun was already down by the time we rolled into Mom and Dad's driveway, and we could see the discrete family groups, bundled in coats and blankets, scattered around the yard, each nursing their respective heat source, beginning to stir at our approach.

I shut off my heated shiatsu seat, currently set to "Kyoto Bathhouse"; powered down the Ford; and Megan and I stepped out into the cold. The stirring I thought I had seen turned out to be misperceived—it was one of my nieces offloading some gas. Like uncle, like niece. Mom and Dad approached to greet us, which was amazing, but again, still weird, because we had agreed ahead of time not to hug, out of concern for their vulnerability more than anything, as they are in their seventies. We didn't want to take any chances, but even just standing near one another after eight months of isolation felt pretty amazing. It was incredible to see them, and my brother, Matt, as well, who had also stepped over to say hello.

Then it got really strange, when my two sisters pointedly did *not* get up to greet us. We were all medium-to-very-good friends, for two brothers and two sisters. We corresponded somewhat regularly, collaborated on gifts for Mom and Dad, recommended books to each other, and visited in person at least a couple times a year, if not more. It was also dark outside, so the lack of facial visibility wasn't helping what I perceived to be strange communication, but still, something, clearly, was up.

We all began to loosely chat, but it was mostly Mom and Dad and Matt and his family, sort of over on our side of the fire pit, and Laurie and Carrie had their family groups over yonder. We all had our pizzas and it was a mostly enjoyable time, but by now my passive-aggressive Catholic upbringing was kicking in. By God, something was off here, and I'd be goddamned if I wasn't going to talk directly around it. Instead of just saying, "Is everything okay?" or "Is something wrong?," I cleverly said overloudly to Laurie, my older sister, who is I guess the most respectable of us four:

"HOW ARE THINGS GOING?"

She is the Library Director of the Three Rivers Public Library in the nearby, lesser town of Channahon, and usually a competent communicator. That night, however, she was not interested in meeting me halfway.

"FINE," she said, implying that she was aware I was being an asshole but was not looking to get into it just now.

"GREAT," I retorted, clearly winning this round. I widened my eyes at Megan to let her know that Laurie was being a total freak and a jerk.

I was about to launch a similar salvo across the bow of Carrie when I caught one of her famous "glances of dismissal," a killing strike perfected over decades of dissatisfaction as the third child of four *and* the only blonde. The Harry Potter character of Severus Snape was rumored to have based his own historically dismissive glances on this Carrie Ann Offerman facial expression. Thwarted in my half-hearted attempts, I shook my head from side to side like Toshiro Mifune probably would have and made a face at Megan that indicated I was way too tough to even care one bit about these stinky butt-heads. We said our goodbyes and I-love-yous and goodnights and headed for our hotel.

My bride was beloved of our family—I mean, imagine growing up with me all these years, and then Megan Mullally shows up. What a relief. But she has not spent enough time around the siblings to have developed the bark-like shell of emotional repression within which we thrive. My smart friend Sarah recently texted me while she and her sister Lynn were watching the crafting show I co-host called *Making It*, to ask how my family felt about my calling them taciturn on the show. I replied with a screen shot from Merriam-Webster's dictionary app which defines *taciturn* as "temperamentally disinclined to talk" and said I thought they'd be okay with it.

"Lynn still thinks your mom called your sister," Sarah wrote back.

"Yes, and then they said very little," was my reply.

Driving away from our ad hoc Thanksgiving pizza clutch, Megan was really upset about the weird behavior emanating from the sisters' side of the yard. Once she described it from her point of view, I also became much more incensed. I had been enjoying the protective insulation of years of mutual sibling abuse, during which if one of us had a stick up our rear end about something or other, they would be left alone until the stick was worked clear, the crabby behavior was acknowledged, and we pressed on in each of our modest endeavors, our familial love unshaken at the foundation. We could occasionally bend one another, but we did not break.

This night, however, was anomalous compared to anything that had come before, fueled as it was by the uncertainty of the pandemic and the absence of clear, consistent messaging from our "leadership." In the Ford, we agreed that, taciturn or not, my sisters were being jerks. We might have gone looking for some TP or eggs to commence some retaliatory vandalism, but our minds were blown sideways when we suddenly received a text from none other than . . . you guessed it—hero of the American alt-rock-mountain-man-music scene Jeff Tweedy. The man who slid several yards down a medium incline and lived to tell the tale. He knew we were heading for a Chicago hotel, and did we want to come by for a late-night sit 'round their fire pit to share loving gazes with his redoubtable family?

We sure did want to do that, since Jeff lived close by, and we truly adore Jeff's sweet-smart-funny-beautiful champion bride, badass former proprietor of Chicago rock clubs, Susie, and their enviably gorgeous lads,

Spencer and Sam. In a surreal reprisal of the scene in Minooka, we bundled into coats and blankets as we huddled around a small bonfire in their yard. I told Spencer how his dad had bragged about him and Sammy on our hiking trip, how they didn't seem to be getting in the sort of trouble one might expect of rock-and-roll sons in their late teens and early twenties but instead touting their propensity for selecting fonts and writing code. Spencer had recently been instrumental in designing the graphic elements for his dad's books, and Sammy had built his own computer from scratch. The two know more about local and national politics than I could ever hope to learn, and they are generously civic-minded, which has everything to do with the quality of their parents.

Megan and Sue got to exchange a few brief pleasantries before Jeff then launched into 117 minutes of re-creating for all present every detail of his "Montana Trials" (his term). I was cajoled into backing up his recollections, bullied, really, until I felt like a veritable Flava Flav tossing out an "Oh, hell yes he did" to every second and fourth verse of Jeff's Chuck D. The veracity of many of Jeff's claims was questioned, mainly by Susie, who for some reason was dubious about the number of blows it had taken him to fell the Stone Giants, how many unicorn colts he had rescued, and other assertions. I was eventually reduced to slowly nodding my head as Jeff spoke, injecting a "That's right" whenever Jeff would shoot me a glance. As the fire died down and the clock ticked past midnight, we roused ourselves from our toasty blanket cocoons and reluctantly said our farewells. All kidding aside, getting to simply be in the same space with dear friends during the long hardship of 2020 was powerfully comforting. There's a lot to be said for commiseration.

The next day I texted my folks and Matt to say thank you and also ask my sisters what the hell their problem was by asking the question of everyone *but* my sisters. I was basically reassured that this was just the usual Offerman emotional repression and that everything was fine. I took their word for it, mostly, but still wasn't entirely convinced. The next obvious step in solving this perceived rift like a grown-up was to remain perfectly silent about it for several weeks before suddenly insisting that the four of us siblings get on a Zoom together.

We did just that, and Laurie and Carrie were a bit taken aback to hear the impression they had made on us that night in Mom and Dad's yard. They also had thought that things were weird, but placed the blame squarely in my lap, for behavior I had exhibited a few weeks prior to our trip, when I was asking about the family's ability to quarantine and/or get tested. I was basing my questions on the perceptions of reality I had formulated from our home lockdown in our very nice house in our very nice neighborhood in Los Angeles, one of two urban centers in America with arguably the finest and most varied available goods and services. All three of my siblings, to a degree, took personally my frustration at the paltry testing capabilities available to them, and even in larger urban communities where testing was more readily available, the different testing types and methods also supplied an inconsistent set of results. In hindsight, the insecurity I was feeling about making the trip undoubtedly came across wrong. "Am I fucking up here?" sounded a lot to them like "Are you guys fucking up here?," and the streams of misinformation flooding news channels and social media weren't helping anybody to feel like they were on solid footing.

I had developed my perceptions from watching and listening to a *lot* of news, via MSNBC, CNN, and NPR, which generally focused on two groups in America, virus-wise. The first was the frontline workers who were legitimately required by society to keep going to work so that our country didn't collapse into total anarchy. That meant healthcare workers, key infrastructure operators (CTA operators, utility workers, etc.), and the providers of necessary expendables like food and gas. The second group was, loosely speaking, everyone else, who should have been staying home, and our government should have been paying them to do so. This was basically the situation that I had put together from watching the news and experiencing it in LA, then ignorantly extrapolating that paradigm across the country, and that was where I had gone wrong when reaching out to my family about our visit.

I was not aware that most of the country, including Minooka, was not able to behave like we were in Los Angeles, for a few reasons. One reason was that we are well-off enough in my house to be able to weather a shutdown for months without needing to worry that our bills won't be paid, or that our ability to afford groceries will cease. This is not the case with my family in Minooka, who all work jobs like librarian, schoolteacher, nurse, paramedic, and farmer. And Matt sells fine craft beers. So, again, like most of the country who *hadn't* won the employment lottery with a lucrative job on television, my siblings and their families had to split their focus between safely avoiding the virus and providing for their families, because again, the government wasn't paying them to stay home like they should have been. Hell, like I said, a lot of the government wasn't even treating the virus like the deadly threat that it was, and many of the working-class citizens of our nation, not to mention those living in poverty, were paying the price.

Laurie, Carrie, and Matt are all probably smarter than me, except Carrie. And Matt. They are all successfully raising kids, which I am not, meaning that they have matriculated through a whole other compendium of life lessons on top of their conventional educations. When I inquired after the possibility of their getting tested and then quarantining like everyone was doing in Los Angeles if they wanted to get together to, say, shoot eight episodes of competition crafting in a barn, it sounded to them like I was saying that they needed to be sure and get themselves good and bleached if they wanted to be near Megan and me, as though I held Megan and myself apart from them, or put us on a different level. Laurie said that she thought, "Oh, wow. Nick has become an asshole."

This was a devastating gut punch to me, because I have always remained close with my family and this was the first time that such a dark miscommunication had occurred. I apologized and clarified how the nuances of the episode had seemed to me, and ultimately I appreciated the wake-up call. They remained pretty stoic, but somehow their silence was friendlier than it had been. I think we were all partly to blame, as well as the generally opaque insecurity of COVID times, but I can't help but feel the most responsible.

This failure on the part of me and my siblings to see into each other's particular bubbles may be yet another symptom of our modern-day lack of nuance, but we certainly weren't getting any help from our nation's pathetic leadership. The Trump administration's massive failure to address the pandemic on so many levels, providing no clear federal plan for safety protocols, mask mandates, or reopening strategies, and worst of all, dismissing the actual danger of the COVID virus, left the entire country frightened, confused, and vulnerable—those of us lucky enough to have survived, that is. Oklahoma eateries were packed with maskless customers, while in Illinois, at least restaurants and bars were closed to indoor dining. We Offermans only had a minor kerfuffle over misperceptions and hurt feelings, but how must the hundreds of thousands of families feel who actually lost loved ones to this disease, knowing that an enormous number of these deaths could have been prevented? One thing I know for certain is that we learned a valuable lesson in my family about communicating and making sure we're on the same page no matter what the news is telling us, especially when there's pizza on the line. Thankfully we changed our leadership on the national level and much has been done to clean up the shameful mess left by the disgraced former president, but we are far from being out of the woods. Just ask Texas.

19

TEXAS

After leaving Chicago, we headed back to Oklahoma, were reunited with the Nutmeg, and finally made it to Austin, one of the greatest cities on the planet, for my money, and certainly one of the most American. From the leaded exhaust of South Congress taco trucks to the cloud of weed smoke rolling out of the Austin City Limits Live theatre and past the Willie Nelson statue across the street; to the haze of mosquitoes hovering over Barton Creek; to the absolutely glorious heat roiling forth from the oak pits at Franklin Barbecue (talk about "Angel Fire"!); to the tangibly putrid tendrils of stink issuing forth from most of the legislation happening at the Texas state capitol, there is truly something for everyone. Everyone, that is, except the true urbanite.

Much like the sleepy Oklahoma City and the groovy Madison, Wisconsin, Austin is the governmental seat of the state, but it just doesn't give me a city vibe. It's apparently a recipe for success, city-wise, to

house your government in the same place as a liberal think tank of a
university. It makes for an overall feeling of civic insouciance, where
serious business is taking place even while hijinks are allowed of all
stripes. The couple times that I've worn an actual suit and tie in Austin,
I immediately wished that I hadn't. Megan and I have worked on a handful of films in town, mostly for our filmmaker pal Bob Byington, and I
know of few ways to get to know a city that are more fun than shooting
an independent film there. We have both also played a few of the charming, storied Austin venues together on tour, me on my lonesome as a
humorist and Megan with her great band Nancy and Beth.

On this trip, we parked the Nutmeg at an RV park called Pecan
Grove, just a hop and a skip from the charismatic and historic swimming
hole Barton Springs. Since we couldn't play a show at the Paramount or
see any of our friends perform, I took the opportunity to go for a long
run around Town Lake, also known as Lady Bird Lake, in the middle of
town. What is actually a section of the Colorado River is circumnavigated by a beautifully maintained trail, with five or six bridge options
that allow one to mix and match one's route along the ten-mile loop.

I have run this trail many times over the years, and every time I do,
I want to find the women and men responsible for it and shake their
hands. No matter the season, it allows one to be out in the weather, and
since the summer can be brutal, it actually has the bonus of a great deal
of shaded distance along the route. I also love to rent a canoe and paddle
all over the beautiful expanse of the lake and soak in the weather and
the bird life. My home in Los Angeles is conveniently proximate to a lot
of great hiking, but give me a canoe on the Colorado any day.

I usually run four miles a day, just in my LA neighborhood, which is
certainly pretty, but it can't match running next to water. Since we were
also able to indulgently load up on smoked meat goodies from Franklin

and Salt & Time, I was relieved to be able to do this old favorite run every day. Running during the pandemic did my mental health much good, because it felt like I was getting something done, even if it was just maintaining my healthy-ish heart rate and waistline.

I say that Austin is so American, though, because the whole rainbow of social stereotypes is on display, if one merely strolls from South Congress north to the capitol building and the University of Texas just beyond. On one end of the spectrum you have your full-on hippie-artisan-folk crowd, ever pushing the envelope in quality crafted items, from coffee to beer to barbecue to spirits to guitars to chain-stitched cowboy garments, and so forth, concocted with a progressive, mindful ethos that maintains straight-ahead eye contact with our natural resources and climate troubles.

Half-married to, or maybe living communally with, this crowd are the pure musicians. Ever since Willie broke away from Nashville and set up shop in Austin in the early seventies, the town has served as a hotbed of incredible singer-songwriters, like Patty Griffin, Gary Clark Jr., and Jerry Jeff Walker (RIP), and scores of incredible, dependable session players whose names you may never learn, but to whose sounds you have most definitely tapped your paw.

Then there are the filmmakers and actors and tech freaks and entrepreneurs. One little start-up that you may have heard of is having a decent go of things, and they are called Whole Foods. Now, if the true organic and health food purveyors, as well as the other regenerative farming adherents, are on the violet end of the spectrum, then by the age-old slogan of ROYGBIV, I suppose I'd place Whole Foods (or, again, "Whole Paycheck") in the green middle, unfortunately, because that's their whole shtick, that they want us to think they're considerably greener than they are. In some ways they are a step up, quality-wise, from your local straight-up corporate grocery chain, but they are still a massive national corporation (now actually owned by Amazon, even!), and they behave like one. They are simply not focused on local produce, which is going to be the only way we will rescue the few small farms remaining across our nation. I suppose it's going to require legislation, demanding that our meat, eggs, and dairy, as well as our fresh greens and vegetables, can only travel so many miles. Doing this in a way that pays the growers fairly without breaking the consumers' bank accounts doesn't seem that crazy, so long as we focus on the common good and not the lobbyists' demands, or Amazon's bottom line.

Continuing along the rainbow, we arrive at the red end, which is brightly shining from the statehouse. I'm uncertain how Greg Abbott, the governor of Texas, could fail his constituents any more than he has during his tenure, but wealthy white folks seem to like him fine. Speaking of, he threatened to fine local officials if they—get this—enforced local mask mandates during the pandemic. Because, freedom. Politics over people. Whether I'm in Minooka, Oklahoma, or Austin, I feel like I generally get along with everybody one-on-one, in person, but then I learn about shit-bags like Abbott, or the other baby Trumps running states like Florida and Georgia, and I wonder how we got here. Or I guess I know how we got here, but I can't believe we're *still* here. I had a perfectly friendly interaction with a couple of masked pedestrians in Oklahoma City, then watched them walk into a Mexican restaurant and take their masks off and throw their heads back and laugh and laugh, completely oblivious to the actual goddamn situation. In Austin, I left our friends' studio and walked around a corner downtown to see some members of Austin Open Carry with their action-hero AR-15s slung on straps as they stood in line at the Chipotle, and after I finished whispering my silent thanks to them—for protecting our mild, medium, and hot sauces from, presumably, marauding Black people and Mexicans, and I guess

Antifa?—I silently kept walking, because brandishing a firearm of any sort in public is not a neighborly gesture. The gents in the burrito shop dressed up for I guess *Walking Dead* cosplay have very strong feelings about the second amendment, they think, so I don't want to be in their vicinity in case they begin to feel like someone is trying to do a tyranny on 'em. Look, I can't speak for them. Maybe they're not complete idiots? Um. What I am smart enough to know is that I, like all humans, am stupid, so I don't want to have a gun around me, because those things tend to *frequently* kill people who didn't have it coming. Not to mention, after about fifty years of life and counting, I have never once failed to procure a burrito using nothing but my charm, and money. Anybody who thinks they need a fire-stick to buy food might just not know how to do eating right? If we're going to continue to evolve as a people, which is my fervent hope, that progress can only be hampered by the cowardly gesture of bringing a gun to bear on the conversation. Austin truly does have it all.

* * *

After a few weeks visiting with friends in Austin and chasing some javelinas around Marfa, we rolled all the way down to Big Bend National Park on the Mexican border and parked the Nutmeg just uphill from the Rio Grande. This is an arrestingly beautiful park, with a variety of gorgeous topography comprising its vast acreage. West Texas is wonderfully desolate to begin with, but the road into Big Bend just grew more and more lonely until it seemed like perhaps we had left civilization truly behind.

This was our first time staying inside of a national park, and it definitely had its pros and cons. Among the pros were, obviously, the commute. I was able to step out of our trailer and go running down along the

Rio Grande, or follow a trail up to some hot springs, or choose from a few other pastoral desert choices. In the arid climate of Arizona and Texas, the ubiquitous cottonwoods show up anywhere near fresh water, and I was never sorry to see them. Their soft, lightweight wood is not worth much to a woodworker, but they sure do make some nice shade.

Megan and I would walk down a trail that peaked on a high promontory over the river, from which the sunsets were about as romantic as you would care to see. An additional pro to this visit would have been the charming village of Boquillas, Mexico, which could only be reached by crossing the river in a small rowboat. The cash-flow custom of American tourists is the main revenue of this remote town, so we were dismayed to learn that the crossing had been shut down because of COVID. We were also selfishly bummed because a dinner of homemade real-deal, I mean *verdadero,* Mexican food sounded like a pretty amazing date night out in the middle of over a million acres of Chihuahuan desert. Since the Rio Grande itself is the border between our two countries, I was curious where that put the border line, specifically, and I was gratified to read that our land extends to *"the center of the deepest river channel as the river flowed in 1848."*

First thing every morning, a park ranger would come by on their rounds, inspecting the RV area to make sure everybody was behaving, and picking up the occasional piece of litter, although 'Streamers, and all campers, are pretty conscientious about keeping Mother Nature's parlor tidy to begin with. There was a little store with laundry and shower facilities (closed for COVID), where one could also fill up one's gas tank.

To me, this store—this one specifically, but also this store as a concept—has always been one of the greatest moments of civilization. If you are lucky or wise enough, or both, to be living in an idyllic fashion à la Aldo Leopold, sleeping at the shack with loved ones, food to eat, songs to sing, fish to catch, and plenty of nature in which to occupy one's days, then you will only occasionally, maybe once a week, need to "get to town," for milk or eggs, or if you're anything like me and Megan, for a Snickers bar or an ice cream. Childhood family vacations at our fishing cabin in Minnesota were like this; at the little store in the woods on Sundays after church, we could get a treat each, which made the 1978 introduction of the Whatchamacallit candy bar a mind-blowing, life-changing epoch. It was followed up a couple years later by the advent of Big League Chew, which was literally the answer to my prayers.

My cousin Ryan and I were born six months apart, so we spent a lot of time together, playing sports, riding bikes, break-dancing, performing in the school jazz band (on trumpet and tenor sax, respectively), and emulating our dads and uncles and Grandpa Mike as they executed the labors that the farm required. Grandpa Mike chewed Red Man tobacco, a brand that Kit Carson might have enjoyed, complete with "Indian Chief" in full headdress logo. He would fetch a wad . . . pack . . . spit . . . which we thought was simply fantastic. This weird, smelly, shredded black ball of leaves seemed so adult, and the ceremony of pulling out the pouch, shoving the cheek full, and spitting was obviously the coolest behavior among the options presently available to us (especially spitting, which was confusingly forbidden for children with nice, clean child spit but okay for old guys with gross ashtray spit).

One summer day when we were five or six years old, hanging out with Grandpa as he sat on the front steps getting his boots on, he asked us if we wanted some Red Man. Ryan and I looked at each other, saucer-eyed, clearly aware that Grandpa Mike was fucking up big-time, but trying to play it cool before he realized his mistake.

"Sure," I said, a hard-boiled picture of nonchalance.

"Fuckin' A," agreed Ryan, probably.

He let us each pinch out a little boy–size wad and put it in our mouths, as he instructed us to simply chew it like chewing gum. We did, quickly finding ourselves blinking and frowning at the insanely pungent and foreign taste, somewhere between cloves and diesel fuel. It wasn't long before we both dropped feebly down onto our bottoms in the grass, moaning in discomfort at the nausea his prank had induced. He cackled his delightful laugh and told us never to get hooked on tobacco.

So that was a very dirty trick that you might think sounds a bit brutal, and you would be right. We were cured of our desire to become tobacco connoisseurs of either the plug or cut variety, but he left behind in our hearts a gaping hole that we tried to fill with all manner of gutter dross: Twizzlers, Smarties, Circus Peanuts . . . garbage, all. Some candies were quite enjoyable, but they just weren't engineered to travel in the pocket of an active kid. We were distraught, thinking we might as well throw in the towel and become stupid adults, when out of nowhere arrived Big League Chew. The gum itself was actually pretty crappy, for the first few years, anyway, but it mattered not at all. It could have been hay straws and we still would have whipped that pouch out of our pockets with the greatest of élan. Here was a gum that looked and spat like the real thing, that was totally legal and didn't make us puke! (PS–tobacco in any form is a horrible, cancer-causing product that is just as, or much more, addictive than most narcotics. It should absolutely be strictly controlled, but, you guessed it, money.)

Anyway, the little store in Big Bend was perfect. They had a really impressive selection, actually, of outdoor and camping gear, with high-quality brands. Food-wise, they stocked a nice selection of basics, with fresh, local eggs and dairy products, and most important, a candy bar rack and a nice selection of ice-cream treats. I don't know about you, but despite the economic advantage, I can't buy a box of twenty-four Snickers bars and keep it in the pantry, because no matter how healthy I manage to roll, at *some point* I'll have a moment of weakness (or maybe a day, or hell, a week of weakness) and eat too many. So I love having the middle-woman or -man there at the store—the arbiter of the Snickers—to assist me in acquiring my occasional treat one at a time without going overboard.

I was telling you about the pros and cons. On my way back to the Nutmeg from the store on the first morning, I spotted a very healthy bobcat stalking the campground. It was no great feat of tracking on my account, because the cat was pretty brazenly just casually sitting on the other side of about fifteen yards of grass and big, old cottonwoods. Like it was waiting to see if anybody was going to absentmindedly leave a bucket of chicken or a baby otter out on the picnic table. This feline was, I'm guessing, forty-five to fifty pounds, and was about a third again as large as the couple of bobcats I've spotted around Los Angeles. It was as gorgeous as it was fascinating, and I saw it almost every day, as well as coyote, deer, javelina, jackrabbit, and roadrunner, while out running my daily four miles. As pretty as the bobcat was, though, it was also a significant con, considering we had an adorable nine-pound cotton ball named Clover who was keen to conduct some business twice daily upon her old friend the grass. As long as a grown human was present, the bobcat kept well away, but you can bet your sweet aunt Myrtle I pointed a flashlight up into those cottonwoods quite a bit when Clover was night-tinkling.

Let's get the main con at this location out of the way so we can hit the trails: The actual RV area is pretty bad. It's a big blacktop parking lot, with high concrete curbs and spots for twenty-five campers. Usually the good campgrounds have some kind of green space or buffer between lots, which does a lot to soften the overall feel of one's "yard" and also provide a little distance, and therefore privacy. These lots were nakedly right next to one another, with nothing but blacktop between trailers, which can just be very loud, especially at night, especially with families whose parenting style involves playing movies *extremely loudly*. Now, look, I'm not a total Skeezix, kids, I like to party hearty and rock and roll and brang the noize as much as the next member of the cool club, but you have to realize that this is the very reason for the hallowed "quiet hours" at RV resorts—because you're kind of living up each other's asses. They knew they were violating Quiet Hours. They had just given up.

Even so, this was not the worst of it. These cons were pretty minor when compared to the main complaint of all residents of the Nutmeg, yes, even the dog, and that is: for some reason—faulty engineering, deteriorated gaskets, plumbing ghosts (I don't know?)—the whole lot smelled like shit. One of the great, even imperative, pleasures of the 'Streamin' life is when you set up camp and prop open all of your screened, shaded windows, turning your land-craft into a screened-in porch on wheels, because everybody knows that a breeze wafting through a screened-in porch is a sublime meteorological delight. Well, obviously, if some sewer phantoms (doing my best here) are hitching a ride on your breeze, that is, uh, no bueno. By the way, if you are a Big Bend administrator, or you happen to know one, there is an *amazing* area just a quarter mile down the road to the west with large grassy lawns and more of those wonderfully august cottonwoods. Spend a few bucks, install some more spread-out RV spots, attend to your plumbing troubles (septic exorcism? I'm done), and charge a premium. Please and thank you.

*　*　*

It is probably clear to you by now, dear reader, that I like to lace up my boots and wear out the leather in them by executing long walks.

I feel like I should mention, though, that this is not only true of hiking trails through the mountains and the woods. I have also spent thick, long, savory hours hiking the streets of Manhattan and the other boroughs, Manchester, London, Cleveland, Chicago, New Orleans, Pittsburgh, Atlanta, Toronto, Cape Town, Boston, Seattle, Perth, and so forth. Whether the human rash of fireplugs and billboards has reached the terrain or not, I enjoy observing my immediate surroundings as I trundle through them like I'm reading a good novel. I suppose it's obvious for a place like a national park, but one of the best ways to get a feel for a new city as well is to simply get out and walk it.

In my adult life, one of the richest sources of this brand of treasure has been shooting films on location, because I have been invariably plunked down in some faraway place or other, to collaborate on a (hopefully) fun art project. The magic happens when you realize that you have a random day (or several) off, and you're in a strange city with no vehicle. Rather than plop down on a hotel bed and binge some content, this is when I love to consult a map, on the smartphone or on paper—I adore both—and strike out on foot. I am guaranteed to see some unexpected things in the great big world outside, forcing me to make some decisions that feel somehow more muscular and chewy than those made with the merest manipulations of my thumb on a TV remote.

Given that "walking around all day" is a pastime that lights me right up, imagine the hogshead of childlike wonder into which I was hurled—as if into a giant pit full of those colored balls, except each ball was a uniquely delightful sensation—when I realized that places called national parks existed, and they had gone to the trouble of blazing and maintaining trails by the hundred, and then to top it off, *printing* those trails on a map which a body could read and use to execute a fully feathered pedestrian pleasure-jam. This ball pit had it all: You've heard of eye candy? Well, this cornucopia also brought ear candy, which had every-thing from the Mills Brothers to a burbling brook to the sound of a cowboy steak hitting the searing cast iron, which also crosses over into tongue candy—also just known as "candy." *Nose candy* is a term with a complicated connotation, but these smell-balls were less narcotic and much more straight-up olfactory, like garlic sautéing in butter, lilacs across the yard, and once again, that sizzling cowboy steak.

To the matter at hand: Big Bend had an amazing menu of trails, or "foot candy," from which to choose. I started off with the Ore Terminal Trail, described in the guide as a "strenuous" eight-mile out-and-back. The rocky desert path follows an old tramway that consisted simply of thick steel cables, like an inch and a half thick, strung along periodic massive, sturdy towers built of wood timbers. Historically, along the six miles of cables rolled ninety hanging ore buckets, spaced out so as to deliver about seven and a half tons of zinc, lead, and silver ore per hour. This impressive rig, in operation from 1909 to 1919, brought the ore to a specially built road, where it was then transferred by wagon ninety miles to the railroad in the town of Marathon. Every single detail about this delivery system struck me as impressively crafty and impossibly bru-tal. As a sometime-laborer a century later, I can't even imagine how ar-duous these towers were to construct, just hauling the timbers and *miles* of steel cable across unfriendly terrain with only men and mules to bear the load. Considering how poorly we treat our itinerant labor force even today, I cringe to think of how these earlier workers and animals must have been savaged, because, well, money.

The night before this hike, Megan had whipped up the most amaz-ing pork stew with hominy and roasted guajillo peppers, and for dessert, a Shaker lemon tart. Or perhaps a lemon Shaker tart. The whole blessed mess had been so delicious and fortifying that I was daydreaming about it as I walked along the brown steel cables now lying on the ground, punctuated by the occasional pile of thick, desiccated timbers, like the forgotten skeletons of early-twentieth-century wooden Voltrons. The meal made me think, for the millionth time, how grateful I was to be a partner in this marriage. Like any relationship, it has required vigilance and maintenance, and has certainly had its ups and downs over its first twenty years, but if I ever wonder if I'd be better off without my marriage, all I have to do is think back on the times that I have been away from Megan.

Especially when I was younger, if she would fly to New York for a few days to do press without me, I would consistently consume too much beer; order a pizza or, fuck it, two pizzas; and just instantly revert to man-child mode, indulging in at least three hours of hedonistic fun. Then I would feel the unpleasant repercussions of the binge, physically and emotionally, and I would look around our house—our utterly exquisite, gorgeous, sublime house—and see that it was but an empty vessel when she was not there with me. The dogs and I would look at each other in commiseration, as though to say, "What good is this place if she's not in it?," and they would merely nod and say, "No shit, guy." For these periodic reminders to stay somewhat between the ditches of "living wrong," I have long been grateful, because as I may have mentioned, I'm not always real smart, and I would take all the help I could get.

In that rambling way that thoughts can free-associate on the trail (brain candy), it occurred to me that this admittedly romantic musing on my bride had inscrutably surfaced because I was feeling similarly bereft of George and Jeff. They had been much on my mind, primarily due to our three-way text thread, via which Jeff had been sending us a robust crop of songs over the months of the pandemic, with a prolific regularity that caused George and me to frequently exclaim, "Dude!"

Because Shakespeare is famously supposed to have written some of his greatest works while under lockdowns due to outbreaks of the bubonic plague, including *Macbeth*, *King Lear*, and *Antony and Cleopatra*, Jeff had initially planned to call this collection of pandemic tunes *King Lear*, but eventually changed it to *Love Is the King*. George is a splendid guitarist who dabbles in writing lyrics as well, and there was one text session during this proliferation of Tweedy tunes in which Jeff sent us lyrics and invited us to spitball with him. I was driving my Nutmeg team through Oklahoma and wasn't available to jump in, and frankly, I don't think I would have done them any good anyway, because, come on. It's George and Jeff.

The result of their divine peanut-butter-in-my-chocolate combo was a song called "A Robin or a Wren," and it's just beautiful in the soulful, loving way in which these guys try to do everything. So I guess what I'm saying is that I was hiking along by the remains of this long-defunct human operation that had once mined precious metals from these limestone hills and transported them to the world so they could ostensibly make things better for the people, and I was getting sappy listening to a couple of modern-day humans who seek to mine treasures, perhaps more ephemeral but no less weighty, in the topography of our hearts, and deliver them via much lighter-weighted emotional ore buckets. A sampling:

> *At the last last call*
> *When it's time for us all*
> *To say goodbye*
> *I know I'm gonna cry*
> *Know I'm gonna cry*
> *Because all in all*
> *I'm just having a ball*

Being alive
And I don't want to die
I don't wanna die

So, just like I feel with Megan when she's gone (or similarly anyway, without the soulmate-lovemaking-forever-partners parts), I felt, "What's the use of hiking this magnificent national park trail without the other two members of my tripod? How am I to stand? Without my bromance, did this hike even exist? After listening to the song a couple times, lightly bouncing along to the melody and the warm affection, I used my conveniently located eyewater ducts to clean what must have been an abundance of pollen out of my eyes. I wanted to be with them then, and tell them that the song was moving me powerfully, so I started recording a voice memo on my phone, recounting for them most of what I have just written about here.

Now, I hadn't seen another person for a few hours, so it was pretty surprising as I was recording a relatively free-associated monologue that a guy came around a corner of sorts and without hesitating said, "Hey, Nick, what's up?" I mean, he *just* appeared and had hardly even laid eyes on me, which led me to believe he must have recognized my voice, but whatever the case, it's rather off-putting to be approached by a stranger thus, greeting me as though he knows me.

I said that yes, I was in fact Nick, and he immediately said, as though by way of explanation, that he was a big Wilco fan, that he loved Jeff and had seen him and Wilco a "million times."

"Aha," I said, and asked him his name, which he said was Murphy Johnston, and then, since I hadn't stopped recording the voice memo for Jeff and George, and I thought that his immediate mention of Jeff was rather uncanny, I asked, "How about the author George Saunders?"

"Ahh, nope. Don't know George," he replied, and I think he could sense how great it would have been if he'd brought something more than that to the table. He said he didn't read much, outside of books about parks and hiking trails like this one upon which we were jawing. He asked for a photo, and I agreed, but then had to stop him when it became clear he was just going to shoot me without himself in the frame. I gave him my usual line for that circumstance, which is that he needs to be in it with me, or I'll feel like a zoo animal. He then proceeded to accidentally shoot a few seconds of video of the two of us, which I suggested he could probably sell as a comedy pilot. He told me he was from Arlington Heights, a neighborhood outside of Chicago, just north of O'Hare, and I told him he seemed pretty nice anyway.

The next day I was on a mammoth, looping hike around the Chisos Mountains, with a detour in the middle of the day to summit Emory Peak, one of the highest mountains in Texas, at 7,825 feet. The last 40 feet or so of this climb required some clambering and bouldering up a rock face, which was pretty goddamn exhilarating. I took my time and made certain that every grip and toehold was dependable, but it was still frightening, just enough that I felt vibrantly alive. The 360-degree views at the top were literally breathtaking, and I'm glad I had a few minutes to myself seated up there, enjoying the solitude and some almond butter, before a handful of other climbers crested the rocks.

One truly wonderful silver lining about the pandemic has been the freedom that masks have given me to pass in public undetected. There are many instances which can have their tone completely altered when people recognize me. It's almost always positive, which is very nice, but you know, just think about being in a situation where you want to fully access your emotions, like a funeral or a Japanese sex swing competition, and you can't help but feel partially guarded because a couple people have made it clear that they really want to see how the Ron Swanson actor emotes in real life.

So, when one of my new Emory Peak–mates recognized me, and then was joined by a couple others in requesting photos, I obliged them, and bared myself to them a little, when I said that I had found that last bit of the climb pretty scary, and that I was grateful to share this moment with them. I was satisfied, but then I had to go, because it became weird—they had established me as a selfie-worthy entity, making me a bit more two-dimensional than I am, specifically as my unemotional, granite-willed character Ron, and then I had upended that notion by coming across as sensitive and thoughtful. It was still nice up there, but I wanted to scoot along before someone asked me what Chris Pratt is really like. We were all up there to allow the sensory tsunami of the mountain (life candy) to wash the mold and rust clean from the parts of us we wanted to take back down the trail, and that's just what I did.

20

ARIZONA

As we journeyed from state to state, we usually listened to gripping audiobooks, curated of course by Megan. Alone or together, consuming a nice, long novel is a terrific way to enhance the miles as they fly beneath the wheels of your Nutmeg. Between chapters, we'd also take on board a sizable dose of MSNBC and CNN on the radio, because remember, these were the weeks following the 2020 presidential election, in which Joe Biden and Kamala Harris had handily routed the opposition, but the Republicans were continuing to spout all manner of crazy shit, including what was being referred to as "the Big Lie"—the disinformation that the election had somehow been unfair, illegal, illegitimate, you name it.

These things seemed potentially dangerous, so we wanted to keep abreast of the doings of the dum-dums. Thus we subjected ourselves to an extremely teeth-grinding amount of advertising on both of these news stations that repeatedly made us loudly exhort the ad agencies and the companies themselves to reconsider the absolute garbage they were paying extremely good money to have broadcast across America.

There were many entrants in this event, and we were able to really dig down into their syntax because the networks (via Sirius) played the same spots over and over ad nauseam. Mike Lindell, for example, the MyPillow clown who has gone on to much greater fame as a far-right-wing donor and batshit mouthpiece of the "Stop the Steal" movement, was definitely a runner-up with his risible "revolutionary" pillow and bed linens—specifically his claim that his sheets were so extraordinary because he had discovered a heretofore unknown type of cotton in Egypt. *"Grown only in a region between the Sahara Desert, the Mediterranean Sea, and the Nile River. Its long-staple cotton makes it ultra-soft and breathable."* I don't normally indulge in the slang that the kids are slanging around social media but LAUGH ON LOUD, you asshat. I don't begrudge anybody the opportunity to make and hawk their wares, but if your methods include babbling this brand of bullshit into my sphere? Please take a long walk into a deep Wisconsin lake.

The unequivocal winner, however, of the race to the bottom of my patience and goodwill was an ad from WesLend Financial. It featured a belligerent-sounding fellow named Wesley Hoaglund urging the listener that now was the time to secure a loan to either purchase a home or refinance the mortgage on their current home based on the existing market trends. Now, I don't know about you, but when my wife and I are managing our finances and we want to make a move of some sort, but we're a bit ignorant and therefore curious to learn more about our options, it has honestly never occurred to us to *flip on the radio* to see if that's where the answers might lie. But that content is merely the setup for the final punch line in the ad, when the speaker literally says this— to convince you to get in bed with him and his company, entrusting the most important purchase of your life to this guy on the radio, he says, *"It's the biggest no-brainer in the history of mankind."*

Next, there was a company called Blinkist. Oh, sweet Franz Kafka in the Bardo help us, I'm sure the folks at this company are perfectly nice and all, but this product really feels profane to me. If there are people doing jail time for possessing some marijuana, then the Blinkies, as I assume they must fashion themselves, should perhaps be made to work in an Amazon fulfillment warehouse, with no bathroom breaks. Oops, I repeat myself. Is there a worse existence available to the modern-day American? If so, let's give them that.

Blinkist.com is a site, an app, a cadre of dystopiants who provide the service to you of condensing thousands of the most popular nonfiction books into fifteen-minute versions. You read that right. They could literally claim to save you the time of reading the CliffsNotes of a given title.

"Want to read books but you hate reading books?"

They have a commercial in which a woman proudly states with a straight face that she reads one hundred books a month. She even singles out a wonderful recent favorite of mine, *The Hidden Life of Trees* by Peter Wohlleben, and says that she liked "reading the book" on Blinkist so much that she's going to read the book. I'm not making this up. This wonderful, elucidating title from a German forester is all about the impossibly intricate web of fungi and other microorganisms that exist in the root beds of a forest community, and how the tree-citizens thereby communicate with one another and even make transactions in the economy of their metabolisms. It is an imperative text that illuminates how broad and deep the gulf of human ignorance remains, but here is one tiny increment of progress provided by cranking up the magnification on the microscope. "Does that sound good to you? Great! Then let us crank the lens way, way in the other direction!"

The audio version of that book is listed at seven and a half hours, and Blinkist wants you to prefer only fifteen minutes of that. And it exists, so people must be buying it? I daresay it has me hopping mad. OMG! (I believe this is "Other Mitten, Guys," cuz they try to shake my one mittened hand but then I say OMG so they pull off my other mitten and I'm giving them the finger.) Unadulterated stupidity for sale, and advertised during the news programs from which I would hope people were growing *better* informed, not worse. It smacks of a similar phenomenon that has been profoundly bothering me for some years now.

In the business of film and television, depending upon your genre and your delivery system, people are attempting to create entertaining works of art, to one degree or another. Whether that means a devastating, Oscar-winning documentary about a Middle Eastern war zone, or a big studio comedy film about a farting nun, or any one of the thousands of offerings now available on broadcast and streaming platforms, by and large we are all trying to deliver our own brand of medicine to an audience. Let's take an episode of *Parks and Recreation*, for example. A couple hundred people utilizing their God-given talents and plenty of elbow grease spend so much time and effort writing a script, rewriting the script, finding locations, designing sets, building sets, dressing sets, painting shit; same for props, designing wardrobe, building wardrobe, shopping for wardrobe, fitting wardrobe; same for hair; same for makeup; same for lighting; same for greens—there is a whole department devoted solely to making sure all the plants/trees/grass/flowers look right, or maybe they bring in a dozen fake trees, then special effects shows up to lightly sprinkle the whole scene with snow machines. I mean, just successfully scheduling all of this is literally a whole department of several amazing organizers/mother ducks, then we need all of the people required to run cameras and the dollies upon which the cameras ride, and the sound department recording everything success-fully, and a crew to cable together all of the cameras to monitors that can be viewed in "Video Village," and also a DIT (digital information technician) to monitor and curate the quality of the actual digital content on the recording drives, oh, and drivers to get all the gear and people everywhere, and craft services and catering to make sure everyone is fed and not crabby from low blood sugar, but if you do get sick from some bad clams, we have an on-set medic, and we have producers making sure that all of these operations are happening within the budget that is supervised by a team of accountants, all while the casting department is auditioning and selecting the guest cast, and the script is rewritten again, and all of this is happening before we roll one minute of "film."

Then we shoot the episode, requiring all of the above departments to be flawlessly orchestrated while the director and actors and stand-ins and stunt performers execute the scene work, even while the literal armies of grip and electric crews manage to *not fuck up* the scene; it's just wild.

Then we have just as much happening in postproduction, with a crew of editors, and all the cleanup crew—color corrections, sound mixers, sound editors, ADR producers, not to mention any CGI or other visual or audio effects. Added to all of the above industriousness nowadays is the COVID compliance safety crew, making sure everyone follows protocols, even the dum-dums who don't think they need a mask or a vaccine.

Okay? That's a brief overview and I'm probably leaving out thirty-seven departments. Now, for me personally, I spent my adult life working very hard at learning to effectively interpret a script for an audience in a pleasing and effective manner, which in the case of *Parks and Rec* often meant a lot of silent grimacing and eating of savory foods. I have had worse gigs. Nonetheless, just like the rest of the whole teeming team, I care *very much* about the quality of my work. It brings me to tears, just thinking about it. If you don't have work that makes you feel that way, then you might be missing out. I think that we had at least a bit of what the Leopold family felt at their shack when we were planting our seeds of comedy and pathos at that quality program. I can't speak for everyone there, but they sure came across as exceptional professional artists. Speaking for myself, I just wanted nothing more than to give our audience twenty-two-odd minutes of escape from their realities; to succeed, in this crazy moment in this crazy world, in locking people's focus onto our little comedy show so that we might delight them by our efforts.

With that, we have finally arrived at the point of this digression. Imagine feeling this way about your show, and let's say the show is going to air on a Thursday night at eight p.m., and the network's publicity department contacts you to ask if you will "live-tweet" the show. Just think about that for a second. Your employer is asking/ordering you (depending on your place on the call sheet) to encourage your audience to *look away* from the show to your simultaneous social media postings. Because success is currently defined by the number of likes and retweets, the corporation is made to so value their accumulation of "views" (*Will it go viral? Can we get it trending?*) over the integrity and efficacy of the content that they're willing to cut off your storytelling at the knees.

There's another related trend with which you may be familiar, and this one really makes me shit little green apples—at the end of a broadcast show, during what are often the most pivotal moments of the resolution, or the denouement, a little figure of a character from the next show about to air in a couple of minutes will appear, maybe cartwheeling across the bottom of the screen, with some language, like *"Coming Up*

Next: Skippy the Clown!" I understand that this shameful practice is driven by the need to keep eyeballs on your channel in this age of tiny attention spans with a near-infinite array of choices, but ruining your product thus does not seem like the wisest choice. It's like serving a seven-course meal, and just as the diners are about to savor the last bite of each delectation, the morsels are slapped from their mouths, and the next offering is unceremoniously dropped in front of them. No, thank you. Please.

All of these examples make me ashamed of us. They make me want to somehow pressure-wash the caked shit off the fenders of my soul. I think and talk and write a lot about our relationship with the obvious versions of nature, like parks and forests and trails and gardens and farms, for example. Badgers. But these distasteful interactions bring to mind another way that we neglect our natural relationships, and that is simply with one another.

So much of capitalism hinges upon our propensity for laziness. A guy named Wesley Hoaglund makes a radio ad that essentially says that if you don't finance a loan through his company, you're totally stupid. I mean, what don't you get? *"It's the biggest no-brainer in the history of mankind!"* If he is able to pay for radio ad time in which he is able to sound this way, it must mean that some people are calling the number. I'm conjecturing here, but I guess they might do that because it's *easy*. Instead of doing things in what we should all know to be the right way (i.e., doing the homework, researching and weighing options, exercising prudence, and minimizing personal risk), especially because a home loan can make or break the life of a family, we dummies are so susceptible to the easy choice.

I know I'm certainly guilty of this. After years of missteps, living without a credit score or medical insurance or *car insurance* (I would leave dealer plates on my vehicle for years), I was goddamn lucky to realize how juvenile this behavior was before it really bit me in the ass. Now I know that the ultimate success of any serious expenditure, be it a mortgage or an Airstream or a new woodshop dust-collection system, or a health or dental issue, demands that I be honest with myself. If I need a loan or outpatient surgery, I first determine who is going to give me the best advice. Then I ask them all the questions I can think of, because in this day and age, the small print never ends, and I want to know all the pros and cons of any such decision.

Most important, I do these things in person. That's the inconvenient part that radio salespersons like WesLend Financial are playing upon—it takes time and effort to get oneself in front of a benevolent somebody's desk, but that, I think, is the key to this idea. When you see a person, and interact in the real world, in real time, I believe that you then care about them, and they you, in ways that can never be replicated over the phone or via videoconferencing, and certainly not by text or DM. This is obviously a sweeping generalization, overlooking oily car salespersons and glad-handing politicians, but it's one of the tenets I employ to filter the filthy music of consumerism out of my channels as best I can.

Our next stop after Big Bend was in Tucson, a nine- or ten-hour haul, but we wanted to drive northwest along the Rio Grande—a gorgeous, gorge-ish stretch that added a couple of hours to the drive. We stopped at around the halfway point for an overnight at El Paso Roadrunner RV Park, which was perfectly nice. I love the functionality of this type of park—it's in a medium-okay part of town, just off the interstate, with nothing remotely pastoral to recommend it. It's simply a clean, safe, functional, affordable place to park your Nutmeg and plug her in, and the community bathrooms (a.k.a. Daddy's Thunder Closet) were laudably clean and comfortable.

Catalina State Park, our destination, was pretty much right in Tucson, just north of town, on the west side of the Santa Catalina Mountains, nestled up against Coronado National Forest, and it was lovely. It made all the difference in the world to have some distance between the other campers and us, especially since the buffers were covered in assorted succulents and shrubs dotted with birds and the occasional little ground squirrels and rabbits, also known as badgers.

I picked up where I had left off in Texas, hiking the many excellent trails of varying terrain and difficulty, marveling at the platoons of saguaro cacti—the stereotypical tall, armed sentinel I always picture when somebody says *cactus*. We actually enjoyed some intermittent squalls, which was nice since I had my rain jacket to keep me and my snacks dry. A couple of times around the full moon I arrived at my trailhead an hour or two before sunrise, and the desert terrain was so well illuminated that I was able to perfectly see the trail.

The morning of New Year's Eve was one truly magical example—the moonlight was so bright I felt like I was walking in a strange solar eclipse. It was also quite cold, in the low forties. I had plotted a course on my map the night before, setting my sights on a fifteen- or sixteen-mile day, heading up the Sutherland Trail to the back side of Mount Lemmon. The route had some varying degrees of difficulty but was mostly moderate for the first few miles, and then pretty strenuous once the trail turned more steeply uphill into Coronado National Forest. I had an invigorating experience, stopping a few times to catch my breath and deplete my treat stores.

After the sun had passed its noontime apex, I began to tire a bit, wondering how much farther I would get before turning back. There were still a few miles between me and the top end of the trail, where there existed an observatory and a ski village, and I had half hoped that

I would make it up there to find maybe a charming coffee shop or little pub that was inexplicably ready to serve me despite the pandemic. (One cool thing about hiking is that you burn a lot of calories, so you can have a beer or two halfway through, and it's much less deleterious to your constitution. This is also my tried-and-true method for running marathons—I allow myself to stop in the pub for one pint per mile. I've never made it past the first mile, but I mean, I feel good.)

Alas, neither coffee nor Guinness was in the cards for me that day; in fact I was starting to grow a bit confused about where the trail had gotten to. Clumps of catclaw, brittlebush, and mesquite were suddenly occluding my way forward, and I wasn't able to really spot any clear trail or the tree blazes that should have been marking it.

Just then I was somewhat startled by what sounded like a large critter some way up the hill beyond me, making intermittent rustling noises through the brush, then falling eerily silent again. I've been in this game long enough to know that the more it sounds like a rhinoceros barreling through dry leaves, the more likely it's a chipmunk or an industrious scrub jay. Still, when I'm tuckered out and chilly up on a mountain, many miles from the nearest oat milk latte, animal noises register a little differently on the danger scale. Fortunately, the mystery varmint didn't keep me in suspense for very long, as it suddenly gamboled clear of the juvenile ironwood and acacia thicket, revealing itself as a young, healthy male specimen of the *Homo sapiens* variety.

His footsteps went silent again as he was scrutinizing his smartphone, and then he trudged another ten yards. I hailed him and he expressed a companionable relief to have the opportunity to apply the old idiom "two heads are better than one" to our current predicament of having lost the path. His stopping and starting was explained by his use of a GPS program on his phone that was helping him steer back to the

WHERE THE DEER AND THE ANTELOPE PLAY   297

poorly marked trail. It turns out that he had set off even earlier than me, and he regaled me with the wonderful moonlit visions he had taken in on his ascension up the mountain that morning.

Usually in a situation like this, I'll exchange pleasantries with the rhinoceros and then bid them a pleasant day as I return to my solo reverie, but sometimes, like in this instance, when the day has been legitimately arduous, it can suddenly become a substantial comfort to have a companion for the last few hours of the jaunt. Putting our combined thinking caps on, we were able to regain the trail pretty handily, although still using our feet for walking. Handily. With reinvigorated spirits, we turned our boots to bear us back down the hill.

As we got to chatting, I was pretty quickly taken aback by the serendipity of this friendly stranger's being dropped into my timeline. Check it: Esteban hailed from Appleton, Wisconsin, but had earned his degree in microbiology from—you guessed it—the University of Wisconsin at Madison. When I asked him if he knew about Aldo Leopold, you would have thought I'd asked Elizabeth Warren if she knew about tax codes, he rattled off so much excited exposition.

When he served as the school's Microbiology Club president (!), at the school's Discovery Center they would set up demonstrations on Aldo Leopold Day for kids and parents alike, showing off a group of microbes called rhizobia that live in the soil and engage in a small economy between bacteria and plant, whereby the rhizobia use their ability to pull nitrogen from the air in a process called "nitrogen fixation" and "pay" that nitrogen to the host legume in exchange for setting up shop in a "nodule" in the plant's roots. This discovery, although over a century old, is eliciting a great deal of thrilling new research with agricultural applications, and—I cut him off there.

"Sorry, friend, but your content is getting a little too good for my book—I'm more about making generalized statements and then fulminating on some personal opinion or other without really considering all the sides to the argument. You know, without nuance."

He took it amicably and I relayed that this rhizobia situation sounded uncannily like a symbiosis in Chicago's Pilsen neighborhood in which I once had the pleasure of participating, except instead of nitrogen, I was securing *weed* for my host, and instead of a nodule, he was providing me with a *futon*. I was sincerely gratified to talk roots and fungi with Esteban, as this was precisely the subject matter of the splendid, aforementioned *The Hidden Life of Trees,* which a woman used Blinkist to read one hundred times in a month, if memory serves. This "wood-wide web" is also featured in Richard Powers's incredible Pulitzer-winning novel *The Overstory,* which posits the enlightened notion that we humans might do a much better job of continuing to exist on this planet if we were to study and emulate the economy in which the trees have so successfully participated since time immemorial.

We also talked Madison, and the coveted local beer from New Glarus known as Spotted Cow, and I said, cutting him off again, that I wasn't interested in perpetuating the argument over whether it's a cream ale or a farmhouse ale. All's I know is, it's good. He let it go; broke off a mesquite branch and swung it violently through the air several times, like he was beheading a small dragon; then tossed it down, took some deep breaths, and regained his equanimity. He was a real cool customer. Esteban was tickled pink to hear my backstage bratwurst story from my humorist debut at UW Madison's Rathskeller, or at least he pretended to be with well-reared politeness. When it comes to manners, it's always Midwest for the win.

Now here's the kicker, as he had thus far buried the lede: He was currently working for a company in San Diego called Illumina that had commercialized the technology called "sequencing by synthesis" (a.k.a. Illumina SBS Chemistry), which is what allows us to identify and maintain surveillance upon the COVID-19 variants that continue to loom over us. This Wisconsin soil nerd-angel had fallen from agrarian heaven right onto my public preserved park trail (a.k.a. John Muir's life's work) to illustrate the direct link between Aldo Leopold's life's work and the very scientific knowledge that can identify and track the current deadly virus in its multiple guises, thereby saving innumerable lives. Synchronicity, much? And what, pray tell, is the sports team mascot at this vaunted "Big Ten" Wisconsin university? Ladies and gentlemen, I give you the humble *badger*.

Well, shit. I was somewhat flabbergasted to have one of the top-tier scientific brain types here all to myself in this time of national confusion. When so many of our fellow Americans were allowing misinformation and superstition to influence them in making painful, sometimes fatal decisions about the virus and the ways to protect ourselves against it, here was a welcome dose of the cool, crisp logic derived from years and years of repeatable scientific experimentation. As I have often attested, we'll never know everything. Knowledge—all information—the universe—the Grand Economy—is ever expanding, and the mysteries that remain are some of the wonderful things about being human, especially in my job, because nothing sparks the imagination and the suspension of disbelief better than good old *darkness*, but it's that very abyss of ignorance that makes the proven facts of repeatable science so goddamn welcome.

Esteban carried between his ears a lot of comforting intelligence from the front lines of the COVID battle regarding the impending vaccines and their astonishing efficacy. Hearing the hard, fast facts from him directly instead of filtered through the palatability gauze of a news channel brought the same sense of comfort one gets from the cable guy or gal who is there in person actually solving your problem hands-on, versus your trying to discuss the issue with a random help line operator by phone or email.

I asked him a question that had been occurring to me over the last four years, but especially since the pandemic had begun. Did he think our species' propensity for killing each other (quickly, like in war or genocide, or slowly, like with systemic racism, including the wealth gap, real estate redlining, the incarceration system, and so forth, as well as our indifference to our responsibility for climate change, in addition to this newly obvious penchant for actually killing ourselves, with the dum-dums screaming their defiant ignorance as they spit a deadly virus into each other's faces)—could this be Mother Nature striking a balance? Like, the plague itself can easily be seen as a population equalizer, but on top of that, how is it that our human organism can blindly reason itself into shooting itself in the foot or worse?

He told me about a great book by Richard Dawkins called *The Selfish Gene* in which Dawkins extensively argues that the idea that altruistic behavior would somehow be good for the survival of the species is fallacious—it simply stems from human beings' desire to attach a morality to our behaviors. In truth, in Darwin's fight club, it's the self-serving, aggressive, competitive traits that best serve a species' chances for perpetuation—okay, I had to cut him off again. I told him he had to take it down a notch or somebody at Dutton was going to make me start citing his shit with footnotes like a real writer.

That was plenty enough science for me, and it served nicely as a conversational springboard into musings then about "*What a piece of work is man*" and the conundrums presented by the particularly human dichotomy of greed and selflessness. We are a people who can produce a Leopold family and a Rebanks family and have them inspire an entire watershed and the world beyond with their attention to the mutually beneficial methods of agrarian farming, and then simultaneously see our modern agricultural schools completely funded by the food corporations, racing in the other direction with all haste toward the singular goal of the almighty dollar. Will we be able to turn the boat of our nation and our planet around in time to save ourselves from engendering an extinction event? Things are bleak from many points of view, but still I am hopeful about our chances. As I said to Esteban, "Once my new book hits the shelves, that should fix everything."

We spent the rest of the descent talking about gear—he was pitching me on the effectiveness of hiking poles while I attempted to sell him on clip-in bicycle shoes—as well as how much we both adored Conan O'Brien. I thanked him sincerely for his tolerance of my eager questioning and wished him Godspeed on his drive to San Diego, then went to find Megan back at the Nutmeg.

She'd made these incredible pizzas on focaccia crust, to which we gave a proper holiday sendoff as sundown approached on New Year's Eve. We were sitting in our comfy camp chairs under our comfy awning while our fairy lights twinkled on the Nutmeg. It was pretty nice, if you're into romance and picture-perfect, purple sunsets. And pizza. Across the "lawn" area, about forty yards off, we noticed our cute neighbor couple who looked to be in their late sixties or early seventies, messing about behind their camper. I had discovered their names to be Pat and Judy. He was tall, regal, and slightly round, and she was relatively tiny and birdlike and pretty.

We had remarked upon them the day before when we saw them park their tiny little bubble camper that was not much bigger than the queen-size bed it housed, and set up a couple of chairs, coolers, a tabletop propane grill on the picnic table, and what appeared to be a five-foot-tall wooden saguaro cactus, painted green. It also had little white Christmas lights draped on it. Sorry, holiday lights. All of these items were surrounding a ten-foot square of linoleum, or something like it, its corners held securely down by four gallon jugs of water.

Just as we finished cleaning up our dinner dishes, we heard music starting up over at their spot—it was "When a Man Loves a Woman" by Percy Sledge. We scooted our chairs closer together and snuggled up, holding hands and making sure that Clover had a comfortable perch on our laps, as Judy and Pat began to dance. The surface they'd so carefully laid out was their dance floor! They were wearing dancing shoes. Hers looked like character shoes that a dance instructor might favor, and his looked like burgundy suede, built for jazz.

I had previously seen this phenomenon in my own parents as they seemed to glide about the dance floor at wedding receptions, their feet barely touching the ground, but these two lovebirds were truly exceptional. From Judy's carriage and form, Megan immediately identified her as a former professional dancer, and we agreed that the two of them must have done some class together because Pat was no slouch, either. As the sun sank below the jagged skyline and their cactus lights began to take full effect, they glided and sashayed, two beauties moving as one, thrilling us where we sat as though we were secretly spying on a Fred and Ginger rehearsal.

The next day Pat and I were both packing up our campsites, and I told him that we loved their dancing, and Megan was especially moved, being the former ballerina in the house. He shyly shrugged, thanked me, and said they had been doing that together for more than forty years. I said sincerely that their moves looked quite youthful, not to mention

they must have been somewhat spry to be getting along in such a wee camper.

"You know," he said, "it gets a little tight in that thing sometimes, a little close, but then she just asks me to go for a walk, and I'm glad to do it. Usually, though, we just get along."

"I know what you mean—twenty years in and the rare fight doesn't ever seem to stick very long. I guess we picked right. We're lucky enough to love each other."

Pat smiled. "Well, sure. It's pretty nice, ain't it?"

21

SEDONA BLOWS

If you don't know Sedona, Arizona, perfect. My first impulse is that I would like to keep it that way. Nothing infuriates me more than when some "tastemaker" publishes the details of the amazing hole-in-the-wall burrito stall near your woodshop, rendering it forevermore unavailable because of the now line around the block you don't have time to go stand in because you're trying to run a business.

So, Sedona is not that great. It's too crowded, and you probably won't like it. The rock is all red, so . . . boring. We went there anyway, because we love to be disappointed, and I was hiking a trail that I don't think you would care for, but I was having really a pretty wonderful time, not because it was gorgeous, but because I am a creative person. This route required some bouldering and some spiderlike scrambling up a couple of sheer rock faces that had just enough incline that I was only able to ascend by staying flat, nose to the rock, as I scrabbled up. If you're not familiar with extreme Alpine adventuring, they call this "free soloing," which some of us do just for ourselves, Alex, for the thrill, even if a film camera is not trained upon our prowess.

Once I had crested this garbage trail, I sat on a rock and had a cup of tea that was so goddamn roborative that I think I morphed into Jim Carter for a minute (Mr. Carson from *Downton Abbey*, a paragon of proper comportment), gazing out upon Sedona's notoriously blasé vistas. With my tea (Portland Breakfast by Steven Smith Teamaker), I savored a massive hiking cookie (Mr. Carson would have of course called it a prodigious constitutional biscuit) packed with oats, chocolate, nuts, and protein. My indulgent solace was suddenly shattered when two young men on mountain bikes came catapulting around the corner, flying smoothly through the air until they touched down and zipped around the next bend and out of sight. The whole episode took all of five seconds, and everything was surreally quiet except for the breeze whistling past these riders, and the "zzzzz" of the freehub bodies in the rear tires. I reflected that I had seen a few small instances of tire tread tracks in different places on my way up here but hadn't really given them much thought until I actually saw these bikers. It was wildly impressive on this underwhelming trail in a location that you should not visit.

I pressed on to the back side of the mountain, and you know, can we just take a minute to talk about trails? The trails themselves are such a huge part of the draw for me, even in a visual butthole like Sedona. I'm talking about the actual physical makeup—the construction of the walkway itself, which is one of the oldest creations, perhaps the oldest, of creatures on the planet. As we wake from our sleeping spot and amble to our tinkling spot, then stroll on to the blueberry patch, and then back to the napping and smooching place after all of that exertion, and we do this again and again, day after day, our route becomes traced into the soil, and eventually inspires a person in New Jersey to invent the toll road.

Paths, roads, trajectories, crossroads . . . their symbolism fuels our human narrative, and a great deal of emphasis is placed upon the life choices that ultimately determine whether or not we manage to stay on the "right" path. Over my fifty-one years, I have taken on board a lot of messaging, usually from people trying to sell me shit, about "chasing my dreams" and "reaching for the stars," and basically being as ambitious as possible. And maybe that route to that definition of success works for some people, but I can't say that it's really been my experience. I personally do a much better job at feeling successful by making smaller moves, and reading the organic signs that life sends my way.

Thoreau wrote, *"Pursue some path, however narrow and crooked, in which you can walk with love and reverence. Wherever a man separates from the multitude and goes his own way, there is a fork in the road, though the travelers along the highway see only a gap in the paling,"* and I feel like this is the quote that people think that Frost's "The Road Not Taken" is trying to be, missing the rather sharper point of that famous poem. Where Frost is pointing up our human penchant to revise or rationalize our own decision-making histories, Thoreau is merely advising us to pick a lane, which I take to mean "get to work making what appeals to you, and choose your turns and straightaways by paying attention to the idiosyncrasies that organically appeal to you."

Flipping my gaze back onto the real-life physical manifestation of this topic, it's the "narrow and crooked" path that delights me the most, like when the way winds downhill through old-growth trees so that over the years a sort of staircase has developed using the exposed roots of the trees, or the many sections of trail that utilize nature's stones to create stair steps, or the old English phenomenon known as a "holloway," which is when a well-worn path is flanked by rows of trees whose branches arch to join each other above the path, creating a visual tunnel that thrills the imagination.

Above and beyond the natural path peccadilloes, I also adore all of the amazing construction and maintenance that has gone into the trails we enjoy. I'm especially aware of it when I'm miles into a mountain trek and I come to a footbridge, built with timbers or concrete or steel, or maybe a set of dozens of steps up a steep cliffside. As I said while hiking the ruins of the old ore tramway in Texas, I can't help but recognize that some hardy souls had to haul these materials all the way out/up here, and then put in the hours and days of labor required to achieve their designs far from running water and electricity. So that we may safely enjoy them, the many, many miles of enjoyable paths on private and public park land require some degree of maintenance and caring attention, and I am deeply grateful to the ladies and gents responsible.

I had to do a little homework to discover that a "gap in the paling" refers to the spaces between slats in, like, a slatted fence or picket fence. I like that notion of Thoreau's quite a bit, that whatever attracts a body to fork off the path on their own is but a blip to the rest of the world, going past too fast or distracted to notice what lies through the slits between fence pickets.

Apparently, I wasn't the only traveler to be taken in by the crappy offerings of the Sedona outdoor-scape, as I presently came upon another lone biker cruising up the hill toward me on a mountain bike with fat balloon tires. We were in a dry streambed, with an assortment of rounded river stones populating the trail, strewn generously about and varying in size from golf ball to baseball to basketball, but the fellow simply pedaled steadily up the incline and swerved hither and yon without an apparent care in the world.

"That just doesn't seem possible," I said as he passed within a few feet of me.

He simply laughed and proceeded up the trail and out of sight.

I was duly impressed by the athleticism required to ride in this fashion, and thought again of the moments earlier in the day when I had scrambled up a rock face only to discover a tire track in a small deposit of dirt along the stone trail. This then made me recall further my time in the redwood-forested hills of Santa Cruz when I was running the wonderful trails there and I had some encounters with cyclists. In that setting, the young mountain bikers had set up earthen jumps along the trail, engineered at the bottom of steep hills so that a rider could gain the utmost downhill speed before being launched off the ground. The result was some pretty remarkable airtime, which culminated in a precarious landing that required a quick swerve to avoid being thrown off the trail into a tree.

The first time I witnessed it was nearly my last, as I came running unwittingly from the other direction around a bend, and a woman on the side of the trail said, "Heads up!" just before her companion came flying on his bicycle literally higher than my head. She was shooting video of him on her phone, and I weakly exclaimed and half ducked, as the bike landed well past me. I was frightened and they were embarrassed, but they apologized and I suggested they bring little signs to post, or perhaps some version of yellow crime scene tape, to slow oncoming traffic.

Some years ago, while hiking the mountains above Santa Barbara, I was fully frightened by two mountain bikers in full stormtrooper-style body armor and helmets, who came barreling past me in a fashion that made me dive off the trail to avoid being hit. I managed to yell, "Hey!" before they vanished down the steep trail.

So obviously, I like to utilize trails much more slowly and simply than some cyclists I have known. I don't begrudge them their trail time, even those who are apparently in it *solely* for the thrill of the gaps in the paling. I'm down with adrenaline-inducing fun-times, and have enjoyed a variety of them over the years, but (uh-oh, here comes Mr. Carson the Edwardian butler again) I feel like we could all use a refresher on our manners. If I am going to water-ski on a lake, I will do my best to stay within the allotted zone and far from any "no-wake" zones, where swimmers and canoeists depend upon the lack of violent boat-waves for safety and quietude. Similarly, if I'm biking on a mountain trail that is most frequented by pedestrians, I would hate to be so thoughtless of others as to go tearing around blind corners. It all continues to come back to remembering that none of us is an island, and that we really do have to think of others in the ways we use, well, everything.

I continued down the back side of this trail, thinking these incredibly deep thoughts and wondering if I should bother sending them to Mensa or, I don't know, the Dalai Lama? MIT? MI6?

My unspeakably ugly trail (never visit here, if you're smart) was tracing the right bank of a sizable dry river wash, and eventually, a rough, rocky back road emerged across the wash, flanking the left bank as I loped ever homeward. Before long, I began to hear the growl of an off-road engine powering its way up the trail, eventually drawing near to me on the other side of the riverbed. Unfortunately I was to discover that this was only the first of several of these vehicles that would be my intermittent-but-constant companions for the remaining few hours of my hike.

They were extra-long, pink jeep-type vehicles from a "tour" company creatively titled Pink Jeep Tours. Behind the front seat of each open-air truck were housed two or three bench seats, so they could carry maybe six to ten passengers per vehicle. Before the engine came into earshot, I could actually first hear the driver guide elocuting over a loudspeaker system to his wards mere feet behind him, to give you some idea how obnoxiously loud this operation was. The first one brought me up short, and I just stared as they trundled slowly past my location and on up the road.

The first driver was seriously speaking the following words, at the volume of an auctioneer at a farm estate sale: "*I don't care where it is, I just love to get out in nature and sit with the sounds and smells, to get away from civilization.*" I'll let you run the math on that one real quick, before hitting you with the next jeep's narration, maybe twenty minutes later: A passenger asked, "*Are there any gold mines out here?*" And the driver answered, "*I don't think so, maybe south of here. You can pan for it in Oak Creek, though, my neighbor got a ton panning but in the nineties.*" And then as they passed from hearing, the passenger said, "*Have you ever seen that show?*" Um. Okay, so I was in enough disbelief at how dumb this whole scene was, but also how sublime their snippets of dialogue were, that I got out my phone and made a voice memo, for which I'm so thankful, because otherwise you could not ever credit the rap emanating from the third jeep:

"*I'm talking about, you know . . . it's the Age of Aquarius. And the Age of Aquarius is about being conscious . . . being conscious of your place in the universe and your impact on those around you, even right here . . .*"

Okay, so I mean, I get it, that I'd been out in the platonic ideal of a meditative natural experience, even in the utter toilet that is Sedona, so at some point I should not have been surprised to have my starry-eyed trance shattered, but you have to admit that this irony-delivery method was pretty goddamn rich.

By the way, it's not lost on me that all of us are sometimes the whiskery guy on the trail and sometimes we're buckled into the back of a pink jeep, and still other times we're the amateur astrologer, rolling out our musings on the Age of Aquarius when the moon is in the Seventh House and whatnot. Only a few years ago, Megan and I took a helicopter tour of an area called Secret Mountain (horrible—zero stars—don't go), which featured heartbreaking scenic beauty wherever one looked, threading through impossible-to-reach slot canyons and culminating in close views of ancient adobe and stone homes of the Sinaguan people, tucked into open cliffside caverns that rendered them otherwise impossible to observe.

This was a highlight of our trip, even our year (despite how shitty everything looked), but I'm sure that simultaneously there were hikers and other people enjoying the serenity of nature who passionately raised their middle fingers at our chopper as it thundered past.

It begs the question, is there a "right" way to "use" nature? If so, what is it? I don't believe I'm any kind of expert, but I can't help imagining that the versions involving walking and bicycles would probably score better than the ones with the helicopter and the pink jeep with Dolby Surround Sound. Just like actual grass-fed eggs from one's own county would score better than those from an egg factory one or two states over. Of course, there are nuances to this argument, such as ensuring that the elderly, the infirm, and the disabled are able to enjoy nature "to an extent," but what is the extent? People in (unattractive) communities like Sedona are deriving their incomes from these jeeps and helicopters and hotels and restaurants, so what about their welfare? Where do we draw the line?

The "pink jeep" version of this experience feels representative to me of an especially American recreation. My parents' generation (Boomers) grew up with such a proliferation of vehicles on the road that there was more than one car for every two Americans, or loosely one hundred million automobiles. In 2020, fifty years later, the United States had 286.9 million registered vehicles. Internal combustion engines are so ubiquitous that it seems perfectly natural most of the time to solve a problem with a gas-powered vehicle. In this way, the pink jeep is not dissimilar to my Ford Expedition—they are both burning fossil fuels to transport a small number of people to their "recreation."

So let's say the owners of the pink jeeps read this book, and they realize that they should find another way to earn a living. And they send me a handwritten apology in a card that also contains a gift code for a nice ice-cream place. Let's also surmise that I succumb to the guilt I feel at the hypocrisy of "caring about Mother Nature" and her "Grand Economy" while burning tons of gas on our road trips, so I give up the Ford and, I guess, park the Nutmeg somewhere hopefully good (obviously not Sedona—gross). Will these actions be enough to turn climate change around? Will the pink jeep people and I be heralded as environmental heroes, receiving even more ice-cream gift credits from Greta Thunberg herself?

Hell no, we won't.

What we need to do is print enough copies of this book, or I guess that kills too many trees, so make sure to use recycled paper and also distribute as many digital and audio copies as possible. This is good, I like reading the book for the audience, and if you're listening right now, thank you for doing your part to shame the loud jeep people and save the planet. If you're reading this on paper, well, I guess you have some thinking to do.

Don't distract me. We take an ass-load of my books and fill all of the newly cleared shelf space in all the schools and libraries, where all the Ta-Nehisi Coates books used to sit, but now they've been burned because of how we can no longer teach critical race theory and a lot of the bad shit we did in the four, five hundred years of (white) human history in this country in which we're supposed to believe everything was cool and nothing we did was wrong, because of God and how good white people are at shit like flawless constitutions and civil rights. Right? We fill the shelf space with copies of my book and add it to every curriculum and then once everybody has understood the revolutionary ideas I have gifted humankind, *then* we . . . will . . . damn it.

Um. Okay, we're going to need some smart people. We take the smart people, and we get *them* to strategize a way to convince our legislators— the people whom we ostensibly *choose* to represent *our* wishes (over the nefariously purchased preferences of corporate interests nationwide) in the way they legislate the laws of the states and the country—that we care more about climate change than white supremacy; that we care more about the health of our farms and farmers and our food systems than we do about being able to wear our guns into more public places. That we care more about people than money.

But I guess that begs the question: do we?

EPILOGUE

Oh, give me a home where the buffalo roam,
Where the deer and the antelope play,
Where never is heard a discouraging word
And the sky is not clouded all day.

These are the opening lines to a poem entitled "My Western Home" penned by Dr. Brewster M. Higley in 1872 or '73 about his life as a Kansas homesteader. The verses were subsequently published in the *Smith County Pioneer* newspaper in 1874. A friend of his set them to music and the song traveled all about the country, undergoing some minor tweaks, but largely staying true to the original until it was published in the 1910 book *Cowboy Songs and Other Frontier Ballads* by folklorist John Lomax. At some point a realist got ahold of the third line, *"Where never is heard a discouraging word,"* and changed *never* to *seldom*, because, I mean, come on, even on the otherwise placid range, they were only human. The new twentieth century was not going to begrudge a pioneer a few cusses over a stubbed toe, or a badger in the henhouse.

Or maybe somebody got within earshot of the Kansas reservations housing the remnants of the Kickapoo, Iowa, Potawatomi, and Sac and Fox tribes—methinks there may have been a clearly audible discouraging word or two issuing forth from the Native Americans trying to swallow the raw deals they had been handed. Another unknown lyricist added this stanza at some point:

> *The red man was pressed from this part of the West,*
> *He's likely no more to return*
> *To the banks of Red River where seldom if ever*
> *Their flickering camp-fires burn.*

An uncharacteristically thoughtful verse, with an air of melancholy, almost as though the writer understands the responsibility of the song's narrator and all they stand for in the disappearance of the "red man."

By the time Bing Crosby recorded his version in 1933, the song was officially known as "Home on the Range," and when it was legally adopted as the state song of Kansas in 1947, the "red man" verse was conspicuously absent, but another original verse remained, slightly tweaked into this:

> *How often at night, when the heavens are bright,*
> *With the light of the twinkling stars,*
> *Have I stood here amazed, and asked as I gazed,*
> *If their glory exceeds that of ours.*

Okay, hold up. This verse just comes right out and handsomely rhymes our hubris, positing the question of whose "glory" is greater—us humans? Or the stars in the firmament? I hope you will permit me another rare LOL, as we dumbshits effectively erased the verse with any sort of self-reckoning regarding the crimes we committed against the Native Americans, and instead mused on whether we were perhaps the most glorious things in the cosmos. This fits pretty neatly into the drawer of songs celebrating the incredibly one-sided achievements of white America, like "America the Beautiful," which is a song full of reinforcement for the Christian God–ordained actions of the conquering, "liberating" American pilgrims and heroes.

The argument that our nation should be allied with any one religion, or religion at all, is simply bonkers. It's about as solipsistic as thinking can get, to somehow try to reconcile the supposed American ideals of diversity and freedom for all with those of your church (or synagogue or mosque, but I believe it's mainly the churches that are pissing in this particular bed). If our national sloganeering and jingoistic jingles don't recognize the varied nuances of humanity by acknowledging our past mistakes (and crimes) against and our present dependence upon said variety, then those refrains are not patriotic at all, they're nationalist. The Catholic Church in which I was raised was big on penance—if they want to impress us with their sincere devotion, why not repent by way of reparations for the presently unanswered sins of our past?

A true national or state anthem should absolutely cop to our iniquities. If America is going to have any hope of one day being great, it will be by finally facing slavery, genocide, domestic terrorism, Japanese American internment camps, and the list of commensurate evils that runs right up to today and into tomorrow. If a person bases their worldview on the lyrics of these old songs, it's not surprising that they could easily end up indoctrinated into the White Power army, even unwittingly. How can a song extol the so-called glories of this nation without mentioning the exemplary heroics of our civil rights activists and suffragists and abolitionists?

The more contemporary Lee Greenwood right-wing anthem "God Bless the USA" (not to put too fine a point on it) includes the lines *"there's pride in every American heart"* and *"I'm proud to be an American,"* statements powerfully ignorant to the quality of life of the majority of his fellow citizens once you add up the minorities, the victims of many stripes of discrimination, and those living in poverty. Perhaps if Mr. Greenwood wanted to improve the accuracy of his writing, for a start he should insert the word *white* in front of each appearance of "American" in those verses, then add the word *straight* between the two. His song also features the refrain *"God bless the USA,"* but I wonder how he and his fans would square the blind braggadocio of his words with this little ditty from our old friend the King James Bible, Book of Proverbs 16:18, *"Pride goeth before destruction, and a haughty spirit before a fall, bitch."*

* * *

The day Megan and I packed up to drive home from our Nutmeg adventure started out pretty unremarkably. We retracted the awnings, battened down the remaining pieces of Megan's brown butter cake, and were just about to switch off the news and bid farewell to the just-plain-unpleasant ass-canker called Sedona, when all of a sudden it was as though these white pride songs had come to life, complete with Confederate flags and angry, violent white insurrectionists on the TV, beating police officers and storming our nation's capitol building. The date was January 6, 2021.

We stood in shock, yea, and awe, and stared for half an hour or so in sheer disbelief. Snapping back into the focus required of a long travel day, nine hours on the road or so, we finished buttoning up and began to haul our Nutmeg west, all the while glued to the radio. You know how it played out, and the unfurling shit-blossoms responsible are not remotely done, either. The insurrection movement, I mean. Which I guess, based on their voting to oppose an investigation into the selfsame insurrection, means that the movement—Stop the Steal, the Big Lie, the January 6 traitors—has now become synonymous with the Republican Party.

Somehow, despite the noble efforts of Megan, Clover, and myself to wallow in some light escapism for several weeks as we traipsed about the Southwest and canoodled on the banks of the Rio Grande in our cute Airstream Globetrotter, wolfing down pasta and enchiladas, the present evil of the indecent leading the blind appears to be going nowhere soon. I silently renewed my promise to myself and all humankind to fix every-thing by writing this lightweight meander of a nonfiction title. (You're welcome.)

A few weeks after we arrived home in Los Angeles, I finally got to try out a new recreational activity about which I had long been curious. My producer pal Marvin had invited me to go stand-up paddleboarding in the Pacific Ocean. As it turned out, we launched the boards near the California Yacht Club in Marina del Rey, which also has a public-access put-in. Now, I'll remind you that I'm a Midwestern lake and river guy, so even just being on this relatively calm water protected from the ocean's swells by a distant breakwater was pretty thrilling. Part of my adrena-line was being generated by the fact that stand-up paddleboarding is a bit of a balancing act that is relatively manageable once you get the hang of it, but it's still precarious. You have to actively stand still as hard as you can.

We paddled out into the main channel of the marina, where the primary danger was riding out the wakes created by the various boats coming and going, which may or may not have fomented some giggles, a few gasps, and perhaps even a squeal of terrified delight or two, as I barely managed to stay out of the drink. A second unnerving factor was the presence of enormous sea lions lazing about the marina, which, although relatively benign, still occasionally enjoyed "playing" with us by popping up in unexpectedly close proximity, which was startling at least, especially when they can achieve weights of up to seven hundred pounds.

The water is perfectly opaque, so it's easy for an Illinois lad to start imagining what might lie beneath the dark surface, while he comforts himself with the thought that H. P. Lovecraft's stories of the Old Ones are primarily centered in New England. Then just as he terrifyingly recalls that Cthulhu's favorite haunt, the sunken city of R'lyeh, is actually held to be in the *South Pacific*, a snuffling monster head the size of a five-gallon bucket breaches the waves a few feet from his paddle and he squeals with terror but then quickly laughs to let everyone (Marvin) know that he is an American Man™, a special type of coward who must pretend at all costs to feel *no* fear, despite how stupid that is in reality.

It was just the right amount of exhilarating to be great fun, and a surprisingly effective workout as well. We made our way the couple of miles out to the huge breakwater protecting the marina inlet, then turned back toward our dock. On our way in we wove in and out of the five thousand or so boats moored in this marina. Marvin said that some of these watercraft were garbage, worth literally zero dollars, or even less, given the cost required to either fix them up or remove them. On the other end of the spectrum, however, were the massive yachts worth in the neighborhood of $75 or even $100 million. I can't believe I didn't fall off my board upon hearing that.

There were dozens upon dozens of these giant yachts, ranging from classic-looking wooden sailboats to shiny, modern fiberglass monstrosities that looked like if an apartment building had a baby with a bullet train. Now, again, I don't want to come across as hypocritical here—I come from a family that owns at least four or five fishing boats, not including my canoe. But I do think there's a demonstrable difference between an eighteen-foot bass boat that has a specific utility (drinking beer) and a forty-million-dollar house that floats. I'm not so much interested in judging these yacht owners, as there are myriad other examples of gross excess in our society, as I am in simply examining this juxtaposition in which I found myself standing. Or, wobbling, to be more accurate.

Looking at a medium-size version of one of these pleasure boats, I was filled with wonder. It had accommodations so deluxe that you wouldn't even know you were on the water. If you could ignore the heave and swell of the ocean, you could just chill on the $20,000 couch and watch *The Abyss* on the big screen, powering through maybe some nachos that the chef whipped up. What does it say about us, I wondered, that somehow our idea of luxury is to take the undeniably enjoyable experience of being on the water, feeling the breeze, soaking in the weather, perhaps catching our dinner, and then wrap it up in extreme comfort and décor until we have turned a boat into a floating McMansion? (Wrote the man with a massage parlor in his truck seat.)

I was standing there literally looking in the windows of these yachts wondering this, teetering on my paddleboard. The other glaring fact that hit me was that *nobody was there*. These boats were all sitting there unused. Marvin's brother works in San Diego as a charter captain on boats like these big ones, and he says that they'll average maybe a couple of weekends of use per year.

This seems crazy, I thought. Here I was having an amazing few hours on the water, enjoying the elements and getting some exercise to boot, all for the price of a paddleboard and paddle, both items which I could make if I needed to. Since then, I have gone back a handful of times for more laps around the marina, and I look forward to going again this week, as a treat for finishing this writing. The objective of our efforts, both that day and since, is not dissimilar to that of a hike— isolating oneself in an envelope of nature where all you need to do is walk—or paddle—to have a terrific time. The sun and the salt water and the exertion leave me feeling great after a long morning paddle, like I've done something positive, even productive.

Now, supposedly, according to the message of capitalism, I should be dissatisfied with my paddleboard, especially when faced with these gargantuan, opulent surrogate penises. The "American way" demands that I shouldn't rest until I have extra millions to blow on a boat like this, so that it can sit here in its (expensive!) mooring, because it's not so much for me to use as it is for me to *own*. There's something to this, I thought, as the occasional smaller, more modest boat headed out to sea past us—people perhaps intending to fish, or maybe perform scientific research on the ocean. The juxtaposition of our responsible *use* of nature with our *ownership* of it was hanging there for me to pluck.

I recalled a conversation between Neil Young and Conan O'Brien on Conan's podcast in which they were extolling the forgotten virtues of playing music on vinyl records instead of digital media. Neil talked about how American it was to need to be able to store thousands of songs on your device, as though that holds some sort of power, but he then added, "*You can only play one song at a time, man.*" Jay Leno's famous hoard of classic cars is worth over $50 million but no one is allowed to visit it, meaning the 169 automobiles and 117 motorcycles serve little purpose. I get it, cars are cool, and I don't begrudge anybody collecting things they like. But I also feel like we can encourage one another to invest in human beings instead of billionaire yachts that remain docked and shockingly expensive hot rods that nobody gets to drive.

Patrick Kavanagh was a twentieth-century Irish poet who was celebrated for the value he placed upon the commonplace and the mundane, and I feel like Leopold and Neil Young would both agree with this idea:

"To know fully even one field or one land is a lifetime's experience. In the world of poetic experience it is depth that counts, not width. A gap in a hedge, a smooth rock surfacing a narrow lane, a view of a woody meadow, the stream at the junction of four small fields—these are as much as a man can fully experience."

* * *

As I'm writing these final pages, the world remains in turmoil. Where the news should be touting the nation's collective achievement of herd immunity by way of mass vaccination, it is instead filled with stories of herd idiocy. Fueled by a fire hose of misinformation and conspiracy theory, large percentages of Republicans are frighteningly "not confident" about the results of President Biden's landslide victory in the 2020 election over their sad boy. Something as irreproachable as the benefit of powerful vaccines is being insincerely questioned on Fox News, not for reasons of legitimate concern, but to score mere political points, even at their viewers' peril. To wit, states with low vaccination rates are loudly cheered at the Conservative Political Action Conference.

Three celebrity billionaires, meanwhile, are truly exploring the question of whether their glory might exceed that of the stars by launching themselves veritable inches higher than they had previously been vaulted, and they still cannot remotely dunk. The entire continent of Africa has received a tragic paucity of vaccine doses, along with many other poor countries in Asia, the Middle East, and Central and South America, but we Americans are so abhorrent as to turn our noses up at this lifesaving medicine until it actually expires and goes to waste, while our wealthiest playboys play rocket ship grab-ass giggle-tag.

I'd like to show Elon Musk, Jeff Bezos, and Richard Branson the world casualty numbers based on other countries' extreme poverty, then ask if they're "proud to be Americans." Maybe we should ask "the twinkling stars" if they're impressed yet? Meanwhile, as a squadron of air force Blue Angels thunders past across the sky during a "patriotic" air show costing six figures per flyover, I'd love for Lee Greenwood to ask a teeming homeless encampment under a highway overpass if they are "proud to be Americans."

Mother Nature is not an American, and she is not proud. She is all creation, so her vibe encompasses all experience, in every size, shape, and color, from the high to the low. Her economy and its successful evolution thrive on diversity, and her children never rest in their glorious participation, reproducing and adapting, so as to grow ever stronger. A farm, therefore, as a mini-version of her creation, just a few-dozen-acres-size scale model, requires as much variety as possible, because in diversity is strength. A proliferation of species sets up support systems in every direction. To depend upon monocultures, on the other hand, is to invest in a fragile system that opposes nature, literally goes to war with her, requiring more and more chemical weaponry, both as fertilizer and as poison in the forms of herbicide and insecticide.

The same Darwinian notion is true of a nation or a state or a county.

A diverse neighborhood is eminently more powerful than a homogenous one. Ben & Jerry's full menu of flavors is gonna crush plain vanilla every time. I also know that if I can manage to keep an eye on my bird feeder and my woodshop and my farmer's market and my family more than my online shopping cart, and if I can simply continue to enjoy my canoe, then I might just remember that actually nobody needs a yacht. It's a daunting project, this remembrance, but since we continue to own a mirror in our household, try as I might to avoid it, I catch the occasional glimpse of myself and am reminded regularly that I'm a dipshit.

You might think that I would not like to be reminded of this fact, but on the contrary, I am always grateful for the knowledge, because it is the starting point. When I recall my fallibility as a human, it comes as a relief to remember that I have still more work to do, and that the work will never cease until my hands give out. Were I to forget my need to attempt good work, the resultant void would create a dangerously empty frame of mind in me which I would need to fill up in my newly idle time, and so I would begin to cast about, based upon the predilections of an idler, for diversions or maybe something shiny to collect, and before you know it I might end up with one of those yachts.

By chasing the work that I deem "good," I instead get to experience astonishing moments as excellent as anything Perseus ever pulled off, like diving into a glacial Montana river with my great friend George or falling together to the earth in mortal wonder as we witnessed our brother Jeff's feats of daring, stamina, and courage in the deep wilderness of Glacier National Park. Although I'll note that as good as those adventures were, I don't think they would have been diminished a whit if the parks were given back to the Indigenous tribes to run. I feel like the work would actually feel better all around, in fact.

Thanks to following the nose on my face—the very nose that I employ to sniff out the avenues of my good work—I have avoided purchasing *any* collectible vehicles of any sort by instead feeding hay in winter to some absolute units of Herdwick sheep and savoring each blown-cool spoonful of ham and bean broth and meeting the Queen of the Belties, who was more than happy to answer James's questions about Belted Galloway cows, and mine about her aerodynamic tits. I have delighted in the work of learning about regenerative, sustainable farming in the UK and America alike, and I have very much enjoyed investigating the beefy, porky, eggy fruits of its grass-fed ambitions. As delicious as these goodies have been, I feel like they could be even tastier, were they to come from Black farmers working land they've received in reparation from the currently extant wealth of the plantations that so dearly and clearly still owe them.

Because of the generosity and patience of my travel companion Megan and our navigator and copilot Clover, my work has taken me to a hard-won confluence of family and a microbiologically educational mountain ramble, with some lessons in future romance and ballroom dancing thrown in for good measure. I know I'll make more mistakes in the years to come, but if I can keep to my narrow and crooked path, I might even try some hiking poles when my knees begin to gripe loudly enough. The bad news is it doesn't look like I'm going to be getting any smarter or cuter, but the good news is that I can find smart, curious, progressive, empathetic people to follow and support, people who are more interested in seeing my smiles than my tears. We must understand that each and every one of us is a cog or a wheel in the ecosystem of Leopold's parlance, and that like it or not, you need me. And I need you, every gorgeous, goddamn one of you, to continue to engender the ethics of agrarianism throughout the world, to save our food systems, our farmers, our civilization, and ultimately ourselves. It's the biggest no-brainer in the history of mankind.

acknowledgments

This book is a couple of years overdue from the date I was contracted to turn it in, so first and foremost I will sincerely thank the generous folks at Dutton books for their patience, without even *suggesting* a lawsuit. They, further, gave no awareness of even the first stone of gravel in their craw whatsoever. To my knowledge, they have not once besmirched my good name in either public or closeted salons. Can you imagine such forbearance?

To her credit, my agent, Monika Verma, at the Levine Greenberg Rostan Literary Agency, only *gently* mentioned this breach of decency on my part every six months or so over the years, until grabbing my wrist in midair as it tried to raise my hand holding a trembling spoonful of corn-crab chowder to my gaping mouth and thus engaging me in that upsettingly long bout of eye contact during a Norma's lunch in late 2019. She said, in an unwavering voice, "It's time to do that book now." Thank you sincerely, Monika, for your guidance, and for the loan of your handkerchief.

My editor is simply amazing. Her name is Jill Something and this is our fifth book together. I am only able to make these books with her patient collaboration and good cheer, so she gets a very large helping of gratitude and affection, even though she was present at what we have come to call the "chowder incident," and she sat by silently as I was brutalized. Nobody crosses Monika Verma.

My production editor, LeeAnn Pemberton, has a brain as big as Yosemite and a heart to match. She has employed her skills generously on each of my five volumes now, and I am always grateful for her remonstrations, particularly when she helps me spell words like *remonstrations*. We have not taken a meal together.

Publicity bailiffs Emily Canders, Jamie Knapp, and Carla Parisi employ almost exclusively carrots these days as they guide me through the stalls of commerce. Thank you.

Dora Mak, my production shepherd, makes sure everything is running smoothly between my quill and inkpot and the hand-set printing presses that dot the Virginia countryside, operated generationally by father-daughter and mother-son teams as they have done since the time of Gutenberg, I can only assume.

Rounding out the Superfriends Dutton team are Christine Ball, John Parsley, Stephanie Cooper, Tiffani Ren, Susan Schwartz, Ryan Richardson, Laura Corless, and Marya Pasciuto, all of whom I warmly thank.

For wrangling the actual printing of the book, thank you kindly to Sheila Ott at LSC Communications, and for executing the cover printing; big ups and a "What's Updog?" to Tami Kaufman at Coral Graphics Services.

Vi-An Nguyen made the cover art as well as the interior illustrations, and I am especially grateful to her because that tone was very hard to nail correctly because of how I am very persnickety. I think the book is simply beautiful, despite involving a representation of my face.

Jeff Tweedy, George Saunders. Georff Twenders, Feff Seendy. They melt together. I love you, brothers, and I thank you, avalanche-style. xo

The Rebanks family, James, Helen, Molly, Bea, Isaac, and Tom. I meant what I said, and I thank you sincerely. See you soon.

Wendell, Tanya, Den, and Mary Berry, and introducing cute up-and-comer Steve Smith. I am powerfully grateful for your generosity and patience with me. I know that I will likely never do a good enough job of regurgitating your estimable works for my audience, but that won't stop me from trying. Thank you.

Grandpa Mike and Grandma El Roberts had two daughters and two sons. My mom was the older daughter, and her two brothers, Dan and Don, still run the family grain farm (without chewing tobacco) together with their ever-burgeoning families (especially aunts Dee and Lyn). Micki, Mom's little sis, is a local librarian and historian, with a fruitful family of her own (especially Uncle Terry). All four siblings are grandparents, and I think the family numbered thirty-nine or so at last count, although babies keep popping up all over the place out on Bell Road and over in Morris, so don't hold me to it. With the exception of Megan and myself, the entire family lives within an eight-mile radius, and we all continue to share a lifelong bond of fidelity, hard work, sweet corn, humility, and neighborly service (Megan, Clover, and I are doing our best from California). They are an exceptional group of American humans upon whose roster I am certainly proud to be listed. I love them all very much.

My three siblings, Laurie, Carrie, and Matt, are great people, and we get along pretty damn amazingly well for four pampered beer fans. Three of us scored a 29 on our ACTs, and one of us scored a 28, so I'll go on the record as saying I think we're all pretty sharp, all things considered. I would also never sincerely accuse any of them of being dumber than me, or worse at anything than me, except maybe funny dancing, and even that contest wouldn't be a cakewalk. I love them very much and thank them for this their brief appearance in the discomfiting spotlight.

My college roommate Mike Flanigan, one of the funniest people I have ever met, is terrifically handsome, sings in a gorgeous tenor, and to date, resides in my top-three all-time Harold Hills. I have long been grateful to him for being a better thinker and exhibiting a bigger heart than me, which allowed me to crib a lot of extra credit by his example over the years. Among his lessons were the vastly superior quality of the health food store peanut butter that required stirring and the hacky-sack maneuver known as *The Jester*. How I loved to announce that move every time Mike would nimbly pull it off. (Clear, loud, Phil Hartman voice) "The Jester!" I wish you could have been there. But the reason Mike gets a paragraph in these acknowledgments is because I first heard the additional verses to "Home on the Range" when he played that tune for me on his guitar and sang those poignant words. Thank you, Mike.

Thank you to Adriana Bellet, for her inspiring creative conversation and factual suggestions.

Thank you, Albena Dodeva, for all of your tireless assistance in keeping me on my feet and out of the doghouse.

Nearly finally, here follows a list of friends (and Alison Pill) from whom I received guidance and inspiration throughout the years during which

I was formulating the content of this book. This sort of list is necessarily incomplete, and I'm certain I'm forgetting plenty of pals. If you are one of them, please hit me up and I'll buy you a beverage, roborative or otherwise. Thank you, with love, to Danny Airstream, Ronnie Aveling, Chris Bagby and family, Dylan Banks, Datri Bean, Christian Becksvoort, Anne Bell, Joe Berardi, the Berry Center, Sally Browder, Bill Bryson, Lee Buchanan and co., Buddy, Bern Chandley, Melinda and Randy Compton, Jon Cunningham, Matt Davies, Michele Diener, Laura Dunn, Rob Radkoff Ek, Megan Fitzpatrick, Mark Flanagan, Joe Foust, Neil G., Peter Galbert, Alex Garland, Martin Garner, Chris Gerson, Jon Glaser, Devin Granahan, Michael Griffee, Steven Gruber, Christopher Guest, Michele Guthrie, Brett Haley, Rhonda and Richard Hefton, Nancy Hiller, John Hodgman, Bill Holderman, Dean Holland, Peter Howard (Hobart), Peter Howard (Occidental), Patrick Laurie, Josh Leonard, Thomas Lie-Nielsen, Lloyd, John Carroll Lynch, Jon Maret, Charney Marshall, Laura McCusker, Robert McFarlane, Dave McNulty, Matt Micucci, Chip Oppenheim, Jane Parrott, Matthew Penry-Davey, Jeffrey James Perry, Alison Pill, Deneb Puchalski, Puddles, Robert Redford, Red-Headed Cop, Allon Reich, Pat Roberts, Diana Rodgers, Morgan Sackett, Sam the Coyote, Shōzō Satō, Christopher Schwartz, Rusty Schwimmer, Jef Sewell, Erick Sharrow, Krystal Shelley, Micah Stock, Demi Sullivan, Linda Sundheim, Todd Tesen, Jesse Thorn, Roy Underhill, Sarah Vowell, Kevin Wade, Sarah Watlington, Daniel Wheeler, Andrew Whitehurst, Clio Wilde, and Thomas Wilhoit.

Last but not remotely least, in fact let's just say "last, but most of all," my splendid life partner and best friend, Megan, *really* put up with the repercussions of me writing a book on a tight, belated deadline. Her patience has been profound. I remain a student of her and Clover, and all the other instructors about the place who remind me to stop and dance every now and again. Thank you, my beautiful bride, and I love you very much. (Banjo kicks in) *"Timeshare Freedom Group—we'll set you free!"* Now, can I please come back in the house?!

*"Ethical behavior is doing the right thing when no one else is watching—
even when doing the wrong thing is legal."*

—Aldo Leopold